DATE DUE			
OCT 2 8 1998			

Nicholas Bacon

Nicholas Bacon

The Making
of a Tudor Statesman

Robert Tittler

Associate Professor of History
Concordia University, Loyola Campus
Montreal

OHIO
UNIVERSITY PRESS

PUBLISHED IN THE UNITED STATES OF AMERICA
BY OHIO UNIVERSITY PRESS, ATHENS, OHIO
COPYRIGHT © 1976 BY ROBERT TITTLER

ISBN 0–8214–0225–0

LIBRARY OF CONGRESS CATALOG NUMBER LC 75–36976

PRINTED IN GREAT BRITAIN BY
W & J MACKAY LIMITED, CHATHAM

Contents

5

Illustrations

Preface and Acknowledgments

It may not be easy to understand today the high regard accorded to Sir Nicholas Bacon by those who were closer in time to his own age. Even among those who had no need of his favour or who wrote after his death, the consensus of admiration rings clear. Ben Jonson, drawing upon Bacon's posthumous reputation, found that he ' ... was singular and almost alone in the beginning of Queene *Elizabeths* times' for his oratorical eloquence and wit.[1] The historian William Camden referred to him as 'the Oracle of the Law' long before that cognomen became associated with Sir Edward Coke.[2] William Cecil depended on his advice for any number of concerns, from the problems of recoinage to the royal marriage.[3] And to Elizabeth herself, as she once reminded Thomas Egerton, Bacon served as the very model of a wise Lord Keeper.[4]

Nearly everyone for whom modern accounts of the Tudor Age have held interest will have met with mention of Bacon at some time. But how remarkable it is that, regardless of the source, the reference nearly always evokes the same image, and one so far removed from the paeans of his contemporaries. Thus we think of jowlish and long-winded Sir Nicholas, most readily identified as William Cecil's brother-in-law or Francis Bacon's father, serving Elizabeth faithfully – if perhaps tediously – as her Lord Keeper of the Great Seal, and delivering windy discourses on her behalf at ceremonial occasions. Yet those who write about that age seem curiously uneasy about omitting their almost inevitable allusion to Bacon, as if afraid to leave out something which, for some forgotten reason, might perhaps prove important after all.

In the pages that follow, I have attempted to explore the meaning behind Bacon's contemporary reputation, and have tried to add the proper dimension to this long-undervalued figure of the Tudor Age. As one who emerged from the modest background of the Suffolk yeomanry, survived the political vicissitudes of the middle Tudors, and rose to the first rank of Elizabethan statesmen during the last two decades of his life, Bacon aptly epitomizes the inspired 'new men' of whom so much has been written. But there is more to him than the successful parvenu, and his personal contributions far exceed his value as a paradigm of an important group. He brought to his political endeavours a distinct philosophical outlook well grounded in the literary and ideological trends of the Renaissance; he championed progressive reforms in education and government administration as well as in his proper *métier* of the law; he served as an ardent and enlightened supporter of Puritanism whenever he could; and he played a crucial role in determining the course of politics in East Anglia following the demise of Thomas Howard. In short, I hope to make clear that, in an unobtrusive manner, and well camouflaged by the paucity of surviving source materials, Bacon's life fully epitomizes many of the central themes of the Tudor era.

Because of the lamentably incomplete sources for Bacon's life, it has proved impossible to treat all phases of the subject as fully as I would have liked. I have on the whole remained reluctant to leap into the dark on the basis of sparsely documented assumptions, but some contentions have had to be gleaned from unverifiable traditions or deduced from circumstantial evidence. Even after extensive use of sources which would, in more bountiful circumstances, be considered marginal, there will always be gaps in the story.

Almost all of those 'Bacon Papers' which have survived fit into one of two categories: personal papers containing estate records and family correspondence, and 'official' papers, consisting of several manuscript volumes by anonymous copyists who sought to preserve for posterity some of Bacon's more important speeches and a few of his state letters. The former category is at present divided into several collections, the main parts of which reside at the Folger Shakespeare Library, Washington, D.C. (the Townsend MSS., L.d. 1–1036), the Norfolk and Norwich Record Office in Norwich (the Bradfer Lawrence MSS., VIIb) and the University of Chicago (the Redgrave Hall MSS.). The manuscript volumes of speeches and letters, nearly all of which repeat the same items, are more widely scattered. Individual volumes may be found in the British Museum (Additional MS. 32,379, and Harleian MSS. 398 and 5,176), Corpus Christi College, Cambridge (MS. 543), the Folger Shakespeare Library (V.a. 143 and V.a. 197), the Henry E. Huntington Library in San Marino, California (Ellesmere MSS. 2,579 and 1,340), and the National Library of Wales (MS. 10,905 E).

In view of the unchallenging image of Bacon which has emerged, and in view of the lack of sources for his life which has fostered that image, it is not surprising that he has yet to have his modern biographer. Yet there have been a few studies of lesser scope which have proved valuable in the preparation of the present work. The first relatively modern observation on Bacon came in the mid-1840s, with an inaccurate and anecdotal but still useful chapter in Lord Campbell's *Lives of the Lord Chancellors*.[5] In 1865 J. Payne Collier, the Shakespearian scholar, published a few snatches of correspondence and provided an introductory commentary for them.[6] But aside from the comprehensive and generally accurate article published in the *D.N.B.* a generation after Collier wrote, nothing further of significance emerged until almost the last two decades. In 1951, the late Miss Gladys Scott Thomson broke that long silence with her article 'Three Suffolk Figures: Thomas Wolsey, Stephen Gardiner, and Nicholas Bacon'.[7] Although Miss Scott Thomson was clearly more interested in Bacon's origins than his career, her article did imply that further research might well be justified.

In more recent years some serious work has been devoted to particular aspects of Bacon's life which, if valuable to the biographer, leaves much unsaid regarding his political career and his intellectual development. These efforts emanated from the University of Chicago, where the availability of the Redgrave Hall Muniments and the energy of Dr Alan Simpson provided the necessary preconditions for scholarly research. The result was a rapid succession of M.A. and doctoral theses, and – the culminating effort – an excellent and full chapter on Bacon's landed holdings in Dr Simpson's *The Wealth of the Gentry, 1540–1660*, published in 1961.[8]

In addition to my debts to these scholars who have contributed to what we know about Bacon, there are many necessary acknowledgments to those who have not been specifically concerned with Bacon himself, but whose contributions to what we know of his milieu, and whose advice and patience regarding my efforts, have made this work possible in the most fundamental sense.

I cannot begin to thank all of those who helped me gain access to the materials upon which this study is founded, but the following have been helpful in that regard well beyond the call of duty: Miss J. M. Kennedy of the Norfolk and Norwich Record Office; Mr A. T. Milne, Mr W. Kelloway and Miss Rosemary Taylor of the Institute of Historical Research, London; Miss Norah Fuidge of the History of Parliament Trust Project; Mrs Sandra Powers, Mrs Esther Washington and their staff at the Folger Shakespeare Library; and Miss Irene Sendek and Miss Judith Appleby at the Georges P. Vanier Library of Loyola College, now the Loyola Campus of Concordia University.

I cannot disclaim my own responsibility for whatever shortcomings may appear in the following pages, but neither can I deny the patient counsel of those who have helped to shape whatever contributions this work may offer. To Drs Marjorie McIntosh, Ernest R. Sandeen, James S. Cockburn, A. Hassel Smith, Elizabeth McCutcheon and Mary Elizabeth Coyle, all of whom permitted me access to their unpublished work, I am greatly indebted. Professors Michael MacDonald of Mt Allison University, James Cockburn of the University of Maryland and my Loyola colleague Dr Maria Philmus have been kind enough to read and comment on individual chapters, and they will know how much I have profited by their reactions.

Professor S. T. Bindoff not only allowed me to take up a session of his seminar at the Institute of Historical Research in 1971 with the thoughts that eventually found their way into Chapter XI, but has commented at great length on the discussion in Chapter VII. Both sections have profited from those exchanges, as have I from the encouragement which came with them. Professor Joel Hurstfield has been a greater source of support than he may imagine. Perhaps his most valued contribution came even before the beginning, when he responded with keen enthusiasm to a letter from a young American graduate student, unknown to him, who sought his advice before embarking on dissertation research concerning Nicholas Bacon.

His subsequent patience with my thoughts in his seminars, both at the Institute of Historical Research in 1968–9 and 1971, and at the Folger Shakespeare Library in 1973, have been of extreme value. Dr James E. Farnell has closely followed this tale in its progress as a doctoral dissertation under his direction to the completion of the work at hand. He has read each chapter with care and insight, helped unravel many knots, and has found words of encouragement to carry me through even the most muddled of my efforts. As my mentor and friend, he has my sincere thanks.

The research for this study could not have been completed without the generous financial support of Oberlin College, New York University and Loyola College, while the writing and final preparations have been rendered manageable by the largesse of the Canada Council. The intelligent and skilful typing of Mrs Margaret Blevins, copy-editing by Miss Deborah Shepherd of Jonathan Cape, and help with pictures from Mrs Caroline Pilkington of the Courtauld Institute have been invaluable resources, for which I am greatly indebted.

Finally, no small thanks are due my wife. Neither unheated bed-sits, one-burner cookers, nor the rigours of budgeting on fellowship ever stayed her patience and good humour as a companion in the quest for Bacon. To her I dedicate this work.

ROBERT TITTLER

Montreal

I

From Drinkstone to Gray's Inn

The area around Hessett and Drinkstone, Suffolk, seems today to be very much a part of the economic backwater of East Anglia. The main roads from Bury St Edmunds to the west, and from Stowmarket to the south-east, dwindle to one-lane macadam threads which wind around the small farms, through fertile fields and copses, and meet again unpretentiously at crossroad hamlets. The villages themselves present the outsider with a timeless similarity. Only their resolute and dignified churches, and the still proud wattle-and-daub homes left by the wealthy burghers of the past, stand as reminders of a livelier age.

Yet if wills, leases, parish registers and the rare scraps of surviving correspondence are any guide, this same area appears to have been the busy stamping-ground of an active and ambitious yeomanry at the beginning of the Tudor Age. True, the farms of that day were smaller if anything than those of today, the wooded areas denser and more numerous, and the roads mere tracks in which the successions of mud and dust marked the seasons. But there are also persistent indications of a fluid property market, a considerable amount of construction, and other tell-tale signs of vitality. Land sales and purchases, leases, and subdivisions of various kinds figure prominently in the wills of many of the region's yeomen. Tool sheds and cottages, farmhouses, barns, mills, and the homes and workshops of local artisans are much in evidence in surviving bequests, as are sums of money for the poor, or for the fine stone churches which still visually dominate each village.

In the primarily agricultural economy of that age this area was one of the most prosperous in the realm. The chalky clay and loam supported large flocks of sheep as it had for centuries, while the well-drained, undulating fields fostered a bountiful production of grain. Taken together, the grain and sheep made

15

this region one of the few parts of the shire to enjoy a balanced farming economy. Unlike the pasture lands which predominated further east, or the grain areas in the central part of Suffolk which lay to the west, the production of the Hessett–Drinkstone area was not sent seaward: the wool went to the ravenous mills of Bury St Edmunds, and the grain to the unproductive fenland beyond.

While most local inhabitants paced out their lives on the roads and paths of the local area, or at best made a periodic trip to Bury, they kept in close touch with the wider world. Itinerant merchants peddling their wares, wool and grain merchants seeking new stores, brass-cutters and stone-masons hunting for work in the churches, errant friars and students coming down at term's end, and the still slow trickle of vagabonds which would broaden into a stream of 'sturdy beggars' in a not too distant age, all imparted to the village much of its characteristic energy.

Among the more ambitious and industrious families of the area were the Bacons. They were, never more than yeomen, despite later claims to the contrary, and their ranks had been thinned by migrations to greener pastures in previous decades. Yet by the accession of the Tudors they had prospered materially as farmers and minor landholders, and held a distinct niche in yeoman society. At the turn of the sixteenth century the family was divided into two closely related branches, each headed by a John Bacon.

When one of the John Bacons of Hessett died in 1513, he was able to bequeath over a thousand head of sheep, a piece of silver and a brass pot to his heirs, a considerable endowment to the parish church of St Ethelbert, and a separate building to be used as an alms-house for indigent parishioners.[1] His namesake and kinsman, paterfamilias of the other Hessett Bacons, died thirteen years earlier, and had been considerably less prosperous. The latter John had moved from Drinkstone to Hessett late in life, and left a few parcels of land in both villages as well as in the nearby hamlets of Tostock and Mildenhall. But he also left the balance of a sizeable loan to be paid off by his executors, and listed few household goods among his other bequests.[2] This John Bacon was Nicholas Bacon's grandfather.

Robert Bacon, Nicholas's father, was a second surviving son, and received a modest bequest which allowed him to retrace his father's footsteps and resettle in Drinkstone. Although he was evidently ambitious for his sons, Robert never achieved very much himself. He eventually left full-time farming to take up employment as the sheep-reeve for the abbot of Bury, but it cannot truthfully be said that he ever became prosperous by the standards of his peers. By the end of his long life he would leave only his modest properties in Drinkstone, a smallholding in Hessett, and a few sheepfolds and other parcels of property in the area. The remainder of his possessions consisted of a few head of horses, several goats and swine, a modest number of sheep, several bushels of corn and malt, some firewood, bedding, and six silver spoons: the last no doubt his prized possessions.[3] In sum, he seems to have led a comfortable enough life in the context of his surroundings, but, as a comparison of bequests makes clear, he hardly matched the acquisitiveness of contemporary and preceding generations of his clan.

Some time shortly after the turn of the century Robert took for his wife Isabel, the daughter of John Cage of Pakenham, Suffolk. It was a marriage of social equals, if not a small step up for the bride. The village of Pakenham lies barely three miles to the north-west of Drinkstone, a comfortable hour's walk. Very likely the young couple had known each other for years, and could only afford to marry when Robert gained his inheritance. Of Isabel we know only that she bore three surviving sons and two surviving daughters, and that she outlived her husband, who died after more than forty years of marriage.[4]

Nicholas was a second son, following Thomas and preceding James. Like their brother, Thomas and James eventually made their way to London where they met with considerable success. All three remained close for as long as they lived.

Thomas Bacon became a salter, and is mentioned as a London citizen and member of the Salters' Company by 1536.[5] He seems to have prospered both materially and politically, for he was able to join with his brother James by 1545 in the purchase of considerable holdings in Suffolk and was elected two years later as an M.P. for London.[6] Upon Elizabeth's accession he secured a new charter for his company with Nicholas's help, and was duly rewarded with the post of warden of the Company in the following year. After the death of his wife, the former Jane Mery, in 1563, Thomas withdrew from his activities and lived on for several years in comfortable but quiet retirement.[7]

James, the youngest of the three brothers, enjoyed similar success. He had become a member of the Fishmongers' Company by 1529, and he too entered local politics: he served as Alderman of Aldersgate Ward in 1568 and Sheriff in the following year. He engaged in various real-estate transactions with Thomas in London and Suffolk, and his will, proved in 1573, indicated substantial wealth in property as well as cash.[8]

In addition, Nicholas had two sisters, Anne and Barbara. They each married capable but unambitious yeomen from Bury, and their husbands – Robert Blackman and Robert Sharp respectively – were later taken on as bailiffs by the future Lord Keeper.[9]

According to tradition, Nicholas Bacon was born in 1509 while his parents were visiting the home of Robert Walsingham in Chislehurst, Kent.[10] Though accepted by Kentish historians and the *Dictionary of National Biography*, the story is suspect on several counts. Numerous sources, well described by Dr Simpson, point to the more logical date of 1510, which must now be preferred. A chance reference to 'children's day, my birthday' in one of Bacon's letters fixes the actual date more firmly: this is presumably a reference to childermas, December 28th.[11] Although the tradition regarding the circumstances of his birth seems odd enough to have been grounded in fact, absence of precise documentation and the weight of logic speak against it. In an age when travel was difficult and vacations rare among yeomen, it is hard to imagine that Robert and Isabel Bacon would be visiting friends in Kent so near to the appointed time of Isabel's confinement. One might even wonder whether they would have had such good friends a hundred miles distant. Robert Reyce, the Jacobean student of Suffolk lore, was no doubt correct in surmising that Nicholas was born in his parents' home in Drinkstone.[12]

The events of Bacon's childhood are little more certain than the circumstances surrounding his birth. The sharp contrast in life-styles between Robert Bacon and his sons indicates some measure of parental ambition. Whatever their hopes may have been for Thomas and James, there are plausible indications that Robert and Isabel envisioned their middle son in clerical garb.[13]

It must surely have been with his father's consent that Bacon entered the Abbey school at Bury, and his attendance there suggests an early source for his later theological leanings.[14] At the time Bacon entered, both the Abbey and its school had moved well into the forefront of the English ecclesiastical reform movement. Bury was one of the wealthiest abbeys in the kingdom, and had one of the few libraries which could boast of more than two thousand volumes – and that at a time when the University Library at Cambridge counted barely three hundred in its care. In recent decades the Abbey had gained many of the biblical commentaries and other writings of the Continental humanists, and it seemed to be very much in the mainstream of the ideological interchange between East Anglia and some of the Continental reformers of the day. By Bacon's time its progressive reputation had already become well established, and only a few years after he had moved on from Bury a group of English radicals in Continental exile – modelled on the Brethren of the Common Life and known as the Society of Christian Brethren – found the Abbey a ready outlet for the clandestine dissemination of its reformist writings.[15]

Bury seems to have served Bacon well as a preparation for the next stop in his educational progress. He went up to Cambridge in 1523 with a Bible Scholarship to Corpus Christi, then called Benet College.[16] Whatever progressive ideas may have been suggested to him at Bury were certainly susceptible to reinforcement in the iconoclastic and intellectually vibrant Cambridge of the 1520s.

By the second decade of the century Oxford had already begun to cede its reputation for intellectual vitality to its smaller and younger rival to the north-east. Erasmus himself, whose presence had done so much to foster that precocity, was able to write by 1516 that Cambridge ' ... may vie with the first schools of the age, and possesses men compared with whom those old teachers appear mere shadows of theologians.'[17]

There had been for some three years prior to Bacon's arrival an informal coterie of young scholars, clerics, and non-student radicals who met together at the White Horse Inn or at the Three Cranes to share their humanist or Lutheran views. This group comprised an impressive roster of England's early protestant martyrs, and included many future architects of the Anglican Settlement. A few of its members, like the acknowledged moderator Robert Barnes, were well-travelled clerics who had found their way to Cambridge. Others, like Matthew Parker, were scarcely more than adolescents and were probably farther from their homes than they had ever been before. The majority of the group came from Clare and Trinity Colleges, although Parker and the older Thomas Dusgate were at Benet with Bacon; several other colleges were represented as well. The devotional exercises of the group, as opposed to its discussions, were held at the newly-rebuilt Church of St Mary the Great, affiliated with and close to Benet College. Although the group was not likely to find comfort in the notoriety widely accorded its views, the knowledge of its activities appears to have been widespread in the environs of Cambridge, and access to its meetings cannot have been difficult.[18]

Nowhere in the few surviving accounts of the White Horse group can mention of Bacon be found, yet there are several factors which suggest such contact. It is hard to imagine that Bacon remained unaware of its meetings, which were held so close to the college in which he lived and studied for four years. Bacon's close and enduring friendship with Matthew Parker – a young but active member of the group – clearly dated from their student days at Benet.[19] Finally, it seems logical that Bacon's background at Bury should have made him receptive to its concerns. Thus Bacon may well have moved on the periphery of that radical circle, strengthening as he did so the protestant convictions which would guide him in later life.

If we take the word of the poet John Skelton, most of these young reformers were not renowned for attention to their studies, but Bacon evidently did not conform to the poet's image.[20] According to University records, he finished third among the baccalaureates in 1527, and had evidently developed the ability for sustained hard work which would mark his professional endeavours.[21] In fact, his obvious scholarly concerns may have kept him from more conspicuous attendance at the White Horse Inn.

Aside from this statistical indication of scholastic achievement, Bacon's future intellectual development suggests that his Cambridge experience established patterns of mind and character that ran deep, and remained with him always. His receptivity to the reformist ideals of the humanists, his sound background in the classics and his enduring interest in educational innovation seem largely to have had their roots in these formative years.

In many respects, Bacon never really grew apart from the University. His closest friends, Parker and Cecil among them, also remained closely associated with it, and allowed Bacon to stay abreast of Cambridge news even when he himself could pay only an occasional visit. The University provided him with support and remuneration for his legal services in the early stages of his career,[22] and later on it educated his sons.[23] He reciprocated as best he could: first as a well-wisher who considered it his spiritual home, and later as a generous benefactor who expressed his gratitude in the form of scholarships, books, and both funds and advice for building the Chapel at Corpus Christi.[24]

In view of his strikingly successful career at Cambridge, it is both puzzling and disconcerting that virtually nothing has come to light about Bacon's activities in the five years after he came down with his B.A. This is the age at which young men of Bacon's time and our own normally make the contacts and decisions which chart the course of their lives. Yet aside from the unsubstantiated, though plausible, assertion that he travelled abroad at some time during that period, the record remains devoid of hard evidence.[25]

What could the young graduate of Bacon's modest means have done that would have left no record for posterity? Almost certainly a return to Drinkstone would have been out of the question. Bacon had been away long enough to have strained his ties or cut them, and the home turf held little to attract him. It is far more likely that he spent much of those years in London, where his brothers were in the process of settling, and where the widest range of opportunities lay open. One suspects that his later familiarity with financial affairs may have had their origin in some commercial involvement during this period. Foreign travel may also have been a part of such experience. It is only certain that he finally chose to undertake a career in the law. The decision made, he probably undertook preparation at one of the Inns of Chancery. Such a course, rendered unverifiable by the lack of admissions registers for Bacon's era, was the normal avenue to study at the Inns of Court themselves. His ultimate admission to Gray's Inn suggests that Bacon probably prepared at Barnard's or the Staple Inn, which were already loosely affiliated with Gray's.[26]

When Bacon entered in 1532, Gray's Inn stood off by itself, north of cottage-lined Holborn, on Gray's Inn Lane. The latter, narrow to the present day, was then bordered intermittently by dwellings in the few hundred yards from Holborn to the Inn itself. Beyond the Inn buildings it was skirted only by the sparse hedgerows which bordered the pastures and fields on either side. One could still spend a pleasant morning following the lane north for a few miles to the hills of Hampstead and Highgate with little evidence of London's metropolis along the way. Even in the Inn's own fields, unconverted yet into the more formal walks of Francis Bacon's day, one could handily fill a hunter's sack with hare or grouse, or surprise the browsing deer.[27]

Despite these bucolic surroundings, Gray's Inn had become a whirlpool of intellectual activity by the turn of the sixteenth century. The hundred or so members of Bacon's day were tightly organized in a virtually autonomous and hierarchical society. At least in theory, they pursued their studies with a regimen that had no equal for its severity in the universities.

In addition to their apparent singularity and earnestness of purpose, the Inns had also become known for other qualities. Many were coming to see in them the foremost finishing schools in England, and those who attended or sent their sons with that in mind hoped that they might acquire something of the etiquette and social graces which were such a pronounced part of Inn life. Still others looked for the opportunity to engage in perhaps the most dynamic and progressive cultural expressions of the day, and indulged with gusto in the masques, revels and banquets which had also come to form an integral part of the Inn tradition.

Although the organization of the Inns was strictly hierarchical, the hierarchy was not at all static. Progress from one stage to the next came through competitive advancement, and was founded on rigorous application to the learning exercises of the Inn curriculum. Only through such progress might one advance from inner barrister to utter barrister – a step which normally took anywhere from six to nine years – and then to the successively more prestigious ranks of ancient, reader, and bencher. This last group included the grey heads who ruled over and set the standards of the Inn, and hence of the whole profession. From their ranks alone came not only the ruling officers of the Inn itself, including the all-important post of treasurer, but also the chief law officers of the realm: the serjeants, court barons and judges.[28]

Because of the variety of motives which prompted students to enter the Inns, and the natural inequalities of initiative, discipline and aptitude among the members, it is extremely difficult to describe the progress of a typical student, or to cite a particular span of years as the normal course of study. The majority never became ancients or benchers, and never intended to do so. Others worked to complete their studies and to go beyond them with the patience and diligence which have always marked successful careers. Thomas Cromwell took ten years to become an ancient. William Cecil took seven, while Francis Walsingham never made it at all.[29] Nicholas Bacon became an ancient in the remarkably short time of four years;[30] although, reverting to a more normal rate of advancement thereafter, he did not become a bencher until 1550.[31] Nor can it be said that Bacon skimped in his preparation to reach the coveted ranks in such a short time, for the qualities of education ideally imparted by the Inns of Court could hardly have been better exemplified than by his subsequent career. His natural abilities to think logically and speak forcefully, to organize and summarize, and to expound eloquently what was on his mind, were all brought to a rapid perfection by his Gray's Inn training.

II

The Young Lawyer, 1538-42

Thanks to the pioneering work of Douglas Bush, W. G. Zeeveld, Fritz Caspari and James K. McConica, one can no longer maintain that Henry's Reformation destroyed humanism or retarded the growth of learning in England.[1] It is now clear that in his search for willing polemicists and able officials, Henry made at least as many careers as he destroyed.

As a distinguished scholar of Cambridge and Gray's Inn and a known supporter of the Reformation, Bacon had a proven combination of talent and congenial ideas which would immediately recommend him to the King. In retrospect, it seems inevitable that the young lawyer should have come to the attention of the court. For his part, Bacon continued to devote much of his time and energy to the activities of Gray's Inn, but he was too able and ambitious to have considered it the summation of his professional career, and too impatient to await the judicial appointment which might in due course have come his way. By the late 1530s, his late twenties, he was casting about for a patron and an office.

He was not to be disappointed in his quest, for he soon came to the attention of those who controlled appointments to the Court of Augmentations. Because of its functions and the circumstances of its creation, the Augmentations was very much in the vanguard of the Reformation. Such a court was so carefully watched over by the King and Thomas Cromwell that its modern historian has found it difficult to imagine that any of its major offices were filled without their intervention or approval. It was therefore more than coincidence that the Augmentations served as a nursery for many young and able officials who would climb to greater heights in Tudor government: Richard Rich, Edward North, Richard Sackville and both Richard and Robert Southwell, like Bacon, were typical in this respect. Many of them were enjoying their first important post at Westminster, and most were brought in by Cromwell.[2] One of these, in all probability, was Bacon.

Bacon's name first appeared on the Court's payroll in the middle of 1538, two years after he had become an ancient at Gray's Inn. Although the exact nature of his services is not at first specified in the treasurer's account book, it is at least clear that he was not merely receiving the royal bounty in a gratuitous fashion from the coffers of the Court, as many did, but rather that he worked for his meagre stipend. For September of that year we find his signature at the bottom of the annual treasurer's account submitted and endorsed by Thomas Pope. Along with Rich, the Chancellor of the Court, Edward North, and two auditors, Bacon had scrutinized the account and found it satisfactory.[3] Another glimpse of Bacon still later in the same year finds him in the role of a young official out to impress his superiors. Having vetted a routine account of rents from the lands of the former Reigate Priory, Bacon questioned what might have been an irregularity in the collection of those revenues. He noted his query at the bottom of the account. The reply, written just below Bacon's note by Gregory Richardson, a deputy auditor, refers to Bacon as 'Mr Solicitor', and assures him, in an ever so slightly condescending tone, that in fact all was as it should have been with the Reigate account.[4]

This revealing exchange is the first reference to Bacon's actual function in the Court. But, although it was not unusual for an official to assume the duties of an office before receiving the official appointment, the title of Solicitor was clearly misapplied, perhaps facetiously, in this instance.[5] Firstly, Walter Henley, who had received the patent for the solicitor's office in 1537, and who may have shared part of his meagre revenues with Bacon as his deputy, did not finally yield the office until March 1540.[6] Secondly, in October 1538 Thomas Cranmer, almost certainly acting on Bacon's initiative, unsuccessfully urged Cromwell to appoint Bacon to the post of town clerk of Calais.[7] Bacon's attempt to find another post entirely at just this time clearly indicates the uncertainty of his position at the Augmentations.

Although Bacon continued to serve at the Augmentations for the next year and a half without an official position, it became increasingly clear that his tenure would shortly become more secure. In June 1539 his salary became fixed at £10 per annum, to be paid on a regular quarterly basis;[8] it was precisely half of Henley's annual salary, and there are indications that Bacon now regularly acted as Henley's deputy. A few months later Bacon had succeeded Henley altogether, and on January 3rd, 1540, he is even referred to as the Solicitor in a list of those who attended a ceremony to welcome the ill-fated Anne of Cleves as she approached London.[9]

Lastly, on March 18th, 1540, the patent of office for which Bacon had waited two years was finally enrolled in the records of the Court of Augmentations. The same device made explicit Henley's surrender of the office, and provided for him the higher post of Court's attorney. As if to reward the new Solicitor for his forbearance, his regular salary was raised on the following day from the £20 which Henley had enjoyed to a full £70 per annum.[10]

The Court of Augmentations was created in 1536 to preside over the confiscation of Church properties, to administer the transfer of such property, and to deal with the dispossessed residents. It was also intended to serve as a court of record for disputes arising out of any property or transaction within its jurisdiction. For its structure and procedure the Augmentations took as its model the Court of the Duchy of Lancaster and, to some extent, the Exchequer. Its ultimate direction rested with the chancellor, but leadership emanated as well from the three other chief officers: the treasurer, the attorney and the solicitor. Together, the four comprised the council of the Court, constituted its full judicial bench, and supervised the operations of the rest of the Court.[11]

Of the three fundamental jurisdictions of the Court – the administrative, financial, and judicial – the attorney and solicitor, as the legal officers, were most concerned with the last. According to statute both officials were to be learned in the law, and for good reason. Their function was originally described as ' ... the prosecutinge and settinge furthe of accions sutes and proces ... as also for thexamynacyon of matters to be examyned herde or determyned in this Courte.'[12] In addition, they were to serve the chancellor and other officials when called upon for their legal counsel in the hearing and determination of cases.

Although they were not specifically charged with attending actual hearings, their responsibilities seem to have made regular attendance virtually mandatory.[13]

While in most instances the functions of the attorney and solicitor were largely interchangeable, the former did take precedence over the latter in several ways. The attorney was referred to as the third officer, the solicitor as the fourth; their salaries were £20 apart; and when the crown figured as a litigant before the Court it was the attorney who represented it, the solicitor merely serving as his deputy.[14]

Translated into actual practice, the statutory description of the solicitor's role could involve him in nearly all aspects of a case. This may best be illustrated by an actual example. In a typical but undated case during Bacon's years at the Augmentations, four plaintiffs brought a bill of complaint against one John Yonge, of Petworth, Sussex, charging him with felling and selling a grove of trees which had stood on land held by the plaintiffs as tenants of the crown. As the land in question had been administered by the Court in the dissolution of Church lands, the case fell within its jurisdiction. Once the plaintiffs' bill had been received by the Court, Bacon examined it in detail, and listed at the bottom of the bill several 'Introgttoryes to be mynystryd to John Yonge upon our Informacon ageynst hym for Spoyle of Wood'. He included such points as the number of trees, their variety and their condition.[15]

In the meantime, Yonge submitted his written answers to the bill of complaint, and conceded nothing at all to his accusers. Bacon received this document and scrutinized it as he had done the first. At the bottom he wrote instructions to a clerk of the Court, whereby the latter was to strike a commission to certify the validity of Yonge's defence 'by the Feast of St Andrew's next'. This instruction was then endorsed by Henley, the Attorney, and by the two clerks who carried it out.[16] Although the remainder of this case has not survived, we may infer from similar instances that Bacon would have received, examined, and acted upon the commission's findings: he would either have thrown the case out of Court without a hearing or scheduled the hearing itself. In the latter event, Bacon may well have assisted in questioning the litigants, and would almost certainly have contributed to the final determination of the case by the full council of the Court.

This, then, with an infinite number of variations, was the nature of Bacon's regular work as Solicitor of the Court of Augmentations. From the frequent glimpses of his notations which one finds in the records of the Court – readily identifiable because of his unique handwriting – it is evident that Bacon attended diligently to his duties, and frequently took great pains even with the minor details of cases within his jurisdiction. These merits were not lost upon his colleagues, and it is no small measure of their esteem that two of the remaining three chief officers, the Attorney General Sir Robert Southwell and Sir Thomas Pope, entered into lifelong friendships with Bacon and remembered him in their wills.[17]

One of the more pleasant aspects of Bacon's new position was the free time he enjoyed between law terms, when the Court was not in session. Although some of his work pursued him from Westminster, he found a substantial amount of time to take on extra assignments in the Court which were not part of his regular duties. These were *ad hoc* functions which had to be performed if the Court was to run as smoothly as it did during regular sessions. Such missions, carried out singly or by a commission formed for the purpose, might involve taking inventories of lands within the Court's jurisdiction, investigating a litigant's claims in a pending case, or scrutinizing a questionable audit. Bacon did not assume these chores out of any particular bureaucratic zeal, but rather because he found them lucrative, and because in the fulfilment of his task he might well hit upon some information of personal value – particularly with regard to property for sale – or have an opportunity to use his influence in a way which might be profitable.

The Court paid well and surprisingly promptly for such missions, and included ample reimbursement for most expenses, including travel and diet, incurred along the way. Thus Bacon received £13 6s. 8d. on two different occasions for helping in the scrutiny of audits, £5 6s. 8d. for 'expenses about the surrender of Wynkfielde College' in November 1543, and £5 in the following year for helping the Earl of Lennox prepare his accounts for submission to the Court.[18] In addition to the sums paid out by the Court, it was a regular practice for a chantry or other clerical institution whose lands were about to be surveyed and confiscated to offer a sum for the due consideration of the officials concerned. It is hard to imagine, for example, that the Solicitor's part in surveying various lands in Huntingdonshire in 1541, or the College of St Katherine near the Tower in March 1546, went unacknowledged by the interests which were so precariously vested.[19] Yet records were rarely kept of such transactions, and Bacon seems not to have been an exception to that general rule. Such missions thus constituted a form of moonlighting which was in the best traditions of Tudor administrative practice: beneficial to the Court and to the office-holder and, at least some of the time, to the third party.

Taken together, and considered in relation to the many other ways in which a Tudor official could turn his post to his own advantage, it becomes apparent that Bacon had indeed been fortunate not to have secured the Calais post he had so recently sought. Yet it must be acknowledged that Bacon's solicitorship was no sinecure. It demanded considerable legal expertise and a larger burden of actual work than most bureaucrats of that age were wont to undertake. As had been the case at Cambridge and Gray's Inn, Bacon seems to have pulled his weight with diligence, and to have gained the esteem of his colleagues in the process.

Despite the assiduous performance of his duties at the Augmentations, Bacon's ambitions led him to seek other outlets during these years. The activity from this period which has generated the greatest degree of notoriety and curiosity is his share in the so-called 'Denton–Bacon–Cary Report' on the Inns of Court. Commissioned by Henry VIII some time between 1534 and 1547, most likely between 1538 and 1540,[20] the Report was never implemented, and in fact comes down to us only through the transcription of the seventeenth-century antiquary Edward Waterhouse.[21] So far removed are we from the details of its composition, in fact, that even Waterhouse's account seems to have reversed the original order of the Report's two sections. Even in this form, however, it is wholly worthy of the attention it has received. In its original form, it opened with a detailed description of the operation of the Inns and concluded with a provocative proposal for the foundation of a new Inn based to some degree on the model of the traditional four.

Assuming that the Report was commissioned after 1538,

Henry's choice of Bacon was quite logical. He had intimate knowledge of at least one of the Inns, his record of attainment at Gray's must have been familiar, and he seems to have been well versed in and sympathetic to the humanist ideas of his day which were so much a part of the Report; and he would already have demonstrated his merit in the King's service at the Augmentations. Although his fellow commissioners are more obscure to us, there is no reason to think that they were not even better known than Bacon in their own time. Nor should we infer that Bacon dominated the trio. Thomas Denton, a long-time member of the Middle Temple, was somewhat older than Bacon and had held a number of minor posts in government. Perhaps of greater importance to the work at hand, he was also an old friend and close associate of Thomas Elyot, whose own ideas on education are curiously similar to many of the Report's recommendations. Robert Cary seems largely to have founded his career on his ties to the Boleyns, although he too may well have had first-hand experience at one of the Inns.[22]

The first part of the Report consists almost entirely of an objective description of the operation of the Inns; their educational programmes, governmental practices and social conventions are treated in detail. It is the single most complete source of our knowledge regarding these crucial institutions, and from Waterhouse's time to our own it has been of great value.[23]

But it is the second and concluding part of the Report which has excited so much curiosity and speculation, for this is nothing short of a radical proposal for the establishment of a new and altogether different type of training institution. This fifth Inn was designed to provide for the systematic training of statesmen and diplomats, and of lawyers with a strong orientation towards such professions.

Its students were to be hand-picked by the crown, presumably from the ranks of the existing Inns of Court, and were to be supported in their studies at the expense of the crown. Although formal learning exercises were to be carried out in much the same fashion as in the existing Inns, the curriculum was geared towards a different end. The students were to perfect French and Latin as spoken languages, and were to be well versed in the Greek as well as the Latin classics – especially those works concerned with politics and statecraft. As with the regular Inns, the curriculum included extensive practical exercises carried on outside the study and lecture hall. But instead of attending moots and sitting in on the regular sessions of the central courts at Westminster, the students of the new school were expected to perform specialized and very practical services to the state. Some were to serve apprenticeships with English ambassadors abroad, where they would perform many of the routine affairs of such missions. Two students annually were to be sworn to impartiality by the privy council and entrusted with keeping an objective chronicle of the major events of the realm. Finally, students were to gain an appreciation of the martial arts through instruction and regular practice with the long-bow and cross-bow (the Report was hardly progressive in its concepts of military ordnance) so that they might go to war as knowledgeable observers and chroniclers of the action.

Although these proposals were never implemented, they are of extreme interest. They indicate the extent to which Henry explored humanist concepts of political education, and entertained views relating to the training of diplomats and statesmen which were quite advanced at that time anywhere outside Italy. Many of the proposals bear the seeds of concepts which did not fully attain fruition until relatively modern times. The idea of complete government support for education goes well beyond the Tudor practice of granting small stipends to promising students. Impartial collection of information and recording of events, while not at all alien to the judicial practices of Tudor England, were considerably more progressive concepts when placed in the context of other contemporary functions of government. They smack strongly of the rationalism associated with some of the more pragmatic statesmen and humanists of the early Tudor age, from practitioners like Wolsey and Cromwell to those like More and Starkey who were also concerned with political theory. In all, the Denton–Bacon–Cary Report stands out as a provocative and surprisingly sound departure from the traditional concepts of professional training.[24]

For Bacon himself, the opportunity to collaborate on the Report was a decided boon, both as a sign of the King's favour and as another feather in his cap. It is impossible to assess the extent of his own contribution, and a good case has recently been made for Thomas Denton rather than his two colleagues as the guiding spirit behind the more innovative proposals of the second part.[25] But it is also apparent that many ideas which appear in this Report crop up again in some of Bacon's later proposals for reform, both within and without the realm of education: his designs for reforming the common law and for rationalizing the finances of the crown, his proposed academy for the wards of the crown, and even the statutes he drew up for the grammar school at Redgrave, all seem, as we will see, to bear a similar imprint in many details.[26] To some extent, no doubt, his participation with Denton and Cary was an edifying experience which may have done much to form or sustain the bent for administrative and legal reform which became so evident in Bacon's later years. But it is also highly likely that the Denton–Bacon–Cary Report bears his mark in many of its recommendations, including the emphasis on the careful preservation of records of state, the obligation of the government to educate those who were likely to serve in office, and the importance of education as a mark of gentility.

Along with his other activities in these years, Bacon still somehow found the occasional opportunity to practise law as a private solicitor and attorney. Although he probably served several clients in these capacities, we have only a sporadic record of one such association. Cambridge, Bacon's ties to which never entirely disappeared, retained his services upon occasion from at least 1540, first as a solicitor and eventually as an attorney. In the first such instance he was paid just 6s. 3d. for what must have been a modest service, but in 1543 he was retained to help settle a sensitive dispute between the University and Sir Edward North, who was by that time Bacon's Chancellor in the Augmentations.[27]

Finally, this early phase of his career saw Bacon receive several modest boons from the crown in the form of appointments to sundry commissions. He served on commissions for sewers in Essex, Surrey, Norfolk and Cambridge in the early 'forties, and received from these sources modest but welcome remuneration.[28]

Apart from these first steps on the path to his long and full career, this same era affords us our first substantial awareness of the other side of Nicholas Bacon: his personal life and private concerns. At about the same time that he began to seek beyond the boundaries of Gray's Inn for a patron and a career, he felt himself far enough along in life to contemplate marriage and, somewhat more distantly, the life of a country gentleman. By the death of his first royal patron in 1547 he had realized the first of those aspirations and was about to realize the second.

Bacon's initial quest for a bride began with a false step, but it remains all the more intriguing for the mystery surrounding it. In October 1536, at the start of his ultimate year as an utter barrister at Gray's Inn, Bacon received a dispensation from the Court of Faculties to marry without banns a woman named Agnes Cosell.[29] Nothing at all has come to light regarding the intended bride; it is virtually certain that the marriage never took place. Among several possible explanations, it is entirely likely that the projected match was the outcome of a youthful indiscretion on Bacon's part. He or one of his brothers may have succeeded in buying Agnes off, thus allowing her to sink back into obscurity without jeopardizing Bacon's reputation.

In any event, a full four years elapsed before Bacon again thought seriously of marriage. By 1540 he had become acquainted with Jane Ferneley, a Suffolk girl of good background and capable manner. This match seemed agreeable to all concerned, and on April 5th William Ferneley gave his daughter's hand to Bacon at the family's parish church of West Creeting.[30] It was just a few months after he had secured the patent for his office at the Augmentations, and the timing probably indicates that this wedding was carefully planned in advance. Although he had waited somewhat longer than was usual to take a wife, Bacon at thirty chose well. Jane was everything that could be expected of a young official's wife. She bore Bacon three surviving sons and three surviving daughters, and reared them for as long as she was able.[31] She helped him establish his first country seat, at Redgrave, Suffolk, and in the few years that they lived there she ran it with a quiet efficiency which suited his exacting standards. Finally, and of critical importance, she brought with her family ties to the commercial elite of East Anglia, whose support was to be valuable to Bacon in many of his endeavours.[32]

Considering Bacon's professional and matrimonial position after 1540, it was perhaps only a matter of time before he embarked on another major pursuit, the purchase of property. Not only was this one of the few ways of investing capital, and still the safest, but it brought with it the accoutrements of the country gentleman which were a virtual necessity for someone with Bacon's professional aspirations. From shortly after his marriage until almost the end of his life Bacon undertook investment in real estate, and exhibited care in its management with a willingness bordering on zeal. Within a dozen years of his first purchases he had acquired a fine nucleus of property in his native Suffolk. Centred on his eventual seat of Redgrave, in the north central part of the shire, he came to hold much of the land in the surrounding areas of Botesdale, Rickinghall, Hinderclay, Wortham, Mellis St John, Walsham-le-Willows and Blackburn Hundred. A dozen or so miles to the south-east, and just a few miles from his adolescent stamping-ground at Bury St Edmunds, lay his sheep-folds at Ingham and the manor of Talbots in Timworth.[33]

Most of this property consisted of woods, meadows and arable land. Except for the latter two holdings, cultivation of grain and other crops rather than the raising of sheep was the principal concern.[34] Bacon administered the land in several ways, keeping little of it for his own use. In the main, he let it out on profitable terms, leaving the tillage to his tenants and the administration to his bailiffs. He retained Redgrave for his own seat, and began building his house there in 1545.

Although these purchases of the 'forties were costly and concluded in rapid order with money that was often borrowed, it is difficult to accuse Bacon of reckless expenditure. That was both contrary to his nature and unnecessary. His in-laws evidently underwrote some of these ventures, while his position at the Augmentations gave him advance notice of attractive properties coming up for sale, as well as an introduction to the fine points of finance and land management. An examination of his lands and their returns in rent, facilitated by Dr Simpson's assiduous research, indicates that, for the most part, Bacon had acquired sound properties which yielded handsome profits under the generally efficient management of his bailiffs and retainers. Only the occasional parcel was resold for ready cash, and speculation seems not at all to have been one of Bacon's motives for purchase. In a later stage of his life he would purchase specific lands for the establishment of his sons, but this did not count as a factor in his earlier acquisitions.

As Bacon did not begin to build at Redgrave until 1545, and as his duties kept him in the London area for most of the year, the newly-weds became urban dwellers in the first years of their marriage. A patent roll entry of 1545 still refers to 'Nicholas Bacon of London', and not until 1549 is there a reference to Bacon 'of London and Redgrave'.[35] Even that is probably the self-identification of an impatient proprietor, for Redgrave was not substantially complete before 1554, and only the last of Bacon's six children by Jane was baptized at St Mary's, Redgrave.[36]

At its completion, Redgrave Hall was not one of the great homes of the mid-Tudor era (see Figs. 1 and 2);[37] it would easily be surpassed by his later seat at Gorhambury, in Hertfordshire. Located midway between Redgrave and Botesdale, it nevertheless appeared from the main road pleasantly set off by a wide lawn and an impressive avenue of trees. The house itself had two full storeys and an attic, all of which appear to have been utilized, and was formed of three sides with an open court to the south. The ground floor included a hall of some forty feet in length, and also boasted a minstrel's gallery, two parlours, a school chamber, and five rooms associated with the storage and preparation of food. On the second floor the living quarters of the servants on the east wing, over the kitchen areas, were set well away from those of the family on the west wing. Unlike homes on a grander scale, it had neither a proper gallery nor much accommodation for visitors. The practical rather than ostentatious values of its builder are reflected in its general lack of ornamentation on the one hand and an ingenious system of running water on the other. Bacon's motto, *Mediocria Firma* ('Safety in Moderation'), carved above the main door as it would later appear over the Gorhambury mantle, is a fitting commentary on the home as well as the man.

For all its modesty, Redgrave meant a great deal to Bacon. It symbolized for him, as it does for us, his attainment of a new station in life, and a distinct break with the traditional status of his family. He took considerable pride in entertaining William Cecil there in 1557 and possibly Matthew Parker two years later.[38] Even after he left it to the care and eventually to the keeping of his son Nicholas, it continued to receive his close attention and concern.

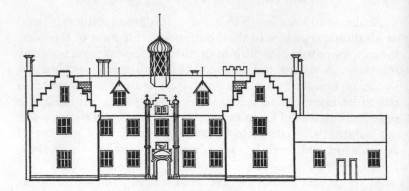

Figure 1 Reconstructed front elevation of Redgrave Hall, reproduced from E. R. Sandeen, 'The Building of Redgrave Hall, 1545–1554', *Proceedings of the Suffolk Institute of Archaeology* (1961), XXIX

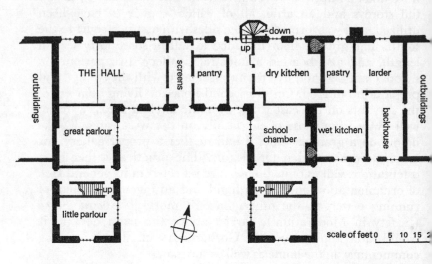

Figure 2 Reconstructed first-floor plan of Redgrave Hall, reproduced from E. R. Sandeen, 'The Building of Redgrave Hall, 1545–1554', *Proceedings of the Suffolk Institute of Archaeology* (1961), XXIX

In sum, these years marked Bacon's successful arrival as a man of stature, and heralded even greater accomplishments to come. His abilities and loyalty had been recognized by the most puissant patrons in the realm, and they marked him as one to be encouraged in the service of the state. In a more personal vein, he had embarked, after a false start and some delay, upon the domestic endeavours befitting his position. His land, family and new-found connections contributed measurably to his own fulfilment, and would facilitate his continued advance. Finally, the construction of Redgrave was a durable and tangible symbol of his arrival in the ranks of the landed gentry: a long journey, in status if not in miles, from his starting point.

III

The Noted Attorney, 1542-58

By the early 1540s Nicholas Bacon had come a long way from the young fortune-seeker who had been proposed for the town clerkship of Calais just a few years before. He had come to the attention of three of the most powerful men of the middle Henrician years, Cranmer, Cromwell and Henry himself, and had received the boon of good lordship from each of them. That patronage, and his own training and abilities, had served as the foundations of his fledgeling career, and seem to have gained for him free and ready access to the highest circles of London and Westminster society. As long as he steered a moderate course in his political opinions and kept clear of the harsh currents of political turbulence, Bacon might well anticipate even greater recognition and wider opportunities to come.

As a telling measure of the recognition which was now his, Bacon was returned as the Second Knight of the Shire of Westmorland in 1542, and took his place accordingly in the Parliament held in that year.[1] Election to parliament in itself, of course, was not necessarily an accurate indication of a person's standing at court; the returns of the House of Commons were filled for centuries with the names of local squires who were unknown both before and after their election. But Bacon's case was different. Not only did he sit as a knight of the shire rather than as a burgess, but he had no local interest or personal influence whatever in Westmorland, and can have come to stand there only through the patronage of a local magnate and, ultimately, through the strength of his reputation at Westminster.

During most of the Henrician era the political structure of Westmorland was dominated by two of the great north-country families, the Parrs and the Cliffords. William, Lord Parr and Ross of Kendal and the future Marquis of Northampton, firmly maintained his family's grip on the Barony of Kendal, roughly half the shire, during this era. Henry Clifford, First Earl of Cumberland, had fought off the Dacres and other challengers to secure hegemony in the other half, the Barony of Westmorland.[2] Although there are no extant returns for the shire in the two Parliaments prior to 1542, each family seems to have secured a shire seat in 1545, and most probably did the same in 1542. Sir James Laybourne (*c.* 1489-1548), who sat ahead of Bacon as First Knight of the Shire in that year, was a man of considerable stature in the area, and was sufficiently linked to the Parrs so that we may safely consider him to have been their candidate.[3] Although no other explanation for his unanticipated election seems plausible, it is at first difficult to see why Bacon should have been the Clifford choice. A more logical course of events would have seen Cumberland's eldest son, or at least one of his chief tenants, elected instead. But the Earl had a well-deserved reputation for a quarrelsome and uncharitable nature. By openly exploiting his tenants and generally neglecting his duties as warden of the West Marches, he lost the loyalty of many of the local gentry and the respect of his two sons. To bring already strained relations to breaking point, he remained loyal to Henry while his sons and tenants supported the ill-fated Pilgrimage of Grace.[4] His choice of Bacon, an obvious symbol of the forces of Reformation through his post at the Augmentations, may be interpreted either as the Earl's revenge upon his tenants, or as his earnest desire to restore the evidence of royal authority in a pronounced manner. Cumberland's long-standing friendship with the King – they had been adolescents together far into the age which is usually taken for maturity – could well have led him to awareness of Bacon's loyalty and availability. Nor, for that matter, is it inconceivable that Henry himself may have initiated the process of patronage for Bacon's seat, and the royal visit to Westmorland of 1541 would have provided an ideal opportunity for such a nomination.

Unfortunately, the paucity of records relating to the later Henrician parliaments prevents us from learning anything of value regarding Bacon's early career in the House. It would have been interesting to see if he took this opportunity to polish the rhetorical skills for which he later became famous, and to know whether he stood out as a spokesman for royal policy.

Within a year of Bacon's election, his erstwhile patron in

Westmorland passed away, leaving the earldom to his son and namesake. When writs for the next parliament were received, the Second Earl did what one would have expected of his father, and kept the nomination for Bacon's former seat in the family by naming his younger brother.[5] But Bacon had no grounds for disappointment. He had ventured nothing so far as Westmorland and the Cliffords were concerned, and in any event managed to find himself another seat.

Bacon's election as M.P. for Dartmouth, Devon, in 1545 seems at first glance to be every bit as illogical and unexpected as his experience in 1542. In the ten parliamentary elections held between 1529 and the death of Mary, he was the only Member to sit for Dartmouth who maintained neither residence nor interests in the area.[6] Almost certainly he was once again chosen for his loyalty to the crown, and perhaps also for the service he might be expected to render at his post in the Augmentations. The Dartmouth delegations of both 1539 and 1547 each had one official from the Court of Augmentations: John Ridgeway in the former case and Richard Duke in the latter.[7] Despite the fact that Bacon, unlike Ridgeway or Duke, had nothing to do with the Dartmouth area, it seems likely that his position in the same Court counted for a good deal. The same may be said for the strength of his associations at Westminster.

Several factors suggest John, Lord Russell, the future Earl of Bedford, as Bacon's patron in 1545. Having held almost no land at all in Devon prior to the dissolution of the monasteries, Russell received an enormous grant of land from Henry during the peak of the dissolutions, and the grant was administered through the Court of Augmentations. Such bounty was not simply a reward for Russell's loyalty: he was expected to assert his political hegemony in the shire, which was one of the less secure corners of the realm, and to keep its political activists in line. The most direct way to accomplish that aim was to control the major shire offices, and that is apparently what led Russell to put forward his candidate – conspicuously identified with the court of Westminster rather than any local interest – as M.P. for Dartmouth.[8]

Again, it is quite plausible that Bacon's name may have been suggested to Russell by the court itself, but this may not have been necessary. By 1545 Bacon seems already to have begun to move in the social circle of which Russell was a part when not in the King's service abroad. This group also included Queen Catherine (Parr), William Cecil, the Duchess of Suffolk, Roger Ascham, John Cheke, and Anthony Cooke, Bacon's future father-in-law. In view of these circumstances, it was quite understandable that Russell should have chosen Bacon, very likely a friend and in any event a known supporter of the King, and one whose position in the Augmentations might be very useful.

Although Bacon's contributions to both these sessions remain unknown to us, his service in parliament marks an important milestone in his career. As with his office in the Augmentations, the circumstances of Bacon's election to parliament in 1542 and 1545 speak eloquently of his reputation as a loyal and reliable upholder of the crown and the forces of Reformation. In both of these instances his nomination was obviously seen as a means of effecting some greater measure of royal authority in areas which had recently proved insecure. At the same time, moreover, he gained a wider recognition among those of a like mind, and thereby increased his chances for further advancement.

The last major step in Bacon's career prior to his elevation as Elizabeth's Lord Keeper came in January 1547, with his appointment as Attorney of the Court of Wards and Liveries. So far as they can be reconstructed, the circumstances surrounding this appointment are complex. Walter Henley, who had moved up to the Attorney's office in the Augmentations after Bacon succeeded him as Solicitor, had become so infirm with age and near-blindness that he could no longer fulfil his office. Although logically Bacon should have succeeded Henley in this second office, the changing of the guard came in an unexpected way. Richard Goodrich, Bacon's friend and colleague at Gray's Inn, was brought over from his post as Attorney of the Court of Wards to succeed Henley, and Bacon went instead to fill Goodrich's shoes at the Court of Wards. Goodrich and Bacon seem to have begun their new offices in the early autumn of 1546, but Bacon's patent for the office was not issued until January 2nd, 1547, and not delivered for another ten days.[9]

The Court of Wards was not officially created until 1540, but its functions were essentially as old as the custom of wardship itself, and much of its machinery had actually been set in motion under Henry VII.[10] Simply put, the Court dealt with the many lands and heirs left by deceased tenants-in-chief by knight's service of the crown. When such a tenant died, both the minor heirs and the lands passed into royal custody and were administered by the Court until the heirs came of age. In addition to its administrative and fiscal functions, the Court of Wards served as a court of record for transactions involving wardships, and as the court of first instance in adjudicating disputes arising from such transactions. Almost all of its judicial business may be classified under three headings: actions brought by the crown against apparent violators of the wardship system, actions brought by individual plaintiffs against the crown or a guardian, or actions brought by the Court as legal guardian, to protect the interests of the wards in its care.

Once he became installed in his new office, Bacon had every right to feel at home, for, like the Court of Augmentations, the procedure and structure of the Court of Wards and Liveries were based on the model of the Duchy Chamber of Lancaster. His new duties as Attorney were similar in almost every way to those he had performed as Solicitor to the Court of Augmentations. The only major difference was that the attorney of the Wards and Liveries performed the duties which were shared by the attorney and the solicitor in the larger Court of Augmentations.

In addition to his part in judging cases argued before the Court, where he was the chief legal authority, Bacon usually served as Attorney in the more literal sense, i.e. as an advocate before the Court. In most such instances, Bacon spoke for the interests of the crown and, when the Court acted in litigation on behalf of one of its charges, it was Bacon as Attorney who would see the case to its conclusion. He might be called upon to perform the dual function of advocate and adjudicator: a delicate task for a man of Bacon's ethical concerns.

The lot of the crown ward had never been happy or even just, and it is much to Bacon's credit, and perhaps among his most significant actions at the Court of Wards, that he demonstrated an active and sustained interest in the well-being of the wards of the crown. His 'Articles devised for the bringinge up in vertue and lerninge of the Quenes Majesties Wardes', first drawn up in the reign of Mary and resubmitted in the more hopeful climate of her sister's reign, was, according to one recent historian of the Court, 'one of the rare indications throughout the history of the Court of any serious interest in the welfare of the wards'.[11]

A telling sidelight concerning Bacon's chagrin at the way in which the wards were brought up came when he considered the prospect of his own children becoming wards of the crown. So distasteful did this possibility appear to him that he later received permission from Queen Mary to circumvent the usual process whereby they would become wards of the crown if they were still minors at his death. Mary granted him special permission to name his brothers Thomas and James guardians instead; they were to raise the children and administer Bacon's lands held of the crown until the children were of age to attain their rightful liveries. Not until 1603, when Robert Cecil was Master of the Wards, did this become a more general practice.[12]

Although it is again difficult to describe the course of a normal case before the Court of Wards, it is frequently possible to observe Bacon's actions in the everyday judicial business of the Court. Clearly, the post was no sinecure, but until the last years of his tenure, when he was considerably burdened by his greater office at the Chancery under Elizabeth, Bacon suffered no deputy to assist him in his duties. He normally attended the Court six days a week during term time for its regular sessions. On four of those days, Monday, Tuesday, Thursday and Saturday, he would generally be engaged in regular hearings. Aside from his partisan duties on behalf of the crown or one of its wards, Bacon's participation at hearings also entailed close attention to the progress of each case as it came up, and a share in drawing up the decrees which announced the determination of cases.

But the more time-consuming and difficult part of Bacon's job did not come on hearing days, for on Wednesdays and Fridays he would have to contend with almost all of the paperwork which came to the desk of the Attorney. Such work included the scrutiny of bills and defences submitted in writing prior to the hearing of a case, the scheduling and planning of hearings, and the writing of the many internal orders which activated the machinery of the Court. The evidence for Bacon's fulfilment of these tedious functions leaves one with a strong sense of admiration for his thoroughness in attending to detail and for his precision in obtaining the most proper form and wording of each order.

In one typical instance, concerning the wardship of one

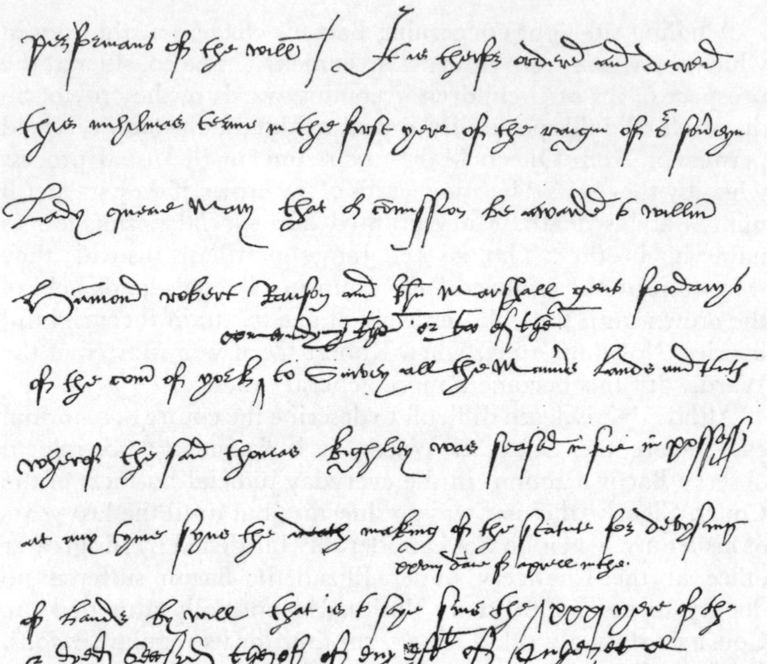

Figure 3   A sample of Bacon's handiwork in a document from the Court of Wards; P.R.O., Wards 1/2/File 51. Side A: Bacon's insertions may be seen between lines 4 and 5, 8 and 9, and following line 13.

Side B: Bacon has deleted the entire paragraph and substituted his own version.

Lawrence Righley of Yorkshire, Bacon scrutinized with close attention an undated order of the Court establishing an *ad hoc* commission to investigate charges involving a concealed wardship.[13] Such an order was a regular and routine procedure used to facilitate the progress of a case, and may even have been drawn up by a clerk of the Court on Bacon's verbal instructions. But here the Attorney took the original order – less than two sides of a sheet of paper – and made on it three major and lengthy additions and a number of smaller corrections which completely changed the nature and wording, if not the intent, of the document (see Fig. 3). What Bacon did was to transform loose and general statements into extended, legalistic, and very precise descriptions of the desired action. Although his duties obviously did not admit of such care with all of the routine documents emanating from the clerks in his office, a random sampling of such orders for one year during the reign of Philip and Mary indicates that Bacon gave such attention, probably on a spot-check basis, to between a fifth and a quarter of even the most routine inter-office orders. Although these qualities cannot have particularly endeared him to those who worked under his authority, they certainly indicate his serious approach to office, and the diligence which he exercised in the fulfilment of his duties.

By modern standards the salaries of Tudor officials were ludicrously small, when indeed they existed at all, but Bacon did not fare badly. The attorneyship of the Court of Wards brought with it potential rewards which could far exceed its official remuneration of £90 per annum. There were fees, gifts and other perquisites of office which pertained to some extent to every Tudor official, and which, in the absence of salaries in the modern sense, served as the prime lubricant in the machinery of Tudor government. Of these rewards Bacon surely had a large share, for the nature of his office made it a natural bottleneck in the flow of such gifts. But the business of wardships itself was a lucrative one for those who cared to indulge. The purchaser of a wardship was normally entitled to rents and other income from the lands of the ward, the choice of spouse for an unmarried ward, or the sale of his marriage. Most of the officers of the Court of Wards engaged in such purchases, and so did any number of people who were in no way connected with the Court.

But the officials themselves often had an advantage in hearing first of wardships which might come up for sale, or in being able to assess the hidden values of a wardship through their inside information. Although Bacon joined with his colleagues in making such purchases, he had also bought a few wardships before coming to his post, and continued to purchase them after he relinquished it. If one considers that no less than five out of the total of his twenty-one wardships concerned young relatives towards whom he felt some familiar responsibility, and that he was not interested in reselling these wardships for profit, it becomes evident that Bacon took but moderate advantage of this opportunity. In a typical year at this stage of his career he probably received about £50 a year from the lands of those wardships in his charge, and from time to time an additional sum from such emoluments as the sale of a ward's marriage.[14]

In addition to the various receipts which accrued from his office at the Wards, Bacon continued to accept *ad hoc* or short-term appointments outside his official duties, which doubtless augmented his coffers even more. Although there are no indications that he pursued his private legal practice in this period, we do find Bacon's name on commissions of the peace for Suffolk and Cambridge in 1547 and for Suffolk alone in 1549,[15] and on commissions to carry out inquisitions post mortem in Norfolk and Suffolk in 1548,[16] to collect part of a parliamentary subsidy in Suffolk in 1550,[17] and to 'enquire of heresies' in 1552.[18] It is interesting to note that these appointments came under Northumberland as well as the Duke of Somerset: an indication that Bacon managed to avoid the vagaries of partisan politics at this stage in his career.

Throughout these years Bacon still managed to maintain a studious interest in the law and an active presence at Gray's Inn. A full three years before his election to the rank of bencher in 1550, his legal acumen was acknowledged by the designation of 'studiant at the Lawe' attached to a quarterly royal stipend in support of his further studies.[19] The implication of that designation far exceeds its face value, for, in the absence of the more hallowed and formal terminology of the university tradition, the Inns used such seemingly commonplace descriptions to denote men of recognized accomplishment in the law. Thus, for example, in Christopher St Germain's contemporary classic

Dyaloges … between a Doctour of divinitie and a Student in the lawes of England, the two figures of the title interact entirely as equals in their accomplishments rather than as superior and subordinate as the title would imply. In addition, if the infrequent appearance of that designation in the usual sources is any indication, it was not a title lightly bestowed.[20]

A further testimony to Bacon's learning came in November 1548, when William Stanford, the Attorney for the Court of General Surveyors, dedicated to Bacon his *Exposicion of the Kinges Prerogative collected out of the great abridgement of Justice Fitzherbert*. The nature of Fitzherbert's treatise, a fundamental document in the literature of prerogative law, had obvious relevance to Bacon's post at the Wards, and was one of the reasons for its dedication. But a fuller explanation of that generous act accompanied the dedication and – like the rest of the work – is known to us through the second edition of 1567. In this explanation, Stanford pointed out that Bacon had studied Fitzherbert directly, and had grown 'above others' in 'the great learnynge that you have'. Further, the author readily acknowledged his own reliance on Bacon's judgement in the year when they had worked closely together as Attorney of the Court of General Surveyors and Solicitor of the Court of Augmentations respectively.[21] This rich testimony is all the more valuable for its apparently gratuitous and sincere motives. When he wrote it, Stanford enjoyed an office which was much on a par with Bacon's, and in fact he seems to have risen much faster in his own career.[22] Clearly there was no hope of securing a patron by means of the dedication, for there appears to be no way in which Bacon could have provided such service to his friend.

As befitted someone of such recognized stature, Bacon was elected by his fellow benchers to the paramount post of treasurer in 1552. He held that post alone for three years, and then jointly with the equally prominent Gilbert Gerrard for an indeterminate number of years thereafter.[23] True to the record he had established in his other offices, Bacon fully accepted the duties and responsibilities of what could, in less diligent hands, have become more or less a ceremonial position. Within a month of his election, and probably largely at Bacon's instigation, we find the Inn selling off most of the clerical vestments and other relics of the old faith which had been lingering in its ante-rooms since the Reformation. Even at Mary's accession in the following year the Inn was notably slow to restore such furnishings. Nor can that lethargy be passed off as mere lack of direction, for at the same time the Inn embarked on a massive building programme in which the considerable sum of £863 10s. 8d. was dispensed over the next four years for the reconstruction of the great hall and other additions and repairs.[24] Both the reluctance with which the vestments of the old rite were restored and the zeal with which this construction programme was undertaken bear the clear imprint of Bacon's incumbency.

As events transpired, Bacon was indeed fortunate to have enjoyed such a sound position in the world of the Inns, and the added security afforded by his post at the Wards, for this stage in his career embraced the troubled mid-passage of the Tudor dynasty, and could well have put a permanent stop to his advancement. But because his attorneyship was not an office of partisan political significance, and because Bacon wisely refrained from making it one, he found it a safe haven in the storms of the Edwardian and Marian eras.

These years also embraced a personal crisis which, if shorter in duration, was much more immediate in its impact. Some time shortly after his order for new gloves for her in October 1552, his wife Jane died, leaving him with six children. Though Bacon was of sufficient means not to have to bear the actual burden of their care and feeding, his sudden widowerhood inevitably posed problems: his children were all under the age of twelve, and one was virtually a babe in arms. It was obviously desirable for him to marry again soon, and, realistic in his personal as well as in his professional life, Bacon had taken a new wife by February 1553. Nor was he to regret his haste in marrying Anne, the daughter of Anthony Cooke of Gidea Hall, Essex, and Westminster.[25]

As a friend of the senior Cooke, and of William Cecil, who had married the eldest of the Cooke daughters just a few years before, Bacon had no doubt known Anne for some time before he was in a position to consider her for his spouse. Chances are that Cecil himself urged the match. In any event, this marriage proved at least as fortunate for Bacon as had his first, albeit in a different manner. The difference, moreover, is worthy of exploration, for it serves as a yardstick for Bacon's progress in the span of scarcely a dozen years.

Whereas Jane had brought with her alliances to important merchant families in East Anglia – in-laws whom Bacon was fortunate to acquire in 1540 – Anne's family travelled in decidedly more prestigious circles, and proved of even greater value to Bacon. Anthony Cooke, and for that matter Cecil, had been associated with the humanist clique surrounding Catherine Parr and the nursery of the young Prince Edward. When the boy acceded to the throne, Cooke and Cecil stayed on: Cooke as a non-titled fixture in the household circle and Cecil as a member of Somerset's personal entourage and then as a privy councillor.[26] Nor did the ties of the Cooke marriage stop there. By the time the rest of Cooke's five daughters had been married off, Bacon and Cecil had gained as brothers-in-law the fashionable London goldsmith Sir Ralph Rowlett, the courtier-humanist-ambassador Sir Thomas Hoby, the diplomat Sir Henry Killigrew, and – after Hoby's death – Lord John Russell, son of the Second Earl of Bedford. One may marvel at Cooke's skilful matrimonial engineering until one realizes the remarkable qualifications of his daughters. Educated in the surroundings of Prince Edward's household by their father and such family friends as John Cheke and Roger Ascham, they were as well trained as any women in England, royal or otherwise. They were also thoroughly at home in the conventions of Westminster society, which was as great an advantage in securing suitable marriages as their cultivated intellects.[27]

Anne herself was probably the best educated and proved to be the most intellectually active of this remarkable brood. She attained fluency in several languages and has been judged even in our own day as one of the foremost Latin translators of her century.[28] She was also well versed in theological matters, and even before she became Bacon's wife at the age of twenty-five she had translated from Latin into English the sermons of the distinguished Continental reformer Bernardino Ochino.[29] Yet it is for her activities in Elizabeth's reign that Anne is best remembered. Siding wholeheartedly with the forces of the Reformation, she provided the masterful translation of Bishop Jewel's *Apologia Ecclesiae Anglicanae*, published in 1564,[30] and then in her own actions went far beyond the moderate settlement which Jewel had defended. By the 1570s she had begun to patronize and shelter at the family home a veritable roll-call of outspoken puritan and presbyterian dissidents, and was recognized for her deeds in the dedications and letters of the Elizabethan radical elite.[31]

Personally, Anne seems to have been every bit as formidable as her activities would suggest. Her extant letters, many of them to her sons Anthony and Francis, bear this out.[32] Friends and family alike looked to her for support, and no doubt Bacon himself had occasion to seek her counsel. When Nathaniel, Bacon's second son by Jane Ferneley, married the ill-trained and illegitimate daughter of Sir Thomas Gresham, he sent the poor girl to his step-mother for the proper finishing.[33] When Matthew Parker angered his old friend Bacon by condemning the latter's open support for his avowedly puritan chaplain, he approached Lady Anne to smooth over the troubled waters.[34] And when her own two beloved sons Anthony and Francis followed in their father's footsteps to Gray's Inn, she warned them so sternly to shun the mums and revels for which Inn life had become known that her admonitions are still recalled in the lore of the Hon. Society. It is said that during the annual revelry known as 'Call Night' Lady Anne's ghost may be seen to ' ... come down as opiate from the catalpa tree that ... Francis planted. Gliding along the grass, alone and palely loitering like Keats's hero, she wrings her lily-white hands and magnolia-like brow. "Alas they mum! They sinfully revel," she moans ... ' and then presumably disappears for another year.[35]

The contrast between Bacon's two wives is thus quite striking, and the difference between them mirrored and complemented his own progress. The young official of the early 1540s needed the acquiescent domestic support which Jane could offer; he had little time for the more intellectual pursuits in which he would later indulge. But by the time of Jane's death, Bacon's status and needs had changed. He was by then an established official who had made his mark in two successive offices, had sat twice in parliament, and was well known not merely to a few patrons at court, but had many friends among the privy councillors, courtiers, and intellectuals of the day. Where he had been the novice investor seeking to purchase a few parcels of land in Suffolk, he now counted his holdings in six other shires – Norfolk, Essex, London, Middlesex, Somerset and Dorset – as well.[36] In this context, his marriage was remarkably apt. Anne fitted comfortably into Bacon's changing lifestyle, and actively helped him to enhance and cultivate his intellectual outlook as perhaps no one else could have done.

Most of this was of course still in the future at the time Bacon took Anne for his bride, but within weeks of the marriage she was called upon to prove her mettle in highly dramatic circumstances. No sooner did the flurry of Bacon's personal affairs subside in the spring of 1553 than a matter of grave concern for his career loomed ominously ahead. Although his apparent desire to place duty before the temptations of political opportunism had seen him safely through the turbulent reign of Edward, Bacon received a full-blown scare when Northumberland's house of cards began to tremble in June and July of that year. Having established a reputation for support of the Reformation which he could scarcely deny, Bacon had serious grounds for apprehension at the impending accession of Mary Tudor. As befitted one of his legal training, Bacon seems never to have doubted the inevitability or legality of Mary's succession, but that conviction hardly made any easier the last weeks of Edward's reign. In his fears, moreover, he was joined and considerably outdone by Cecil. So closely were the fortunes of these old friends and recent brothers-in-law bound, and so strong was their loyalty to each other, that the story of either during this crisis must also become the story of both.

As Northumberland's Principal Secretary, Cecil was more directly on the firing line than Bacon.[37] Despite his open protests, he was compelled in early June to affix his name to the document which altered the succession in favour of Jane Grey. Northumberland's only concession had been to allow Cecil to sign as a witness to the other signatures rather than as an actual signatory himself, but in the eyes of those who might challenge that fine distinction, and in his own mind, he had done the wrong thing. Whatever the outcome of the succession issue might be, Cecil was hard pressed to find cause for optimism. Given control of the crown and the realm, Northumberland could scarcely forget Cecil's reluctance, nor could Mary under similar circumstances deny the fact of his signature. Fearing the worst while the Duke still held sway, and yet eschewing the ready course of flight, Cecil prepared for the imprisonment which he fully expected would ensue. On June 13th he entrusted to Bacon's care a dramatic explanatory letter for his wife Mildred.[38]

Much to his joy and surprise, of course, the blow never came, and Cecil remained in office through the death of the King on July 6th and through the proclamation of the pretender four days later. But having escaped the shoals of Scylla, he now had to face the maw of Charybdis. Although he could not conscionably rally to Jane, he still feared that Mary would think him a traitor. When Northumberland went forth via Cambridge to capture Mary, Cecil and his fellow dissidents on the council seized their opportunity. Meeting at Baynard's Castle in London, they agreed to proclaim Mary as Queen, and to hope for the best if she won. Although a few of them went off on their own to profess their allegiance in person, several delegated Cecil to perform that duty for them.[39]

When he caught up with Mary, probably at Ipswich on June 20th or 21st, he found a pleasant surprise awaiting him which greatly lightened the burdens of his mission: Anne Bacon sat in attendance on the Queen, and Mary had told her that 'she thought very well of her brother Cecil'.[40] Since delivering Cecil's message to his wife several weeks before, Bacon too had been compelled to come to terms with events, and the route of Mary's flight had permitted him no luxury of delay. Having been in southern Hertfordshire when word came of Edward's death, Mary seems to have fled via Cambridge, Newmarket and Bury St Edmunds, through Thetford and across the Norfolk border to Kenninghall. Both that route and her subsequent move from Kenninghall to Framlingham several days later placed her within a few miles of Bacon and his new bride at Redgrave. It could not have been many days after her arrival at Kenninghall on July 8th that Mary received a visit and vow of homage from Anne and Nicholas Bacon, and the former stayed on in the royal retinue at least until Cecil met up with it nearer London.[41]

Bacon's delicate mission to Mary, in which he represented Cecil's interests as well as his own, marks his first direct involvement in the risky world of partisan politics. In the successful completion of his task he was greatly aided by his wife. Not only did Anne accompany him in joining the royal party and professing loyalty to Mary, but she swallowed her Protestant pride and stayed on as a Gentlewoman of the Queen's Privy Chamber.[42] It was a stern test of personal mettle for both Bacons, and one which they passed with considerable aplomb.

Although a good many of their colleagues and friends chose the alternative of flight and an uncertain future abroad at Mary's accession, Bacon and Cecil determined to stick to their careers as well as they could under circumstances which were at best adverse. Mary accepted Bacon's willingness to serve with no apparent reservations, and retained him at his post in the Court of Wards. During the remainder of her reign Bacon avoided as far as he could any further involvement in partisan politics. He conformed outwardly to the Marian reaction, and went about his affairs in a businesslike and unobtrusive manner. In addition to his duties at the Wards he served in the coveted but wholly non-political post of treasurer at Gray's Inn (despite the ban on married men holding office),[43] managed to secure a place on the commission of the peace for his native shire of Suffolk in 1554,[44] and was named to a commission of oyer and terminer in the same shire in that year.[45]

Only in his private life, well removed from the environs of the court, was he able to pursue the ideals and thoughts which were true to his convictions. Although allegations that Bacon and Cecil conspired with Anthony Cooke and other Protestant exiles to co-ordinate a shadow government abroad seem wholly fantastic,[46] Bacon did remain in close touch with his father-in-law, and helped support him in exile by carrying out several financial transactions on his behalf.[47] Both Bacon and Cecil corresponded with a few other exiles besides Cooke, and may well have met, as John Strype reported, in secret prayer meetings at the home of Richard Morison.[48] Aside from these pursuits of conscience, Bacon also found a good deal of time to indulge in intellectual and other personal affairs which he had long been compelled to neglect.

Thus, at least for Bacon, the years of Mary's reign meant a period of marking time. But his preference for emulating the willow rather than the oak cannot be looked upon as one of cowardice or weakness in character: it proves quite the opposite. His outlook and guarded participation in Marian society demonstrates that he had perfected in his own mind the Stoic maxims of moderation and circumspection which later served to characterize and guide his generation of statesmen. Apprenticed in the craft of politics during the turbulent reigns of Henry and Edward, Bacon and his contemporaries had received a first-hand opportunity to witness the practical limits imposed upon personal ambition and the likely fate of those who lusted after power. They also learned the value of a viable state, delicately balanced on the fulcrum of a legitimate and stable succession. Through their observations and experiences they gained a deep insight into the political process of those years, and drew from it an unwritten code of behaviour which would guide them when their own turn to wield power came in the reign of Elizabeth.

In Bacon's case as in others', the development of this *politique* frame of mind followed naturally from his personal background. As a 'new man' who had few resources upon which to fall back in times of adversity, he was bound to follow the Stoic maxims of his 'Senecke',[49] and to trust for his well-being in the clemency of the monarch. As a student and upholder of the English legal tradition he could in no way bring himself to accept interference with a rite as sacred as the succession. Finally, as a government official with a vivid sense of duty, he steadfastly refused to abdicate his responsibilities. Thus, despite the difficulties he found with her policies, he accepted Mary's legitimacy and stuck to his post in her service. Had she outlived him he would no doubt have died in possession of that office, and would have left little more behind than the reputation of a diligent official. As it happened, he outlived her, and joined with a few others in applying the sense of his personal motto, *Mediocria Firma*, to the political and moral values which characterized much of the Elizabethan era.

IV

The Second Age

A mynde I have suche as it is
And frutes thereof bothe yonge and olde,
Not pretyous muche nor all amisse,
But as they be loe here them holde:
I wisshe them better a hundrethe folde:
Ye recreatyons of bothe myne ages,
Goe and sarve hur as humble Pages.*

When Nicholas Bacon wrote in this poem of 1557 or 1558 of the 'recreatyons of bothe myne ages' he may perhaps have referred to his youth and subsequent manhood, but it is considerably more likely that he meant it as a commentary on his life before and after the two momentous events of his forty-third year: the accession of Mary Tudor, and his second marriage, to the recipient of this poem, Anne Cooke. The former provided the occasion, and the latter the intellectual support, for this second age.

During the five-and-a-half years of Mary's reign Bacon continued in his office at the Wards, but despite his open show of conformity to the Roman rite, he found that his Protestant reputation and his own convictions precluded his further advance during that era. But being a vibrant and active man, and having a substantial and secure income to sustain him, Bacon was not content merely to carry out his duties at the Wards during term time and then sit idly by the Redgrave hearth for the rest of the year. Instead, he took advantage of his relative inactivity to cultivate the more personal and intellectual pursuits which mark this second age. And so absorbed did he

* From 'Made at Wymbleton in his Lo: greate sickenes in the laste yeare of Quene Marye' (Stanza 8), in *The Recreations of His Age* (Oxford, 1903).

become in such endeavours as educational planning, classical studies and architectural, scientific and literary patronage, that even with the resumption of a fully active political career under Elizabeth, he kept them up to the end of his days.

Bacon's interest in these pursuits was deeply rooted in his own education, particularly in the formal training and informal ambiance of Cambridge and Gray's Inn. But that background alone could hardly have sustained for very long what obviously remained avid concerns, and it is to Bacon's associates in the intervening years that we must look for the more immediate influences upon his thought. In the late Henrician era and throughout the Edwardian reign, these would almost certainly have included the friends and associates of Cecil and Anthony Cooke – Roger Ascham, John Cheke and Richard Morison among others – as well as many of his learned friends from Gray's Inn: Richard Goodrich, Gilbert Gerrard, Robert Beaumont, William Stanford, and later on possibly the poet George Gascoigne, to whom he would soon be related by marriage. As virtually all of these associations predated his second marriage, it is clear that Lady Anne's role in Bacon's cultural enterprise was complementary rather than instigatory, but her own abilities no doubt made her all the more desirable when Bacon came to choose a second wife.

Probably the most basic of Bacon's cultural pursuits was his fondness for the classics. When the rhetorician George Puttenham came upon Bacon in his study poring over a volume of Quintilian, he found him at a characteristic and pleasurable task, although doubtless most of his contemporaries were content to relegate that noble Roman to the dim memories of grammar school training.[1] During periods of illness, Bacon took great delight in Anne's reading to him from her 'Tullye' and 'my Senecke'.[2] In fact, so great was his admiration for the ideas and style of Seneca that his chosen motto, *Mediocria Firma*, is almost certainly taken from one of the choruses of that philosopher's *Oedipus*, and, as Dr Elizabeth McCutcheon has recently pointed out and discussed in some detail, the Latin *sententiae* which Bacon chose to adorn his gallery walls at Gorhambury were largely Senecan in composition and substance.[3] He turned a poem for Anne in the manner of Horace, with whose works he was eminently familiar,[4] and appears to have supported by his

57

patronage a major translation of Virgil into English.[5] Nor were his literary tastes confined to the Latin classics. He cherished his Saxon Pentateuch,[6] and avidly collected legal manuscripts as well.[7] Presumably at the urging of Matthew Parker, he donated seventy volumes of his own library to Cambridge.[8]

Even that gesture, common enough in itself, came with a special flourish. In casting about for a means of enhancing his donation, Bacon hit upon the notion of a personal bookplate to adorn the volumes and had one designed for the occasion. Bacon's plate of 1574, bearing his arms and motto, and the rather pedestrian inscription: '*N Bacon eques auratus & magni sigilli Angliae Custos librum hunc bibliothecae Cantabrig dicavit*, 1574,'* is the first dated bookplate known to have been used in England, and one of the first known outside the German states where the custom had originated late in the fifteenth century (see Plate 1). Both before and for long after the time of Bacon's plate, in fact, German humanists and culture-conscious princes were the major and practically the only patrons of the bookplate designer's art, in which they employed such eminent practitioners as Albrecht Dürer, Lucas Cranach the Elder and Hans Holbein.[9] Bacon must have learned of the practice through some contact with the German fashion, and may even have employed a German to design his own plate. He evidently continued to use the plate, albeit without the commemorative inscription, for the volumes remaining in his possession. This milestone in the traditions of book collecting underscores Bacon's receptivity to Continental cultural trends and indicates that he was not content merely to adopt the standard cultural accoutrements of the English landed gentleman, but rather sought to exercise his own tastes and creativity.

We also know that, although participation as a theorist or practitioner was beyond his competence, Bacon recognized the value of the sciences, and extended his efforts in their support. Thomas Digges, himself a scientist of some note, fondly recalled Bacon in lengthy and learned conversation with his father, Leonard Digges, whose work on optics and mensuration was carried out with Bacon's patronage.[10] Thomas Blundeville, whose breadth of accomplishment ran to truly Renaissance pro-

* 'N. Bacon, Knight, Keeper of the Great Seal of England, gave this book to the Library of Cambridge, 1574.'

portions, is chiefly remembered for his mathematical inquiries. He too was one of Bacon's protégés, and spent some time as a tutor in the Bacon household.[11]

As contributions to the world of knowledge and intellect, however, Bacon's enjoyment of the classics and patronage of worthy theorists took second place to his ventures on behalf of education. This concern was both practical and theoretical; it persisted from Bacon's student days at Cambridge until he catalogued his final bequests a half-century later. The extent of his share in the Denton–Bacon–Cary report on the Inns of Court is too uncertain to permit fruitful analysis, but his scheme for the education of wards of the crown and orders for the establishment of a grammar school at Redgrave clearly set forth his own ideas.

The Henrician humanist Thomas Starkey, writing about two decades before Bacon, had been the first to comment on the need to provide a better education for the wards of the crown, but after his long association with the Court of Wards Bacon had no need to take his cue from Starkey. Bacon first submitted his plan for the education of the wards of Sir Francis Englefield, Master of the Court of Wards under Mary, and again to William Cecil, who held the same post under Elizabeth, in 1561.[12]

In brisk terms he labelled the existing system as preposterous, for, as he put it,

> The chief thing and most of price in wardship is the ward's mind, the next to that his body, and the last and meanest his land. Now hitherto the chief care of governance hath been had to the land being the meanest, & to the body being the better very small, but to the mind being the best none at all, which methinks is plainly to sett the cart before the horse. And breedeth in deed such an effort as we see, which is that their lands many times are better to be liked than themselves.[13]

His scheme for amending this condition called for the establishment of an academy for the elite among the wards which was not unlike the Denton–Bacon–Cary plan for the school for statesmen. All male wards whose lands brought in an excess of £100 per annum were to be enrolled in the academy at the age of nine, and were to remain until they attained their majorities twelve years later. The curriculum during the first years was to include

French and other modern languages in addition to Latin and Greek. Music, physical education and regular Christian devotion rounded out the offerings for the younger students. As they progressed, the pupils were also introduced to the fundamentals of the common law, horsemanship and the martial arts, all of which Bacon considered necessary training for such an elite group of gentlemen.

In its broad outlines, Bacon's scheme lay in the mainstream of humanist educational theory. His evident concern to educate the whole person rather than the intellect alone, and for relating education to the requirements of contemporary society, echoed earlier theorists from Erasmus, More and Castiglione to Starkey and Thomas Elyot.[14] Yet in the specific details of his plan he picked his own path among the many cross-currents of contemporary theory. Erasmus would have grimaced at the inclusion of military training, Elyot at the choice of group instruction rather than individual, both Elyot and Starkey at the use of wealth rather than birth as a criterion for eligibility, and Castiglione at a course of study which incorporated law at the expense of the dance and other courtly arts. Although it remains in doubt as to whether Bacon adhered to the view, put forward by Elyot and others, that the state is naturally and most effectively governed by the aristocracy, he echoed a good number of theorists in chastising the elite for their neglect of education:[15] 'I may remember diverse gentlemen that gave gladly great wages to their horsekeepers and huntsmen than to such as taught their children, whereby they had very ready horses and perfect dogs, so they had very untoward children.'[16]

Because of the vast difference in outlook between the wealthiest of the Queen's wards and the children of the Suffolk yeomanry, Bacon's orders for the establishment of the Redgrave Grammar School differed considerably from his plans for an academy of wards.[17] But even with education at a more mundane level, some of Bacon's concerns remained constant. Matriculants were to be firmly trained in Latin, and would benefit from the stern discipline which was considered valuable to boys of any station. Like Ascham, who also favoured a moderate approach in such matters, Bacon's legal background led him to prefer 'a man twice whipped than once hanged': a concept anachronistic in that age for its fundamental humanity, and one readily translated to the realm of pedagogy.[18] Regular Christian devotion was again expected of all students and, though the horsemanship and more exalted weaponry taught to the wards were scaled down to instruction and practice in the use of the long-bow, the martial arts were again represented, as they had been in the Denton–Bacon–Cary Report.

Bacon was also one of the refounders and governors of the Grammar School at Bury St Edmunds,[19] and he supervised the new orders drawn up for a grammar school at St Albans, based in part on the plans for the Redgrave and Bury schools.[20] He endowed Corpus Christi College, Cambridge, with six scholarships, and money which he expected to suffice for the construction of the College chapel.[21] Closer to home, he presided over the education of his own children, chose their mentors, and did much to shape the nature of their formal training.

In the education of his own children Bacon appears at first glance to contradict his theories on the education of others', for here he emphasized individual tutorial instruction rather than group activity. But a close look at the curriculum which he had his children follow exonerates him from the charge of gross inconsistency. The same disciplines as were to be introduced to the wards were given to Bacon's sons, and with much the same end in view. Despite Francis's well-known jibe that he should have studied men and not books, the obvious strengths of his own preparation, and that of his brothers, vindicates his father's educational planning. If the self-important Earl of Verulam found it difficult to learn patience and forbearance towards his fellows, the fault lay not in his training.

Bacon's choice of instructors for his children provides the clearest insight into what he felt they should learn. Particularly evident is the strong emphasis on distinctive protestant theology, and no doubt Lady Anne had a hand in this as well as her husband. Of the three chaplains whom we know to have served at the Bacon household, two – Thomas Fowle[22] and Robert Johnson[23] – were among the vanguard of the puritan classical movement in Suffolk and Hertfordshire respectively, while the third, John Walsall,[24] shared their views if not their activism. Nor was this pointed emphasis mitigated when his children travelled abroad. Of the two who did so during Bacon's lifetime, Edward studied with the eminent humanist and reformer

Johann Sturmius,[25] and Francis, who went in the care of the puritan Sir Amyas Paulet, studied with the reformed theologian Lambert Daneau.[26]

Beyond this religious orientation in their early training, the Bacon boys followed their father in receiving the weighty offerings of Cambridge and Gray's Inn. All five of Bacon's sons were sent to Trinity rather than Corpus, because the Master of Trinity was by then Bacon's old Gray's Inn colleague Robert Beaumont, and Beaumont brought to his new charge the fervent Puritanism which he had maintained since his days as a Marian exile. At Gray's Inn, at least two of the sons had the unusual privilege of a private tutor to steer them through the intricacies of legal study: he was Richard Barker, fellow bencher of their father.[27] It is also worthy of note that Bacon manifested concern for at least the rudimentary education of his daughters, although he stopped short of having them emulate Lady Anne's attainments.[28]

In sum, what can be inferred from Bacon's excursions into the realm of educational planning? His views clearly reflect his own grounding in the ideas of Renaissance humanism and the concerns of reformed religion. He seems to have accepted the idea current in many puritan as well as humanist circles that all men and at least some women should receive a basic education. He seems also to have recognized the value of education as a means of social advancement, to which, of course, his own background bore witness. Thus he encouraged the admission of poor boys to the Redgrave School 'before any others', and specified that his six scholarships to Corpus Christi should be used in the same manner.[29] As both the Denton–Bacon–Cary Report and the scheme for the wards demonstrate, he was also concerned with education as a necessary precondition to a well-governed and godly state; this, too, followed the broad humanist currents of the day. In general, he related curriculum to the practical needs of the recipient group and, although he was clearly concerned for the edification of the soul and body as well as the intellect, he left no place for the more courtier-like pursuits which were associated, for example, with Castiglione. Bacon thus approached education as a utilitarian preparation for life, and his views distinctly imply respect for the principles of merit and ethical living. In that sense, the subdued and weighty careers of his two eldest sons, Nicholas and Nathaniel – firm puritans, learned lawyers, capable landlords, and political activists in their regional milieu – would probably have given him as much satisfaction as the more flamboyant and spectacular careers of Anthony and Francis, which he did not live to observe.

As a source of insight regarding Bacon's personal convictions and outlook on life, only his poetry can compare with his educational enterprises. The thirty-five poems and one prayer which have come down to us are not for the most part autobiographical in nature, but they do express strong convictions which further serve to identify Bacon with the Renaissance milieu. Although they were not published during his lifetime, several handwritten copies of the collection have survived, and were finally published as *The Recreations of His Age* in 1903.[30] Unfortunately only one of the poems can be dated with certainty. It seems likely, however, that none of the poems was composed prior to Bacon's marriage to Anne Cooke, and that most had been completed by the accession of Elizabeth.

The poems themselves are arranged in an orderly but not necessarily chronological manner. The subjects of moral philosophy, love, religion, and humorous fables comprise virtually the entire content, although the rhetorical ingenuity of the author somewhat relieves the monotony with which they are treated. The first nineteen poems in the collection constitute the first category, which is marked by an underlying Stoic cast. These emphasize the value of the mean estate, hard work, reason in human affairs, the value of a mind contented by a clear conscience and cultivated by a proper education. Conversely, they condemn malice, ambition, greed, envy and idleness. Where such platitudes may often be taken lightly in the work of others, they are in Bacon's poems nothing less than a confession of faith. Similar sentiments are evident in the six poems dealing with religion, but those themes are somewhat subordinate here to an insistence on personal piety and obedience to God. These six poems are among the most personal expressions in the entire collection. More intimate is the 'Prayer made by Sir N. Bacon knighte Lorde keper of the greate Seale of Engelande' – clearly written after 1558 – in which Bacon touchingly thanks God for the blessings He has bestowed and places in His trust all hopes for future well-being. The nine humorous poems in the collection are anecdotal in nature and draw upon the fables of English folklore for their inspiration: 'Of Jacke and Gylle', 'Of a Fryer and a Marryner', etc. They are among the few surviving examples of Bacon's renowned wit and, one is sorry to relate, are frankly disappointing to the modern mind.

In the espousal of such virtues as reason and moderation, and in the wide range of metrical forms in which the pieces are set, most of the collection fits comfortably into the traditions of mid-sixteenth-century English poetry. In a few of its pieces, however, we find a refreshing taste of the Renaissance, perhaps Petrarchan in flavour, which was still far from common in the English poetry of that time. This is especially true in the images and conceits in 'Of a Lover' and 'Of a Snowe balle', and may suggest Bacon's familiarity with the works of Wyatt and Surrey, either in manuscript or after the first publication of their work by Richard Tottel in 1557.[31] The assimilation of this new style is by no means complete in Bacon's verse; amid images of snowballs as 'balles of wylde fyer' which 'soe hette my desyer', the enchantress is a 'wanton wenche' rather than any Lauraian vision. Bacon's poetry represents a transitional stage between the so-called 'drab age' of English poetry and the full-blown Renaissance style of the next generation. This suggestion is strikingly affirmed in a comparison of his 'Of a Snowe balle' with Spenser's *Amoretti*, Sonnet XXX.[32]

Far less stylistic ambiguity, however, surrounds Bacon's heralded attainments in one of the most ancient forms of cultural expression: oratorical eloquence. His reputation as an orator among the intellectual worthies of the Elizabethan Age speaks for itself. George Puttenham, who knew Bacon personally and whose *Arte of English Poesie* made him an eminent authority on linguistic technique, thought him 'a most eloquent man, and of rare learning and wisedome, as I ever knew England to breed'.[33] Thomas Nashe placed Bacon with More and Sir Philip Sidney as one of the 'chiefe pillars of our englishe speeche'.[34] Ben Jonson, who knew Bacon by reputation and may have read manuscript copies of some of his speeches, compared Bacon to Cicero for his oratorical talents, and concluded that ' . . . Sir *Nico: Bacon* was singular and almost alone in the beginning of Queene *Elizabeths* times'.[35] As fleeting as many elements of oratory may be – only his listeners could appreciate Bacon's gestures, tone and vocal dynamics – several explanations for his reputation are still apparent.

As Elizabeth's Lord Keeper of the Great Seal, and her effective lord chancellor, Bacon was the chief spokesman for the crown in parliament and before the law, where he had ample opportunity to display his rhetorical skill. Fortunately, a fair sampling of his orations has survived. Considering his legal training and practice, the challenge of eloquent persuasion was one which Bacon could well face with equanimity, for much of the training at the Inns of Court centred around just such oral skills. It has even been said that the ability to argue a case rested nine-tenths on rhetorical ability and only one-tenth on points of law.[36] If Bacon was considered a worthy orator, it was due to a happy combination of natural talent and sound apprenticeship, which evidently led him to excel even among men of the law.

Bacon's official addresses as Lord Keeper were rarely mere speeches and were virtually never spontaneous. They were formal pieces, often extending to three or four thousand words, which had to observe the forms befitting the occasion, but which also had to hold the attention of a potentially restive audience. To the modern taste, these addresses are most impressive for their structural qualities: the orderly way in which they balance form and substance, and the logical and methodical manner in which arguments are put. No wonder that the historian of the Elizabethan parliaments has likened one of them to a fine sermon.[37]

Stylistically, they are largely devoid of the Ciceronian bombasts which were waning in popularity and, if they struck those who listened to them as 'well declared and eloquently set out', they bore none of the flowery phrasing or elaborate presentation of that passing oratorical fashion.[38] Bacon's more practical and businesslike approach came right out of his days of mooting at Gray's Inn, and his ability to turn an apt phrase derived more from his natural wit and sense of economy than from any studied attempt to sound the courtier. In consequence, his speeches are marbled with pithy epigrams and rustic allusions as well as by a few of the biblical and classical commonplaces which were found in virtually all learned oratory of the age. Thus, when urging the Parliament of 1571 towards more liberal expenditure, he observed that ' ... the horse must be provided for whilst the grasse is groweinge.'[39] And when explaining why it was necessary for England to take up arms in defence of the Scots in 1560, he reminded the justices in the Star Chamber that 'when thy neighboures howse is on fyer, it is tyme to take heede to thyne owne.'[40] Such folk wisdom was an integral part of Bacon's conversational style, and crops up frequently in the few off-the-cuff pronouncements and personal letters of which we have record. Thus we may note that in a letter to Cecil, whose newly constructed outhouse at Theobalds struck Bacon as too near the lodgings and the larder, he wrote, 'I thynk you had bene bettr to have offendyd yor yey outward than yor nose inward.'[41]

Aside from these flashes of wit, Bacon's speeches were eminently weighty and authoritative and could only have left his listeners with the impression that he meant business. Puttenham's linkage in the same sentence of Bacon's 'rare learning and wisdom' with his eloquence was no mere coincidence of phrasing, for wisdom and breadth of knowledge had long been considered a *sine qua non* of oratorical excellence. In all these qualities, as well as in those which could only be enjoyed by his immediate audience, Bacon's reputation as a wise, pithy and eloquent orator was well founded.

The final accoutrement of Bacon's second age also came in Elizabeth's reign, with the construction of his last home, at Gorhambury, just outside St Albans.[42] Within a day's ride from London, near to Cecil's still uncompleted Theobalds and Bedford's Chenies, and much closer to the centre of Bacon's interests than Redgrave, Gorhambury provided the ambiance of a country gentleman's estate which the Lord Keeper's official London residence at York House could not. His second estate thus became as much a part of Bacon's new age as his second marriage, and reflects the political and intellectual world of the Cooke connections as Redgrave had the provincial and commercial world of the Ferneleys.

Even the style in which Gorhambury was built reflects the character of Bacon's later years.[43] According to the only surviving plan, which treats only the ground floor of the two-storey edifice and which dates from the eighteenth century, Gorhambury was obviously built to favour the interior over the exterior. The façade was wholly asymmetrical, being irregularly broken by turrets and indentations which left little sense of unity. But the extensive and complex interior must have provided every comfort of the age. The ground floor alone included more than thirty rooms and enclosed two courtyards, while a further seven rooms were distributed among three outbuildings. This main floor included a chapel, cloisters running under a second-floor library, and a gallery of 120 feet in length, built especially for the Queen's visit of 1577.[44] None of this ground-floor vastness, it should be added, included the actual living quarters of the family, guests and servants. These rooms were all to be found on the upper storey, and probably numbered between twenty-five and thirty. Taken as a whole, the grand manner in which Gorhambury was built placed it just below the rank of Theobalds, Longleat and Kirby, all of which were completed a few years later, and on an entirely different scale from the homes of the prosperous merchants and lesser gentry typified by Redgrave.

In terms of style, the largest part of the house was executed in a more or less traditional English mode, looking backward rather than forward for its inspiration. To this traditional design, however, there remained one exception: the neo-classical front porch took for its model a recent and distinctly Renaissance form, and in so doing created an enduring place in the architectural history of England. Most probably, as the recent historian of Gorhambury has concluded, it was built by craftsmen who had worked on Somerset House, and was only the second structure of that style in England.[45]

What we know of the intellectual and cultural endeavours in Bacon's self-styled 'second age' is probably the tip of the proverbial iceberg. Just enough has come down to us regarding the activities of the Redgrave and Gorhambury households to imply that much more must remain hidden from our view. At least we can form a broad idea of what underlay Bacon's reputation for sagacity and breadth of vision, and of what amounted to an important dimension to his life and career. Clearly he deserves to be characterized as one of the 'new men' of the Tudor era in the intellectual as well as in the political and social sense of the term. And yet his receptivity to the cultural forms of the Continent as desirable appendages to his native English idiom marks him as more than a servant of social imperatives. Bacon's interests, from education, the classics and oratorical style to poetry and architecture, were held in common with a small number of

67

his contemporaries, and signal nothing short of a subtle re-definition of England's place in the European world. Not for long would that island remain a mere outpost of the Western cultural world.

V

The Lord Keeper

If the culminating years of Bacon's personal and intellectual life began with the accession of Mary and his second marriage, his professional life did not reach its peak until five-and-a-half years later, with the accession of Elizabeth. Both to those protestants who had chosen the path to exile and to the many who stuck it out at home during the ill-fated Marian Restoration, Elizabeth's accession represented nothing less than a rebirth, and one which was all the more welcome for the fact that it was unanticipated until several months before Mary's early death.

The Marian years had not been unduly harsh on Bacon, for he had kept his post at the Court of Wards and prospered both materially and intellectually. But even such a moderately ambitious man as he could not have considered the attorncyship of the Court of Wards as the ultimate step during the prime years of his professional life. He had good cause to rejoice at Elizabeth's accession and at the subsequent return to Protestantism. He heartily welcomed the personal opportunity which it augured and quickly joined in the scramble for influence and office in the new order.

Shortly after Elizabeth came to the throne she began to assemble her advisers. She picked William Cecil only three days after her accession, and added steadily to her government and retinue in the days following. Several candidates, including the incumbent Nicholas Heath,[1] Sir Anthony Cooke,[2] and the Catholic lawyer Edmund Plowden,[3] seem to have been touted for the post of lord chancellor, and Bacon's name is not to be found on the unsolicited list of candidates which Nicholas Throckmorton sent to the young Queen.[4] When plans for the coming Parliament were discussed at court on December 4th, the name of the Queen's spokesman in the Lords was left blank.[5] But each of his presumed rivals suffered in some particular way when matched against Bacon, and none but he enjoyed the crucial support of William Cecil.[6] By December 9th Bacon acted for the Queen in persuading Matthew Parker to accept the See of Canterbury, and, though his temporary ill-health put off the official ceremony of investiture for almost two weeks, his appointment had quite clearly been determined.[7] As soon as he had recovered he was summoned to Elizabeth's temporary court at Somerset House for formal investiture as Lord Keeper and privy councillor;[8] he seems to have been knighted at the same time.[9]

Despite Elizabeth's initial hesitation in choosing Bacon, the choice in retrospect seems so correct as almost to have been predictable. His qualifications were obvious, his principal champion well placed, and he had none of the disadvantages of his competitors. Unlike Plowden and Heath, of course, Bacon was a protestant, and although Elizabeth never shrank from employing Catholics in her household,[10] she shied away from encouraging them with high office. On the other hand, Bacon avoided his father-in-law's rigid and self-righteous protestant stance which Elizabeth found distasteful, and which would have placed overt pressures on her; these she hardly welcomed.[11] In addition, Bacon had proved his loyalty to the principle of legitimate succession even when his defence of that principle entailed considerable risk and unpleasantness. Finally, Bacon promised to be more than a loyal bureaucrat. He had considerable breadth of vision and an indefatigable capacity for work; he was profoundly imbued with the intellectual and cultural currents of his day, and could be expected to offer the full fruits of his intellect and experience to the royal service.

Thus it was that Bacon came to his appointment at Somerset House and received the Great Seal, in its velvet purse and leather bag, from the Queen's hands. Yet even then Elizabeth, always conscious of social form and chary of titular elevations, demurred from allowing Bacon the chancellorship *per se*. For all his manifest abilities and experience, this sheep-reeve's son was only asked to serve as the Lord Keeper of the Great Seal, though by letters patent he was to hold all the rights and responsibilities of the lord chancellor's office.[12] Considering the long road leading to this final advance, Bacon cannot have escaped some sense of frustration at this ironic deprivation: the parliamentary statute guaranteeing the full extent of his powers, which must

have come at his own instigation, suggests no less.[13] Yet he left
for us no expression or other evidence of this disappointment, and
we look in vain for it in his acceptance oration.[14]

Addressing himself to the Queen and others assembled, he
began with the conventional denial of his worthiness for office,
and with a promise of diligence and fidelity 'whereof I truste
there shal be noe wante'. In support of this *pro forma* declaration
he offered a note of considerable candour, confessing that, since
the days of King Henry, he had found ' … suche suertye in all
chaunges and suche quietnes and delighte … that I cannot make
myself beleve, that I can make any chaunge thereof but for the
worse respecting my private commodity.' Considering the
relative ease with which he had escaped the vicissitudes of those
years, this was only a mild understatement. He continued by
professing himself willing to sacrifice all that he had enjoyed
before, and to ' … preferre busines and troble before quietnes
and ease … [in service to] my Souerayne Layde, and my dutye
to my countrye'.

What exactly was the extent of Bacon's new domain, and what
were his duties as the chief legal factotum of the realm? His
official activities far exceeded the boundaries of the Court of
Chancery, although that was doubtless his greatest official concern. He also found himself the presiding officer of the Star
Chamber, the Queen's spokesman in the House of Lords and
before joint sessions of the parliament, the head of diverse *ad hoc*
commissions, and the chief oracle in all affairs of law and order.
When added to the duties of a privy councillor and his full
personal life, such chores made Bacon a busy man indeed. So
great were the burdens of office that by 1561 he felt compelled to
abandon his lucrative but time-consuming post at the Wards.[15]
It was, in any event, a remnant of his past and of little continuing
value to his career.

Of all the offices emanating from his Keepership, however, it
was as head of the Court of Chancery that Bacon had the greatest
opportunity to apply his particular training and expertise. It was
there that he left his most enduring mark as a jurist.

The Court of Chancery in the sixteenth century perfectly exemplified the dilemma of a fundamentally medieval institution
face to face with the demands of a recognizably more modern
and complex age.[16] At the outset of the Tudor era the Chancery

was already a Janus-headed body which performed two fundamental and distinct functions. On the one hand it served as an
administrative office revolving round the use of the Great Seal,
and as a court of record for cases arising out of its administrative
jurisdiction. This was the common law or Latin side of the court:
the precedents of common law were observed, and the records
were kept in Latin. On its equity or English side, the Chancery
served as a court of equity jurisdiction, whereby it heard and
determined cases for which either no remedy could be found at
the common law, or which were being appealed from another
court.

Of these two aspects it was the latter, the equity side of the
Court, which underwent the most dynamic development in the
sixteenth century, and which by the opening of the seventeenth
century had become the chief bastion of the royal prerogative.
Thus the Court of Thomas Egerton and Francis Bacon had come
a long way from the *ad hoc* and uncertain late-medieval tribunal
with which Sir Thomas More had been familiar. This development of the equity side occurred in both a mechanical and a
substantive sense; that is, the procedure and jurisdiction of the
Court grew more formal and precise and the substantive principles of the Court's equity jurisdiction followed suit. As the *de
facto* lord chancellor with the longest incumbency of the century,
Bacon has long been suspected of playing some role in this
lengthy and complex evolution. It now becomes clear that his
actions and orders were indeed of considerable importance in
the growth of both the mechanical and substantive aspects of the
Court's equity side.

The concept of a substantive equity law as distinct from, and
possibly contrary to, the common law followed in its emergence
far behind the practical and *ad hoc* application of unrecognized
equity principles:[17] as it has often been put, 'equity law is
secreted in the interstices of procedure.'[18] Until Christopher St
Germain's treatise *Doctor and Student*, published in 1530, no
attempt had been made to identify the equity jurisdiction of the
chancellor with the Aristotelian concept of equity (*epieikeia*) as
the law of reason.[19] St Germain wrote of this concept in terms of
the conscience of the judge, which could be applied either in the
absence of clear precedents in the common law, or in cases
where the letter of the common law contradicted the laws of

reason.[20] Yet despite the extreme significance of St Germain's work and its enormous influence on Tudor legal theory, it left many problems unresolved or even unrecognized. He had only begun to conceive of equity jurisdiction as something which might form precedents of its own and thus attain the more formal state of substantive law; he had not yet recognized that equity law might oppose or supersede common law. Although he understood that the Chancery practised equity law, he did not yet envision such law in the narrow sense in which it became known: as nothing more or less than the law administered out of the Chancery. That concept was not fully articulated until Edward Hake's dialogue on equity, *Epieikeia*, written at the end of the century.

Bacon's concept of equity, and his application of it in the Chancery, does not deny St Germain's understanding so much as expand upon it. Bacon identified equity with discretion, as did St Germain, but the Lord Keeper expanded its meaning into two related but distinct concepts. In a broad sense, and that which is closest to *Doctor and Student*, he took equity to imply a conscionable awareness of the consequences of a judgement before the law.[21] He began with the premise that a literal application of the law (*summum ius*) could well produce great injustice (*summa iniuria*). Thus the judge must temper his knowledge of the law with his sense of reason. It was in fact a tenet which Bacon frequently followed himself, and which was obviously intended to apply to some extent in all courts, common law and equity alike.[22]

The other sense in which Bacon extended St Germain's concept of equity is less broad and, in view of the coming struggle between prerogative and common law courts, a good deal more significant. This application derives largely from his argument before the House of Lords for the establishment of the principle that peers were attachable for contempt on writs issued out of Chancery.[23] In this sense, equity was construed as a function of the royal prerogative which was designed to give remedy in ' ... causes otherwise than the lawe is, and to helpe the Subiecte in a case where he hathe no helpe by lawe which seemes in reason as greate a prerogative as maye be.'

This was a jurisdictional definition of equity: certain kinds of cases were to be tried before equity courts and to be determined according to the use of equity law. Bacon continued by stating that the Chancery was a prerogative court in which the chancellor represented the delegated voice of the prince before the law: *coram nobis in cancellaria*. In the prince's name, the chancellor could hear cases, render judgements, and execute remedies 'otherwise than the lawe is', and in so doing his authority took precedence over the House of Lords. From this, it followed that, as Bacon put it,

> ... if a Noble man offend against the Queenes Majesties *Prerogative* in one of the highest degrees, his body is attachable by *Law*: and if a Noble man commit a contempt against a decree made in the high court of Chancerie ... he commits a contempt against that *Prerogative* & therefore his body for the same is attachable by Law.

One direct aspect of Bacon's concept of equity may be seen in his singular propensity to judicial leniency in an age when legal severity seemed the order of the day. His dictum that he would rather see a man 'twice whipped than once hanged' was no idle suggestion,[24] but – as many of his own judgements attest – a marked characteristic of his own performance. The sources of this attitude are unfortunately a good deal more obscure than the evidence for it, but we may well have here a humanistic view of human relations of the Morean variety,[25] or an embodiment of the later Stoic view – with which Bacon was eminently familiar – of the clemency of the prince and, by implication, of the law.[26] Perhaps we may also find here an early example of the puritan attack on the arbitrary qualities of equity jurisdiction which reached a climax in the following century.[27] Despite the impressionistic nature of these suggestions, they may well provide valuable clues to the evolution of a particular attitude towards law and society which appears to have taken root in the late Tudor period.

In sum, we can only regret that Bacon never gathered his views on equity into a coherent treatise, or we might have had a worthy companion to the trio of St Germain, Plowden and Hake, whose views constitute the main body of the Tudor theory of equity jurisdiction.

Beyond these contributions to the Tudor theory and practice of equity, Bacon remained essentially a pragmatist and, in his role at the Chancery, this served him well. It has long been the credit and curse of bureaucracy that principles are of little use without both the procedures that allow them to work, and the jurisdictional limits which determine their application. So it was with the Tudor Chancery, in which the development of substantive equity law was more the consequence than the cause of procedural and jurisdictional development. Bacon's contributions to these more pragmatic considerations are perhaps of greater significance to the growth of the Court than his observations regarding legal theory.

The operational problems of the Tudor Chancery at Bacon's accession were legion, and most of them were common to other branches of Tudor government.[28] The absence of proper qualifications in most Tudor chancellors seems fairly evident in view of what we know of them. The lack-lustre administrative direction which resulted seems to have been the rule rather than the exception for most of the period up to 1558, and the Court seems more or less to have run itself during much of that time.

In addition, procedures were all too informal, specialization of function among Court officials was quite inchoate, and even the bureacratic imperative of record-keeping went largely unobserved. The Court's lesser officials enjoyed a vigorous trade in fees, but were often untrained time-servers rather than professional bureaucrats, and were hard pressed to keep up with their work. In short, the Chancery of 1558 was very much the sum of its past: a ramshackle institution in which procedure, jurisdiction and substantive principles had grown, sprawling and unplanned, like the hovels of Tudor Southwark.

As head of the Chancery it cannot be said that Bacon was entirely conscious of all its problems, or that he attempted to solve all those which he did perceive. But it is evident that the period of his leadership witnessed considerable attempts at reform and innovation, and was marked by his acute insight into the operation of the Court. The lion's share of Bacon's reforms in the Chancery may be categorized under three headings. By reorganizing the personnel of the Court, adding a few offices and redefining the responsibilities of others, he made deep inroads into the apparently endemic back-log of cases. By clarifying the jurisdiction of the Court, Bacon helped both to set it apart from other courts and to discriminate among the types of litigants who came before it. Finally, by revising old procedures and instituting new ones he did much to encourage more efficient and professional operation of the Court.

One of the more obvious changes wrought by Bacon had to do with the personnel of the Court. In the hope that more hands – if well employed – would make for less work, he created several new offices for specific functions. Most frequently, these were clerkships created to take exclusive charge of a particular kind of writ which fell within the jurisdiction of the Court. Clerkships for writing writs of protection for hospitals and charitable institutions, and for writing licences permitting the alienation of lands, were created in this manner.[29] On the other hand, Bacon did not favour the creation of new clerkships without due consideration of their usefulness, and upon one occasion he had to refuse a suit from Sir Francis Walsingham to create a clerkship for a friend because that addition would not benefit the Court.[30]

Several longstanding classes of officials in the Court had their functions clarified considerably, while the officials themselves were frequently admonished to assume a more professional attitude towards their work. This may be seen in the three different sets of orders which Bacon drew up regarding the group of clerks known as the cursitors.[31] Among other things, these orders described the precise responsibility and jurisdiction of these clerks, and dealt in detail with such concerns as their punctuality, dress and fee schedules. Although the cursitors may be traced at least to the reign of Edward III, such regulation had never before been accomplished. A similar act of clarification appears in a detailed set of orders governing the enrolment of indentures and recognizances by the six clerks and clerks of the petty bag. By this procedural revision of 1573 both sets of officials were combined under the new title of clerks of the enrolments, and the business of enrolling such documents underwent strict redefinition.[32] Over the course of Bacon's twenty years at the Chancery, orders of this type had considerable impact in turning time-servers into bureaucrats and instilling in them some sense of professionalism.

It is also worthy of note that Bacon's concern for professionalism and proper qualifications in the officials of the Court did not stop with such minor posts as those of the clerks and cursitors: it extended even to the masters. The eighteen masters known to have been appointed by Bacon were exceptionally well qualified for their posts. All but one – and the exception was a former Lord Mayor of London – had considerable legal experience and at least a doctorate in the civil law. Five had doctorates in both civil and common law, and several ranked with the foremost jurists of the age. Finally, although Bacon did not hesitate to boost the fortunes of puritan justices on the commissions of the peace, he does not appear to have considered the religious affinity of those whom he appointed Masters in Chancery. To have done so with officials of such prominence would have jeopardized the pretence of religious non-alignment which, as will become apparent, Bacon attempted to maintain in the environs of Westminster.[33]

Bacon also effected several important steps towards clarifying the jurisdiction of the Court of Chancery.[34] Such efforts dealt with the types of cases which Chancery should accept, its relations with other courts, and its authority over specific types of litigants.

In 1565 Bacon began to define the types of suits which he felt inappropriate for Chancery. As a result of his orders of Trinity term in that year, the Court would no longer accept suits involving less than six acres of land, except where the monetary value exceeded 40s. per annum. All such cases pending at that time were to be dismissed immediately and, by implication if not by order, were to accrue to the Court of Requests. In cases involving purely monetary values, Chancery would consider only those whose value exceeded £10.[35] It is difficult to know how many cases were thus dismissed, but there can be little doubt that in setting such limits, Bacon placed the jurisdiction of the Court on a firmer footing, which should have done much towards expediting its operation. Later attempts to restrict the types of cases which Chancery would consider, such as Egerton's orders of May 1596, fell within the broad guidelines first established by Bacon a generation earlier.[36]

Much of Bacon's attention to jurisdictional problems centred around the relations of Chancery with other courts. Some of his measures were effected not as part of a preconceived design, but rather in reaction to specific instances of what he saw as frank abuses of Chancery jurisdiction.

The question of a Chancery litigant's freedom from arrest by a writ out of another court furnishes a case in point. The principle of temporary immunity from arrest for a defendant before the Court would seem an elementary point in a mature and orderly judicial system. When Bacon came to office in 1558, however, a person who received a subpoena in Chancery might very well be attached for the same or even a different charge through writs issued out of another court. When such a situation arose in 1560, Bacon gave orders to the effect that any litigant should enjoy freedom from arrest under those circumstances. At the same time, his orders strengthened the authority of the writ of supersedeas out of Chancery, whereby that Court requested the transfer of a case from a court of first instance to its own jurisdiction.[37]

Nor was this the only occasion upon which Bacon strove to defend the Chancery's jurisdiction from apparent incursions of other courts, for in 1561 he successfully fought off jurisdictional claims by the Lord Warden of the Cinque Ports, and upon several occasions denied pleas of privileges from the Exchequer.[38] Taken together, such precedents established a distinct policy whereby the Chancery fought for what it considered to be its privileges in relation to other courts, and later Lord Chancellors like Puckering and Egerton took their cue from Bacon's lead.[39] At the same time, however, it would be erroneous to assume that Chancery under Bacon's direction necessarily assumed a hostile attitude towards other courts. More often than not, Bacon operated on the principle that a major function of his Court was to support the due process of other courts, both local and central. For example, he supported Justice Dyer's ruling regarding the jurisdiction of the Chamberlain of Chester, and personally helped to affirm the jurisdiction of the University of Cambridge.[40]

In his efforts to revise outdated or imprecise procedures Bacon achieved similar advances. He made considerable changes in the important procedures for taking testimony *in perpetuam rei memoriam*, whereby a commission of the Court went to take viva voce testimony from litigants or witnesses who, because of their state of health or poverty, were unable to attend the Court at Westminster in the usual manner.[41] In another instance, Bacon successfully curtailed abuses in issuing writs of certiorari, one of the most common forms of initiating an appellate hearing in the

Chancery, but an action which traditionally lent itself to un-scrupulous abuse by plaintiffs.[42] In still another, as we have seen, Bacon provided a lengthy reform of the much-abused practice regarding enrolment of recognizances and indentures.[43] In these and other ways, therefore, Bacon's two decades in the Chancery were a period of formalization and modernization, and remain something of a watershed in the long development of the Court.

Although his overriding concern with the Court of Chancery absorbed most of Bacon's energies in his official capacity of Lord Keeper, there are several indications that he found time and had the perspective necessary to deal with the problems of legal administration on a much broader level than the jurisdiction of any specific court. Two proposals which Bacon made in the last decade of his life bear out this impression. If accepted at the time, they would have had the effect of providing for supervision of the justices of the peace and of facilitating the application of the laws of the realm.

The idea of establishing commissions of visitation to check up on the activities of the J.P.s was voiced in the address which Bacon delivered at the closing of Parliament in 1571, and again in virtually the same form at the opening of the next Parliament.[44] The concept was frankly based on the common ecclesiastical practice of diocesan visitations. It responded to the constant need for the government at Westminster to supervise the implementation of its policies, as well as the administration of law and order, throughout the realm. During the Elizabethan era the government generally placed its hopes on the justices of assize and the justices of the peace to accomplish these ends, but its expectations were not always met.[45] For some years prior to this plan of 1571, Bacon had voiced his concern for the enforcement of the law in addresses to the justices about to depart for their circuits.[46] Although Bacon's suggestion was perhaps myopic in its assumption that much civil disorder stemmed from the slackness of the J.P.s, such slackness was in ample evidence, and Bacon was not out of line with his contemporaries in his approach.

In another case, Bacon's concern for the proper interpretation and application of the law manifested itself in a proposal for the codification of statute law: the 'Devise how the statutes of this realm are to be ordered and printed, if it shall so please the

Q Matie and her Counsell'.[47] Redundancies in the statutes were to be eliminated, statutes were to be edited for better understanding, and the whole corpus of statutes was to be abridged and arranged in a convenient digest. Such work would be carried out by a commission of legal experts to be drawn from the benches of the Inns of Court. Bacon even appended a list of candidates for that task.

For his diverse duties as Lord Keeper Bacon was well rewarded, both by way of official salary and fees, and through the sundry gifts and perquisites which readily found their way to his purse. Of these two fundamental sources of income the former is by far the easiest to estimate, although it is based on remuneration from at least three distinct offices, the Chancery, the Star Chamber, and the Court of Faculties. From the Chancery itself, Bacon received an annual total of £547 15s., except during leap years, when the addition of one 23s. per diem payment made the total £548 18s. This sum is based on payments of £419 15s. as the total per diem stipend at 23s. per day, £72 for his wine allowance, £40 for robes of office, and £16 for sealing wax.[48] The Star Chamber brought in £500 per annum, based on a flat stipend of £300 and an additional £50 for each of the four terms in which Bacon sat. The total from these constant sources of income was £1,047 15s. a year. Additional fees from both of the above offices and from the Court of Faculties as well brought in a further amount which varied from year to year but, if Professor Simpson's reckoning of Bacon's own accounts is correct, it averaged no less than £260 per annum for the years for which Bacon's records survive.[49] When taken together, Bacon received an average of just over £1,300 per annum from the various official receipts pertaining to his offices as Lord Keeper. Although it is virtually impossible to calculate what he may have received beyond these regular sources, such additional and legitimate emoluments as presents, customs, annuities, fines and brokerage fees for the numerous offices under his control probably raised his income from office to about £2,500 per year: unequal to the great fortunes of the day, but a tidy sum for an early Elizabethan officer of state.[50]

One must inevitably wonder whether a judge who gained such wealth through his offices remained scrupulous in the performance of his duties. In view of the relations between

Tudor officials and their public, which were notably informal by our standards, and the ill-defined notion of official impropriety, officials easily and commonly engaged in corrupt practices. Then, as now, judges were particularly liable to offers of bribes or gratuities, and allegations of wrong-doing were as lightly and commonly made as they were difficult to refute.[51]

Like other judges and high officers of state, Bacon enjoyed virtually unlimited opportunity for corruption, and was accused of such indulgence on at least two occasions: once by a source which remains anonymous to us – and which may have been anonymous to the accused – of exacting fines which rightly pertained to the crown, and once by the respected Catholic lawyer Edmund Plowden of undue partiality on the bench.[52] In neither case do we have specific details of the charge. Bacon felt sufficiently stung by the former to issue an impassioned rebuttal,[53] but his earnestness may have been prompted as much by the natural sensitivity of the allegation as by its possible veracity. So far as we know, his protestation of innocence seems to have satisfied the Queen. Plowden's charge, made by a brilliant advocate and perhaps the foremost legal mind of his generation, may understandably have been little more than an attempt to discredit a public figure whose lack of sympathy for recusant causes had become well known. It may also have borne overtones of personal rivalry, for tradition has it that Elizabeth passed over Plowden in favour of Bacon for the post of Lord Keeper in 1558.[54] Whether or not this is so, it is clear that Plowden never received the recognition in Elizabeth's reign which he had good reason to anticipate, while Bacon, a lawyer whose reputation was certainly not greater than his in 1558, rose to the foremost judicial position in the realm and remained there for two decades.

It must also be acknowledged that the broad context of Bacon's career leaves one with some scepticism regarding such charges. Bacon's stoic attitude towards avarice is well known, as are his frequent admonitions to younger or lesser justices directed towards maintaining the integrity of the bench. He seems to have avoided involvement in the notorious corruption of the Court of Wards, especially in the 1545–50 era, and was in no way implicated when several of his fellow-officers were purged for malpractice in that period.[55] A few years later he chose to ignore the sundry devices for concealing wardship and elected instead to treat openly with Queen Mary to avoid wardship for his own heirs.[56] Finally, under Elizabeth, he took great care to eliminate a pernicious source of corruption in his own court when he regulated and monitored the fee scales of the clerks in Chancery.[57]

A striking example of Bacon's impartiality in the face of very personal interests may be found in the form of a suit brought for his arbitration by the Borough of Beccles, Suffolk, against his kinsmen William Rede and Thomas Gresham. This complex dispute went back to 1540, when Bacon's brother-in-law William Rede purchased extensive fenlands within the borough's boundaries. Both the conditions of the purchase and Rede's attitude towards the townsmen's use of the land had served to create a longstanding and bitter feud. By 1576 Rede's interests had devolved upon Gresham, his son-in-law, and his grandson, William Rede the younger. It is difficult to imagine that the burgesses of Beccles were unaware of Bacon's connection with the defendants, and it says a great deal for his contemporary reputation that they nevertheless asked for his assistance. They were not to be disappointed: Bacon commissioned justices Manwood and Monson to consider the case, and when those worthies upheld the interests of the borough against Rede and Gresham, Bacon duly promulgated the decision.[58]

When these aspects of Bacon's career are considered, and when it is further acknowledged that only two allegations of wrong-doing have survived against one who not only had his share of political foes but who also sat as a judge in both the Star Chamber and the Chancery for two decades in an age when such allegations were commonly voiced, it is not difficult at least to suggest Bacon's fundamental integrity in office.

Clearly, neither of those charges seems to have cast much of a pall over Bacon's reputation with his contemporaries or his successors, for aphoristic tributes to his sagacity and virtue in office overshadow all other claims on his behalf. When Sir Thomas Bromley was sworn in as Bacon's successor he anticipated Thomas Fuller's well-known quip ('It was difficult to come after Sir Nicholas Bacon and *not* to come after him') with the comment that he would 'succeed one in whom all good qualities did abound ... whereby my want and insufficiency shall be made more manifest'.[59] Elizabeth still held Bacon up as a model to Thomas Egerton, her last Lord Keeper,[60] and Edward Hake, writing around the turn of the century, extolled 'the profundity of judgment and also the integrity of Conscience that was to be seene in oure *Sir Nicholas Bacon*'; he placed Bacon in that respect with Sir John Fortescue and Sir Thomas More.[61]

In sum, it is apparent that Bacon introduced important reforms in the operation of the Chancery which brought about some considerable degree of modernization, while at the same time his experience and perception led him to an advanced notion of the equity jurisdiction of the Court. He remained sensitive to the demands of his society upon the judicial system, and was able to carry his concern for the due administration of law beyond the confines of his own bailiwick in the Chancery. He accepted the patronage system of his age for what it was, but seems to have avoided the excesses which characterized his most successful son and many others. His perspective of the place of the Court of Chancery in society, coupled with his distinct sense of professionalism in office, set Bacon's administration apart from its predecessors, and made it a landmark for those who followed. Only upon the achievement of Bacon's years at the Chancery could the mature equity court of Egerton and Nottingham be founded.

VI

Religion and Foreign Affairs, 1558-63

Among the privy councillors appointed in the opening months of the reign, Bacon ranked with the statesmen rather than with the courtiers. The distinction extended beyond the possession of office or lack of it; it amounted to a generally high level of expertise and intellectual weight which was not evenly distributed among the Queen's advisers. Bacon's sagacity in the law coloured much of what he did and lent an authority to his voice which was shared by only a few others. But the range of his interests and activities far exceeded the boundaries of legal affairs, and led to a knowledgeable involvement in a great many concerns of the council. That involvement, moreover, was innovative as well as informed.

On most matters which came before the council, Bacon was naturally allied with William Cecil.[1] Despite their occasional disagreement and at least one dramatic falling out over a matter of policy, their common outlook and long association assured their close rapport. Sir John Mason (although he was not always trusted by the rest), William Petre, Walter Mildmay, and the Earl of Bedford and Marquis of Winchester among the peers, often shared the viewpoint of the two brothers-in-law on major issues.[2] These figures by no means constituted a formal group, but together they feared the threat of a Catholic restoration, the claims of Mary Stuart, and, after a few years, the political and marital aspirations of the Earl of Leicester. In a more positive vein, they looked forward to the Queen's marriage to a protestant or at least an acceptable Catholic, were generally conservative on fiscal and social policy, and – save for Mason and Petre – were more or less receptive to a vigorous protestant settlement of religion. Despite the numerous points on which

84

they did *not* coalesce, it is thus possible to recognize a significant degree of cohesion among these councillors, with Cecil and Bacon often forming the nucleus of the group.[3]

In the individual expertise of its members, the council was marked by considerable diversity and was on the whole a remarkably astute and well-balanced body. When it dealt with military matters, the debate often turned on the advice of the peers: Clinton, Arundel, Howard of Effingham, Sussex; later Norfolk, and Robert Dudley, who was named Earl of Leicester in 1564, added their voices. Nicholas Wotton, Ralph Sadler, John Mason, Thomas Parry and Cecil were adept at diplomacy and foreign policy, while several of the earls – Shrewsbury, Derby, Bedford, Pembroke and Northampton among them – were counted specialists on Ireland, Wales, and the outer reaches of the realm, where they often held great personal sway. Financial and other domestic concerns were usually entrusted to Winchester as Lord Treasurer, Richard Sackville as Under Treasurer, Parry as Household Treasurer, Mildmay as Chancellor of the Exchequer, and Bacon. Cecil, with no apparent limits to his areas of competence, soon emerged to co-ordinate much of the activity of the whole body, although not for several years would he gain acknowledgment as the council's dominant figure.

Bacon enjoyed his greatest influence in these financial and other domestic affairs. His associations with the Courts of Augmentations and Wards allowed him to draw upon a wealth of observations and experience in the council's financial and economic deliberations, while his background and his office made him the pre-eminent legal authority of the time. He presided over the council when it met as a court in the Star Chamber, and maintained close contact with both the justices of the peace and the justices of the assize who, between them, did much to administer government policy throughout the realm. He served as a natural liaison with the Inns of Court and, through them, with the chief legal officers and theorists of the realm.

The three most important issues facing the new Queen and her council in the opening weeks of the reign were the determination of a religious settlement, the ominous – though by no means new – alliance between France and Scotland, and the compound problem of the royal marriage and succession. Of the three, the first was the most pressing. The Queen might still marry, and although Mary Stuart and her husband, Francis II of France, would shortly lay claim to the English throne, they had not yet taken that provocative step. The religious settlement could not, however, be delayed, and Elizabeth dropped broad hints in this regard even as she made her way to the opening of her first Parliament. She waved away the monks who came to escort her and bade them snuff out their tapers, for she could see well enough without them.[4]

With few exceptions, the early appointees to the privy council were either protestants of a moderate stripe or *politiques* whose religious views, if any, lay well hidden from public view. Bacon, who favoured a strongly protestant and even puritan course in his private life, had long ago learned the perils of ideological extremism, and went to considerable lengths to mute his convictions in the environs of Westminster. This was of course especially true when he spoke in the name of the Queen, the House of Lords or the privy council. Except for a few notable occasions when he dropped his guard, one might easily have concluded that Bacon, like his Queen, had come to consider religion primarily in secular and political terms. Even Elizabeth, who relied on his advice on religious matters from the start of her reign but whose personal contacts with Bacon had formerly been slight, may not at first have perceived the nature of Bacon's true loyalties.

One of the first decisions of an ecclesiastical nature which the Queen had to face was the appointment of her Archbishop of Canterbury. The ultimate selection of Matthew Parker placed a wise and sensitive statesman on the throne of St Augustine, and was one of the most fortunate royal appointments of the entire reign. Yet despite her long association with that veteran churchman, going back to the days when he served as her private chaplain, Elizabeth did not choose Parker before consulting Cecil and Bacon.[5] The latter had not yet been knighted or named Lord Keeper, but his word was deemed so valuable that the antiquary John Strype took him for the prime mover in Parker's nomination.[6] While Strype's claim seems extravagant, it is clear that Bacon supported Parker before the cautious Queen, and then spoke in her name to overcome Parker's deep and sincere reluctance to accept the post. Bacon first presented the Queen's offer on December 9th, 1558, and the two old Cambridge friends debated the issue back and forth in letters and conferences for a full nine months before Bacon secured Parker's assent.[7]

While Parker struggled with his conscience, Elizabeth's first Parliament and the episode which has come to be known as the Westminster Disputation had come and gone. The future Archbishop attended neither; Bacon presided at both. Parliament opened on January 25th, two days later than originally scheduled so that the Queen might recover from an undisclosed indisposition. Bacon's opening oration, presumably intended to describe the reasons for calling the session, must have disappointed those who sought an idea of Elizabeth's intended religious policy.[8] He couched all references to ecclesiastical matters in vague and ambiguous terms. The assembled members were merely instructed to proceed with humility, presence of mind and proper reverence towards the making of a settlement. They were to avoid 'contentious, contumelius, [or] approbius words as heretic, schismatic, papist, and ... like names and nurses of seditions, factions, and sects ... ' Apart from the implication that they were not to have a Roman settlement, little of a more positive nature could have been gleaned from the Lord Keeper's words, which accurately reflected the Queen's apparent indecision.

The most that the Queen and council seemed prepared to do was to present a supremacy bill to the House of Commons on February 9th, in which a formula for church structure was suggested. It said nothing of dogma or practice.[9] Left to their own devices in the absence of more decisive government direction, each of the main factions in the Commons sought to gain its own version of a settlement. The strong puritan force sought to invoke the spirit of Geneva, while others fought for a more moderate or even noncommittal bill. The debate raged on and off for most of the session, and by the approach of Easter, and with it the anticipated termination of the Parliament, it looked as though the conservatives had maintained control.[10]

At the eleventh hour, the reformers received an unexpected fillip. Some time on the eve of what was presumed to be the final day of the session, the Queen thought better of allowing it to end with so little having been settled. If nothing else, a termination at that time would have placed the burden of making a decision squarely on her shoulders, and that was a responsibility she did not welcome. When the members assembled in the morning, expecting to be met by Black Rod, they were greeted instead with the announcement of an adjournment until after Easter.[11] As if to compound the joy of the protestants, it was also announced that a debate would be held during the adjournment in which the champions of both the Edwardian and Marian factions of the episcopacy would have their say. The debate was to begin on the following Friday, March 31st, and would be chaired by no less a figure than the Lord Keeper.

The Westminster Disputation seems to have been conceived by Elizabeth as a means of allowing the protestants a chance to rally support for their position in an open debate, so that they could gain sufficient momentum to achieve the passage of their reform programme when Parliament reassembled. Thus, Elizabeth had not only decided to permit a truly protestant settlement, but was now determined to encourage it.[12]

It has proved impossible to determine with any certainty what part Bacon or, for that matter, Cecil played in this parliamentary debate or in the Queen's sudden decision to convene a disputation at Westminster. We do know, however, that Sir Anthony Cooke, their father-in-law, was one of the acknowledged leaders of the puritan force in the Commons, and we also know that someone – probably Cecil – wanted Cooke's presence in Parliament badly enough to have secured him a seat before his return from the Continent.[13] We may also assume that the brothers-in-law favoured the rather moderate demands which the puritans expressed during the anxious Commons debates of February and March. It is thus reasonable at least to suggest that Bacon and Cecil, whose respective positions more or less precluded their direct partisan involvement in Parliament, encouraged Cooke and his cohorts in their efforts, and may even have urged the Queen to adopt the device of the Easter disputation.

In any event, the idea of an open debate proved an excellent means of implementing Elizabeth's apparent design. Not only was the opportunity of the Easter recess a fortuitous convenience, but, as Bishop Jewel of Salisbury pointed out, the Catholics could have less cause for bitterness if they were put down in the course of a debate among churchmen than if their programme had been scuttled in Parliament by laymen or by government action.[14] Elizabeth's choice of Bacon as her moderator is eminently reasonable. Only a layman might appear to be impartial, and a judge all the more so. Only the Queen's spokesman and a man of Bacon's stature could take the chair if the confrontation was to enjoy the degree of publicity and prestige which it was intended to receive.

On the appointed day, each side was represented by eight spokesmen who were to debate three pre-announced points: the use of the vernacular in church services, the authority of the English Church to determine its own rites and ceremonies, and the all-important question of the mass.[15] The format specified that each side would read a prepared statement on each point, and one point would be debated on each of the three days of the disputation.

Either by mishap or design, this arrangement had not been communicated to the Marians. When they appeared on March 31st they brought with them no statement to read. Bacon rather grudgingly allowed them to speak extempore on the opening point if they would submit their written statement at the next session. But when the Marians brought forth their statement at the second session, on April 3rd, Bacon changed his mind and refused to allow them to read it. Instead he insisted that the debate turn to the second point, implying as he did so that the first had been forfeited. The Catholics grew angry and, although reluctantly conceding the first round, they balked at discussing the new topic. As 'defendants' they demanded the right to have the last word rather than the first. Bacon denied that request, and when they countered by refusing to continue altogether, he threatened them heatedly: ' ... and for you shall not that we shall hear you, you may perhaps shortly hear of us.' At that retort the meeting came to an abrupt end, and later in the day the Lord Keeper's threat was fulfilled: two of the Marians, the bishops of Winchester and Lincoln, were put in the Tower.

The government's hastily prepared official account of the proceedings was a shabby attempt to mask the Lord Keeper's patent bullying.[16] He is described as having 'gently admonished' the Marians and is said to have had no alternative but to dissolve the meeting in the face of their obstinate unwillingness to proceed by predetermined rules.

While it is clear that the government scenario as directed by Bacon was not meant to yield a Marian victory, or even a fair hearing, the intended victims managed to create a trap into which Bacon plunged headlong. Sensing quickly enough the real motives behind the disputation, they skilfully gained the martyr's image at Bacon's expense. His *ex cathedra* outburst can only have been an embarrassment to the government and, although the privy council was willing to support his actions after the fact, both in its statement and in its rapid follow-up to Bacon's parting threat, that outburst was obviously a spontaneous instance of personal conviction vanquishing an official pose of impartiality. Never again would Bacon let his guard drop in such an ill-considered manner, but the effect had been felt. Catholics both at home and abroad henceforth marked him as one of the arch-heretics of the reign, while the protestants in parliament and elsewhere now knew him more than ever for a friend.

Despite the fiasco at Westminster, the course of events in Parliament after the Easter recess fulfilled the government's hopes of a settlement. A final version of the Supremacy Bill, substituting the title of 'Supreme Governor' for 'Supreme Head' and in other ways reflecting more protestant values, was finally approved by both houses with little delay.[17] A Uniformity Bill, including a Prayer Book founded largely on the more radical version of 1552, was introduced into the lower House for the first time on April 18th. It passed its third reading the following afternoon, and was soon approved in the Lords.[18] When Parliament closed on May 8th, Elizabeth accepted both bills.[19]

Bacon's closing speech on this occasion included praise for what had passed and admonitions for future conduct.[20] The members were asked to encourage obedience to the settlement which they had so admirably, wisely and freely worked out. He cautioned them that:

> ... greate observacon and watche [must] be had of the withdrawers and hinderers thereof, ... amongst theis I meane to comprehende aswell those that be to swifte as those that be to slowe, those I say that goe before the lawe or beyonde the lawe as those that will not followe.

They must take sharp heed and impose correction upon those

who nursed sects and seditious tumults, for good government could rest only on unity and obedience. It was, in sum, a message delivered from a position of strength, and implied the government's intention fully to enforce the legislation which it had encouraged in the session.

These two episodes in the making of the Elizabethan Settlement, the Westminster Disputation and the debates of the parliamentary session, allowed Bacon all too little opportunity either to speak his own mind or overtly to influence the course of that Settlement. For the most part he spoke on behalf of others, as was expected of the Lord Keeper, and – except for the outburst at the Marian bishops – only the choice of words was his own. But if his position kept him from joining his father-in-law and others in a frontal attack on religious conservatism, he did find opportunity to nudge the direction of policy gently from within, just as he had done in advocating Parker's appointment. Such opportunities usually came through requests for advice by the Queen or privy council, in the form of *ad hoc* committees, or by the insertion of a personal thought or proposal in the midst of a major speech. Close scrutiny of some of these instances adds dimension both to Bacon's convictions and his subtle means of working on their behalf.

In the summer of 1559 Elizabeth established commissions of visitation to administer oaths of uniformity and to survey the extent of religious conformity in each diocese. Bacon sat on the commission for two dioceses which would shortly become synonymous with puritan nonconformity: Norwich and Ely. He may also have had some influence in the selection of his fellow commissioners, for we find his father-in-law, Sir Anthony Cooke, on the same committee. Not only was Cooke, an Essex man, unfamiliar with the dioceses of Norwich and Ely, but he received very few posts from Elizabeth herself, for she appears not to have liked his rigid and dogmatic manner.[21] With the probable connivance of Bishops Cox and Parkhurst – both returned Marian exiles – the commission cited no instances of protestant nonconformity in what was obviously a highly coloured and inaccurate report. This bias can easily be accounted for by the open puritan sympathies of several commissioners, but if Bacon had chosen to exercise the kind of diligence upon which he founded his reputation, or for that matter if he himself had followed the injunctions which larded his recent speech before parliament, the final report could not have been the same. It was also at this very time, of course, that Bacon had begun to employ the avowed puritan Thomas Fowle as his household chaplain at Redgrave, in the diocese of Norwich.[22]

Another instance of Bacon's subtle intervention in the religious matters of these years came as a personal interjection in his speech at the opening session of the Parliament of 1563.[23] Here he broached the subject of rural deaneries: a radical protestant concept with far-reaching implications.[24] As Martin Bucer had defined it, the rural deanery was a sub-episcopal level of ecclesiastical administration founded upon the model of the apostolic Church, and more recently adopted in several Continental reforming groups of his own age. The rural dean was to carry out frequent diocesan visitations and help to educate the clergymen to their duty in preaching the gospel. In many ways the functions of this office approximated to those of the prophesyings which later became such a central part of the puritan programme in Elizabeth's reign. A rudimental system of rural deaneries had been adopted for a time under Edward VI, but Bacon's plea for its reinstitution in 1563 was among the first references to the issue by a layman under Elizabeth; his advocacy shortly preceded the time when the puritan zealots of the age would place the issue in a passionate and controversial context. In 1571 the puritan-dominated Convocation picked up the issue with considerable zeal.[25] In the context of the resulting notoriety of the idea, Bacon's second reference, in his speech at the opening of the Parliament of 1572, was considerably more courageous than his first.[26] As was the case with many ecclesiastical issues, Elizabeth steadfastly refused to consider it. But if these efforts fell upon deaf ears at Westminster, they do at least indicate to us the manner in which Bacon strove to balance his official stance of impartiality in religious controversy with his deep-seated personal convictions.

Among the other important issues upon which Bacon spoke out in those early years of the reign was that of foreign relations, and here Bacon spoke as an amateur rather than as an expert. Yet even in these concerns his voice carried substantial weight at the council board, and his pronouncements often had telling effects.

At the outset of Elizabeth's reign the age-old rivalry between England and France, reinforced by the hostilities which had only recently drawn to a close, marked France as the perpetual foe and single greatest threat to English security.[27] Spain, the other great power of sixteenth-century Europe, had remained on amicable diplomatic terms with England since the marriage of Philip and Mary, and was not an immediate threat. The wartime alignments of these three states remained substantially in force even after the conclusion of the Treaty of Cateau-Cambrésis in April 1559.[28] Although nominally at peace, France continued to harass England through Scotland. Philip, fearing the prospect of an Anglo-French rapprochement, offered encouragement to Elizabeth, and restrained papal inclinations towards her excommunication.

In one sense, Elizabeth held the balance of strength between the two great powers of western Europe. Closer ties with either France or Spain would tip the scales, and very likely lead England once again to war. But not all the cards lay in Elizabeth's hand. As long as she refused the Roman rite she could never be assured of genuinely secure relations with either France or Spain. It was a point which she could hardly ignore. Her most feasible course of action seemed to be to play off each side against the other as a means of obtaining the basic preconditions for English security. At her accession, those preconditions were the neutralization of a potentially hostile Scotland, and the recognition of her succession in Paris and Edinburgh as well as in Madrid. Although the Treaty of Cateau-Cambrésis made a pretence of accomplishing these ends, any confidence in the viability of its provisions was shortly dispelled in all but the most optimistic circles at Westminster. In the opening months of the reign the future of Scotland and Mary Stuart, both tied to French aspirations, seemed to hold the key to English security.

With the exception of a *pro forma* and sentimental call for the recovery of Calais issued in his opening address to Parliament in 1559,[29] Bacon's first statement on foreign affairs as a privy councillor came in regard to the increasing French pressure on Scotland. In the course of her long absence at the French court, where she had been brought up and over which she briefly ruled as Queen, Mary Stuart's Scottish kingdom had largely thrown off the mantle of the Roman Church and had adopted in its stead a Protestantism of the Genevan mould. The climax of the Scottish Reformation came when Mary's regent government created sufficient repression to provoke a full-scale protestant rising in May 1559. She well knew that religion alone was not the only point at stake; a protestant Scotland would be difficult to rule, and would be the natural ally rather than the potential antagonist of its English neighbour. Modest aid from south of the border, mostly at Cecil's urging, encouraged the Scottish lords, but it also provoked Mary openly to flaunt the arms of England as her own. Her brazen assertion, a direct violation of the Treaty of Cateau-Cambrésis, naturally received firm support from her French in-laws, the Guises. As if that were not sufficient to raise the level of diplomatic tension, a scant four months elapsed between the signing of the treaty in April and the open preparation of a French invasion force for Scotland.[30]

The months that followed brought with them one of the most severe tests of diplomatic skill which Elizabeth would face. French intervention in Scotland would gravely imperil the Anglo-Scottish border. Yet to oppose that intervention with more overt action could be to provoke direct hostilities with France which England could ill afford.

During the summer and autumn months of 1559, Elizabeth, Cecil and a few others shared a clandestine and limited commitment to send modest amounts of aid to the beleaguered Scots.[31] At the same time the Queen continued to proclaim her neutrality to the diplomatic community at Westminster, and most privy councillors had only the vaguest idea of what was afoot during most of this time. But in early November, when the rumoured appearance of a French invasion fleet off Eyemouth, above Berwick, made it clear that halfway measures would no longer suffice, the matter came fully before the council board.[32] It was greeted neither with calm nor unanimity. The best course of action was debated for nearly six weeks before a decision could be reached.

Those militants who followed Cecil's line of reasoning were in the majority from the start. They argued that France meant to conquer England in one way or another, and that if she were not stopped in Scotland she would have to be fought in England itself. They took as their immediate mandate for direct intervention the frequent requests for aid which had been forthcoming from the Scottish Lords of the Congregation: requests which culminated in the unpublicized visit of Lord Maitland of Lethington in late November.[33]

Bacon does not seem to have been in on the full details of the aid to the Scots until November when he found out with the rest of the council. He had considerably less expertise in foreign affairs than those who were a party to the secret – Cecil, Clinton, Parry, Pembroke and Sadler – [34] and there had been no particular reason to reveal to him the full situation. But as the matter came before the council board, Bacon followed the issues with rapt attention. When the time came for the more cautious heads to state their case, including Arundel, Parry, Petre, Mason and Dr Wotton,[35] it was Bacon who emerged as their spokesman. In his speech of December 15th,[36] he argued that England was unprepared, militarily, economically and in terms of national unity, to offer substantial and open military support for the demonstrably weak and disorganized Lords of the Congregation. As if that were not enough, he continued, England could not anticipate support for such a venture from any other state in Europe. Finally, he expressed grave reservations in principle about supporting the Scots, who were, after all, rebels in arms against their rightful monarch. Presumably he felt that it was incumbent upon Elizabeth, whose own claims to rule were still fragile, to refrain from aiding the overthrow of a fellow monarch.

In a more positive vein, he suggested that the best course lay in temporizing on the question of direct military intervention, while continuing to encourage the Scots in the modest manner of the previous months. At best, he judged, it would take France two campaign seasons to prevail in Scotland, and many things might transpire in that time. The French might well find the going too tough for them to continue, or the Scots might after all give a good account of themselves in battle. In the meantime, England would undoubtedly have a better chance to prepare for any undertaking that might be required at a later date.

Although subsequent events might justify epithets of timidity for Bacon's attitude, he founded his views on a thorough and realistic evaluation of England's total position, both at home and abroad. As we will later observe, he had close familiarity with the economic and financial state of the realm, and was no doubt correct in his assessment of England's strength. His hesitation in supporting a revolt against the principle of legitimate monarchy was timely and very applicable to Elizabeth's own position, and was firmly founded on the accepted political wisdom of the day. But despite the fervour of his remarks and the validity of many of his points, Bacon's view did not prevail. By Christmas Eve, Cecil had won him over with most of his fellows, and only the stubborn and erratic Earl of Arundel remained unconvinced.[37]

Once he had thrown in his lot with the hawks, Bacon reverted to the role of spokesman for the Queen, and when Elizabeth finally concurred with the council's recommendations, Bacon took to the podium to present the policy to the realm. He defended it vigorously at a meeting of the justices of the assize and some of the justices of the peace in the Star Chamber.[38] In order that the 'coniectures of busye braynes mighte be the better satisfied' he explained to them the Queen's expectations that they would carry the news of the decision to the grass-roots level, and expounded the policy at length. Experience had shown that it was best to be prepared for an invasion and not to place much trust in French promises. Even at that moment France was preparing a large force to fulfil her designs in Scotland, and England had already lost Calais for lack of proper preparation. Once they had mastered the Scots, it would be vain to hope that the French would not set their sights to the south. He concluded with the common wisdom that ' ... when thye neighboures howse is on fyer, it is tyme for thee to take heede to thyne own.'

As Elizabeth followed her resolve in sending troops to Scotland in the early months of 1560, it rapidly became apparent that the decision which had taken so long to reach had been correct. Their bluff having been called, the French shortly acknowledged that they had bitten off more than they could chew. In March they surprised many observers by proposing a negotiated settlement.[39] The council considered the matter with great deliberation, and, despite reluctance on the part of some, Cecil left on the last day of May at the head of a negotiating committee to meet with the French representatives at Newcastle.[40] In the time it took him to arrive at his destination and settle in for the talks, several events came directly or indirectly to his attention which would have a significant bearing on his mission. The Spanish fleet had been destroyed at Tripoli by the

Turks;[41] Mary of Lorraine, the Dowager Queen of Scotland who ruled as Mary Stuart's regent, was reported near death;[42] and the Scots' siege of Leith had again failed to dislodge the French from that stronghold.[43]

Bacon seems to have spent those eventful days away from court, visiting his sister-in-law Mildred Cecil at Theobalds and resting at Redgrave. Nevertheless he remained abreast of the latest news as it came to the council at Westminster. On June 17th, the day he heard of the Dowager's impending demise, he sat down to relate his thoughts to Cecil at Newcastle.[44] Although he may not have been aware of it at the time, his letter also served to reassure Cecil that his detractors on the privy council were not taking advantage of the Newcastle mission to conspire against him. Leaving the amenities for the end, Bacon quickly addressed himself to the matters at hand:

> ... because you shuld not be ignorant what I thynk of the mattr now in yor handling, I have thowght good to let you understond that yf I were in yor place & saw cause to geve credytt to the advrtysment of the myseryes of ffraunce, of the hard happ happenyd to kyng Phylypp of the want of lythe, and of the deth of the dowager then wold I agre to no end but to sooche as for thys present shuld delyvr Skotland clerly from the ffrenche (the dutye of there aleagyance savyd). Ageyne of the other syd yf I did perceyve cause of dout in these advrtysemnts then shuld thys sentence rule me *Quando cum potest fieri r[edi]vis id velis r[e]drpossis*.[45]

His advice was as sound as it was timely, and when Cecil negotiated the Treaty of Edinburgh in the weeks that followed, he acted well within its spirit.[46]

Following their withdrawal from Scotland, the French underwent a rapid sequence of political difficulties of their own. After young King Francis died in December 1560, the nation experienced the first outbreak of the hostilities which would collectively become known as the Wars of Religion.[47] Gone for three decades was the time when France could long maintain a united political front in Scotland or against the English. Instead, English intervention came to be thought of as a likely factor in the determination of French affairs.

This was immediately evident in August 1562, when the Prince de Condé offered Elizabeth a chance to regain the long-lamented Calais in return for aiding his Huguenot campaign against the House of Guise. If Elizabeth would consent to garrison and maintain Newhaven [le Havre] and Dieppe he would exchange them for Calais when he captured it himself. Sensing in this the sort of arrangement which had allowed her to aid the Scots and further England's security at the same time, Elizabeth concurred with the plan, and the English forces soon began their occupation. It was to prove a hasty and ill-considered decision.[48]

Not only did the Huguenots fail to be as generous as Condé with what they saw as their rightful territory, but the Prince himself soon fell upon hard times. When his army collapsed and he was captured at Dreux in December, Elizabeth's forces were left high and dry at Newhaven.[49] The assassination of the Duc de Guise in the following February further united the French factions, and for a brief time they could present a solid front against the English enclave.[50] In May came an even more deadly foe: the plague appeared in the garrisoned town and began to pace its rounds. Within weeks the situation became nearly untenable. Although the initial casualties were soon made up by fresh reinforcements, the futility of holding out soon became evident to many.[51] Yet to abandon Newhaven after the loss of Calais would be an even greater blow to English honour.

Bacon had railed against the loss of Calais in January 1559,[52] and although he had demurred for a time against hostilities with France later in that year,[53] his initial reaction to the Newhaven campaign recalled his earlier bellicosity. In a memorandum on 'ffrench matters written by the … Lorde Keeper on Whitsunday 30 May 1563' he used the format of a dialogue to speak out clearly on the issue.[54] Instead of keeping Newhaven as a hostage for Calais, England should open a real offensive against the French to take their ancient garrison directly. He reasoned that no hostage would mean as much to the French as Calais itself, and he suggested that England would do well not to expend useless energy on limited objectives. He reiterated what everyone must already have recognized: France did not mean to abide by the treaty of 1559, and the longer England allowed her to retain Calais, the harder she would be to dislodge. As for the prospect of surrendering Newhaven without the return of Calais, he feared for ' ... what it might breede in the handes of the people'. He counted on the conviction that France would find it difficult to oppose an English campaign in view of her domestic difficulties, and assumed that she intended to starve Newhaven's defenders into submission. He admitted that it would be an expensive venture if his advice were accepted, and recognized that the Queen could expect little from parliament. But he suggested that she might raise the needed money by the sale of crown lands – a daring suggestion in view of his knowledge that such sales had not always been successful in the past[55] – and selling about £1,000-worth annually could be justified if it would secure the desired end. If his opinion fell upon deaf ears, he hoped that the French meant to stick to their treaty obligations after all, for great dishonour would accrue to England if she did not.

These thoughts came at the end of May. By June the ravages of the plague upon the garrison had become still more serious, and unspoken thoughts of abandoning the venture grew at Westminster. Yet in some quarters confidence, or the inability to admit defeat, remained. Sir Thomas Smith, one of the two English ambassadors serving in France at the time, wrote to Cecil as late as July 4th to say that the French knew that they would never take Newhaven.[56] Cecil had held that opinion even before he heard from Smith, and now he became adamant. Although Elizabeth herself showed signs of giving up her firm resolve to keep the town, Cecil wrote on the 15th to announce still another dispatch of fresh troops.[57] By that time it had become plain to a great many at Westminster that the retention of Newhaven was a vain hope. Elizabeth shortly opened the matter to her council at Greenwich.

The debate hinged to a large extent on the strength of Cecil's defence of a steadfast course. If he could carry sufficient support among the uncommitted his views would prevail. Bacon allowed others to speak while he assessed the issues and the alignment of the councillors. At last he broke his silence and delivered what proved to be the decisive opinion. In a speech which later drew a stinging rebuke from Cecil, he tacitly discounted his loyalty to the Secretary and urged consideration of surrender.[58] Fortunately, a diligent note-taker has preserved the speech for us. Bacon foresaw the consequences of his suggested course of action and would not treat them lightly, but he saw that the garrison's days were numbered. It was possible, he allowed, that faulty leadership was as much to blame for the crisis as the plague, and as a preliminary step he proposed that more information be gathered regarding the precise situation. But if such a report indicated that the cause had truly been lost, he advised Elizabeth to instruct the ambassadors to sue for the most honourable surrender possible. As a final note, he reminded all present that the French were not to be trusted.

Happily, the anonymous recorder of this meeting did not rest with the conclusion of this speech, and for once we can follow up on the effects of Bacon's counsel. Elizabeth was impressed, and asked the others for their approval of his plan. Many indicated their support and, although there were a few abstentions, no one responded when dissenting views were invited. Cecil, who remained unconvinced, was dumb-struck at Bacon's boldness, and poured out his wrath to the Lord Keeper in a letter the next morning.[59] It was one of the few instances of friction between Bacon and Cecil in an association lasting more than three decades. The council's mandate sufficed for Elizabeth; she thanked Bacon for his sound advice, and ordered Thomas Randolph on a fact-finding mission to Newhaven. When Randolph confirmed the Lord Keeper's pessimistic message, surrender orders were issued without delay. Evacuation was well under way by July 31st.[60]

In these early years Bacon was not steadfast in pursuit of particular policy goals. Such consistency on matters of foreign policy would come later, when greater experience enabled him to maintain a broad overview of England's position in Europe. But despite his evident vacillation regarding involvement with France, England's financial ability to sustain hostilities and her proper relation with the Scots, Bacon seems even in these initial essays into foreign policy to have maintained a firm grip on certain realities. He bore a general distrust and animosity towards the French, took strong pride in being English, and maintained a vigilant concern for financial considerations as a determining factor in diplomatic decisions. It is further apparent that although foreign affairs was by no means Bacon's *métier*, and although he was frequently absent from the council when such considerations arose for discussion, he kept himself very well informed on such matters and did not hesitate to speak his mind.

Participation in these pressing issues of Elizabeth's first years did not take up much of Bacon's time. His interventions do, however, indicate to us something of his personal approach as a councillor, and suggest the weight with which his counsel could be received. The sensitive balancing of his personal convictions with the political requirements of his office, the ability to remain informed and offer cogent advice even on issues outside his principal sphere of competence, and the obvious ability to act independently of even his closest friend and ally, were to be enduring characteristics of Bacon's involvement in Elizabethan politics.

VII

Social and Economic Policy, 1558-63

When the privy council dealt with matters of domestic concern – finances, commerce, law and order, or the administration of justice and governmental authority throughout the realm – Bacon spoke with truer expertise and much greater authority than when he dealt with any other issue. Although these less dramatic areas of concern have not received the attention accorded by modern historians to such problems as the marriage and succession or the vagaries of Elizabethan diplomacy, they were perhaps even more crucial to the contemporary state of English society. Bacon's activities in this broad area establish him as one of the architects of Elizabethan social and economic policy.

It would be nearly impossible to treat Bacon's role in domestic policy-making during the early years of the reign without extended reference to Professor S. T. Bindoff's important attempt to identify Bacon as the guiding hand behind the Statute of Artificers of 1563, one of the longest and most important pieces of social legislation of the entire century.[1] Considering the significance of the Statute, and of Bacon's presumed role in the long series of events which led up to it, an evaluation of Professor Bindoff's masterfully crafted essay encompasses virtually the whole of Bacon's involvement in the creation of domestic policy during the first four years of the reign. In brief, Professor Bindoff's thesis is as follows.

Seeking to prepare a programme of economic and social reform for the opening Parliament of the reign, on December 23rd, 1558, the government named a committee 'For consideracion of all thinges necessary for the Parlyamente'.[2] The commissioners were nearly all career lawyers: in addition to the judges and serjeants at law *en bloc*, they included Chief Justices Browne and

Saunders, the Attorney General Edward Griffin, the Solicitor General Richard Weston, the bencher and long-time member of Gray's Inn Richard Goodrich, Sir Thomas Smith – the only non-practising lawyer or jurist – and the Lord Keeper who, as the only privy councillor, served as chairman. To this group, whose function had never been conclusively demonstrated, Professor Bindoff assigns the collective authorship of a document which emerged early in 1559, and which is known as the 'Considerations delivered to the Parliament, 1559'.[3]

This intriguing document presents nothing less than a comprehensive and wide-ranging programme for social and economic reform. Its recommendations may be arbitrarily arranged into three basic categories: regarding classes of people, including vagabonds, husbandmen, merchants, apprentices, schoolmasters, nobles, law students, labourers and servants; classes of commodities, including gold and silver, haberdashery, wines, sugar, leather and shoes; and diverse economic and commercial institutions, such as the Steelyard, the English Staple at Middleburg, commercial licences, iron mills, the navy and the fishing industry. Despite apparent government interest in the recommendations of the 'Considerations', and the formulation of parts of these recommendations into bills by committees of the Commons,[4] nothing of its substance was approved by that Parliament.

Left at the end of the session with no programme for economic and social reform, Professor Bindoff suggests that the government fell back on existing powers and statutes to effect certain changes, albeit in an unco-ordinated manner, during the next few years. He cites such efforts as the Northamptonshire wage assessments of 1560, the great recoinage of 1560–61, the plans for the better execution of justice in the shires and for the reduction in the number of J.P.s, and the distribution of an abridgment of the statutes for use by those magistrates.[5] Finally, he continues, the government introduced into the Parliament of 1563, the second meeting of the reign, a social and economic legislative programme which was based both on the 'Considerations' of 1559 and the sundry reforms of the inter-parliamentary years. Out of that programme, and after a great deal of debate and amendment, emerged the Statute of Artificers.[6]

Through all these factors Professor Bindoff perceives the connecting link of Bacon's guiding hand.[7] He draws a line from the Lord Keeper's known membership of the committee of December 1558 to his known or presumed interest in many of the points in the 'Considerations', which is alleged to be the handiwork of that committee. He cites in support of this observation 'the proposals to foster education ... of nobility and gentry; to restrict entry to the profession of law; to punish bankrupts and perjurors; and to give every shire its own sheriff'; and concludes that 'all these have a Baconian ring ... '[8] He then observes that one of the two parliamentary committees which considered these proposals was headed by Bacon's father-in-law Sir Anthony Cooke, and that Bacon was associated in one way or another with several of the government's inter-parliamentary reform measures.[9] Finally, he suggests that the actual making of the Statute in the Parliament of 1563 was engineered by Bacon – who was excused from his Chancery duties during that period 'on the Queen's business' – through the co-operation of two of his judicial associates: Thomas Seckford, Master of Requests, and William Cordell, Master of the Rolls, respectively the chairmen of the first and second parliamentary committees to consider the government programme.[10] Any assessment of this impressive and intricate hypothesis is indeed a challenging task, but as so much of Professor Bindoff's argument rests upon the nature of Bacon's activities between 1558 and 1563, it cannot be shirked. In general, what has come to light regarding Bacon's career does much to vindicate his presumed role in the making of the Statute of Artificers, but not always for the reasons put forward by Professor Bindoff. In addition, much can be added which lends credence to other aspects of his thesis, for Bacon's involvement in the domestic concerns of these four years far exceeds what has commonly been realized.

Bacon's membership of the committee of December 1558 is undeniable, but it seems difficult to link the responsibilities of that committee 'For consideracion of all thinges necessary for the Parlyamente' with the 'Considerations delivered to the Parliament' of 1559. The word 'Consideration' appears to be misleading here, for its appearance both in the title of the committee and the document have suggested a linkage between the two. The *key* word in the committee's descriptive title would appear to be 'all', for the 'Considerations' can by no means be construed to encompass 'all' of the government's expectations from that Parliament. It dealt exclusively with economic and social matters, and entirely omitted mention of other vital aspects of the government's programme: a bill for doctrinal uniformity, a bill for the royal supremacy, the grant of a subsidy, and so forth.[11] Beyond this semantic hint of the December committee's true function, we have only the membership of the body to work with. It cannot be a coincidence that except for Smith, an acknowledged expert on English law and government, all were career lawyers and jurists. When Professor Bindoff's acknowledgment that two of the members were Catholics soon to be demoted is joined with the facts that none of the economic experts of the privy council sat on the committee and that only Bacon, sworn to the privy council just the day before the committee was formed,[12] was a councillor at the time, it is indeed hard to imagine that such a group would be asked to design an entire legislative programme for the first Parliament of the reign. One can only conclude that the committee of December was conceived with an altogether different purpose in mind. Its composition and title suggest no more than that, once the writs of election had been sent out on December 5th, this committee was intended to advise the government and the young and inexperienced Queen of the legal technicalities and traditional forms involved in holding a parliament, and in repeating or reaffirming the legislation passed in previous reigns.

Once the connection between the committee of December and the 'Considerations' is thus brought into question, the suggestion of Bacon's participation in the latter can only rest on his known views and their affinity with the specific points or general tenor of the latter document. Here the claims of a 'Baconian ring' must come under close scrutiny.

Like the Statute of Artificers, the 'Considerations' is a reactionary and repressive document.[13] It seeks further to segregate the social classes, and emphasizes that the humbly born ought not to expect advancement in emulation of their betters. It seeks to prevent certain classes of people from engaging in the free purchase of land, from the right to attend the Inns of Court, and from the employment of tutors for their children. For their part, nobles are enjoined to keep their status unassailable by educating their children in the service of the state, and are accorded the exclusive privilege of education in the common law. In sum, the 'Considerations' reminds its readers that 'generation [i.e., birth] is the chiefest foundation of inclination'.

There can be little doubt that a good many of the specific subjects treated in the 'Considerations' were of more than passing interest to Bacon, and a few points in particular do appear to bear his stamp. He did take considerable interest in the education of the peerage[14] and, as Professor Bindoff also observes, expressed that concern in his proposals for educating the Queen's wards, very close indeed to the time at which the 'Considerations' was drawn up.[15] On the other hand, and of perhaps crucial importance, no one's life could better have exemplified the specific attitudes which that document sought to vilify and prohibit than did Bacon's. He was, as we know, of yeoman extraction, a graduate of the Inns of Court who purchased a great deal of land and carved out a handsome career for himself very much in emulation of his betters. He educated at least three of his sons with private tutors at one time or another, both before and after 1559, and sent them all to Cambridge and Gray's Inn.[16] Finally, though he did emphasize the importance of educating the sons of the nobility – not in itself a novel idea among educational theorists of the Tudor era – he had also made provision for the education of the poor in the grammar school at Redgrave,[17] and would leave six scholarships for poor scholars at Corpus Christi College, Cambridge.[18] Not even the Denton–Bacon–Cary Report, in which he had at least some share, discriminated between well-born and humbly born students; instead it recommended crown support for all.[19] It might be suggested that, having climbed the greasy pole to considerable heights, Bacon adopted the traditional attitude of the newly successful in seeking to block the advancement of others by a similar route; but no independent evidence, either from his poetry or prose writings or from his actions, does much to support such a contention. There are indications that Cecil or one of his followers may have had a hand in drawing up the 'Considerations', and here one cannot easily brush aside the role of Anthony Cooke, but it is difficult to imagine that the Lord Keeper himself had much to do with it.

Not until the government's inter-parliamentary measures were introduced to bring some order to the economic and social problems of the realm does firm evidence of Bacon's role emerge, but here there is abundant evidence to confirm and even augment Professor Bindoff's suggestions. Not only does such evidence support the suggestion of Bacon's involvement with the Statute of Artificers, but it points as well to his crucial participation in a majority of the government's domestic innovations during this early part of the reign.

The nature of the government's interest in domestic reform after the Parliament of 1559 can hardly be better exemplified than in the speech which Bacon delivered to the justices of the assize in the Star Chamber at the end of Trinity Term, 1559.[20] The meeting came on the heels of the Parliament, and this was just one of the speeches that the Lord Keeper regularly made to the justices before they departed to ride their circuits. He used this occasion, as he used others like it, to explain the particular concerns of the government so that the justices might carry forth and implement its policy in their jurisdictions.[21]

After a lengthy prologue in which Bacon sought to impress upon his listeners the consequences of the diligent or lax performance of their duty, he reached the substance of his remarks. Of particular concern to the Queen and privy council were three responsibilities which fell to the justices:

> The ffirste in thavoydeinge of all forcible assemblyes ryotous demeanours, frayes, and assaultes, and of all seditious rumores tales and newes, and in the discoueringe with speede all manner of conspiracies and confederacies and in the diligent searchinge out and austeare punisheinge of felonies and murders and suche like mischiefes. The seconde in bannisheinge ... all forestallinge,* regrateinge, and engrosseinge, and ... also all champerties,† mainetenaunces and embraceries, for where theis remaine and be, there

* *Forestalling*: intercepting goods before they reach their destination; specifically, the buying up of goods at wholesale prices with the hope of reselling them more dearly. *Regrating*: selling goods at retail after purchasing them at a lower price. *Engrossing*: buying in quantity or wholesale.

† *Champerty*: an illegal device whereby a party not otherwise involved in a law case agrees to help a litigant in return for a share of the spoils of victory, usually in the form of property. *Maintenance*: an act of unlawfully aiding a litigant, i.e. champerty. *Embrasure*: an attempt to corrupt justice.

peace and concorde (whereof ye oughte to be up holders) cannot dwell. The thirde and laste in the diligente enquire-inge hereinge and determininge of all manner of offences contrarye eyther to the common lawe or anye statute lawe of this Realme examinable and determinable by you by vertue of your comission.[22]

These remarks of June 1559 constitute one of the first public expressions of social and economic concern by the Elizabethan government, and several of Bacon's points would find their way into the statute book in subsequent parliaments.[23]

When one turns to government action on financial issues in those early years, Professor Bindoff is quite correct in dwelling upon the great recoinage of 1560–61,[24] but that was not the first or indeed the only step taken to bring financial order to the realm. Nor was it the first action in which Bacon played a part. Among the earliest priorities facing the privy council before it could effectively utilize the apparatus of government was the need to survey the precise state of revenues held by, or due in payment to, the fiscal bodies of Westminster. This undramatic but essential chore was first recognized in the same privy council meeting of December 23rd which established the committee for the Parliament. Bacon, Sir Richard Rich, Lord North and Walter Mildmay were then empowered to 'understand what lands have been graunted from the Crown in the late quenes tyme'.[25] This was an attempt to gain some idea of the revenues from crown lands, including wardships and other feudal dues, which might be forthcoming to the royal coffers. Bacon was the chairman of the committee and its sole privy councillor.[26]

After the parliamentary subsidy had been voted and accepted by the Queen in the spring of 1559, Elizabeth sought to augment her coffers beyond what she had dared to ask of her subjects. She named several of her councillors, including Bacon, to a com-mittee for the sale of crown lands.[27] If we may judge by the July report of that committee, the scheme was not immediately successful. Bacon, Sackville and Winchester then felt compelled to inform her that she would be well advised to suspend the sales altogether.[28] That counsel did little to comfort the Queen in her visions of penury, and she looked about her for a more vigorous course of action.

Some time later Elizabeth received a comprehensive memorandum on a means by which she could take stock of the royal revenues, and she seized upon the plan with zeal. This scheme comes down to us anonymously, although there is no reason to think that the Queen received it in that state, as a 'Remembrance howe to proceede to the understandinge of the State of her Mati revenue & the reformacon of unnecessarie expence thereof.' The extant copy survives in a collection of Bacon's speeches in the British Library.[29] Apart from this coincidence of location, there are several indications that Bacon was indeed its author. He was obviously interested and involved in its subject, and only a person of his station might presume to deal with something as sensitive as the Queen's revenues or to request access to all the necessary records concerning them. Finally, the provision by name for participation of the three chief financial officers of the realm – Winchester, Sackville and Mildmay – all of whom are referred to in the third person while the report is written in the first person, would seem to preclude their authorship. By process of elimination, Bacon's involvement appears highly likely. As for the date of composition, internal evidence indicates only that the report emerged some time between March 25th, 1559, and June 1561. The importance of the 'Remembrance' lies not so much in the originality of its suggestions, many of which were not new, but rather in its scope; its recommendations encompassed nearly all major revenue-collecting offices in the central government, both within and without the Household.

In brief, the 'Remembrance' asked that the Queen appoint two separate committees to carry out complementary surveys of revenues and expenditures in different fiscal bodies. The first committee was to investigate the amount of revenue which had come to the Queen at her accession, and what had been taken in since by the Exchequer, the Tower, the Court of Wards, and the Duchy of Lancaster. Once these figures had been obtained, they were to be compared with records of expenditure during the same period, so as to ascertain the present state of finances in those institutions. Beyond that, the commissioners were to make projections of anticipated receipts and expenditure for several years ahead, so as to facilitate planning. The offices of the suggested commissioners, treasurer, under treasurer, and chancellor of the Exchequer respectively, and the provision that they were to receive full access to the records of all the institutions named, indicates that the report was not meant to be taken lightly or fulfilled half-heartedly.

The second commission was to be made up largely of the Lord Treasurer and unnamed officers in the Exchequer. It was accorded an even more demanding and sensitive task, for it was to deal with the finances of specific individuals as well as with government institutions. These commissioners were to assess the value and incidence of the royal pensions, and to examine in the same manner as the first committee the victualling of Berwick, the financial condition of the Admiralty, the household chamber, the wardrobe, the mint, the costs of Queen Mary's funeral and Elizabeth's coronation, and the accounts of the Queen's agent in the Low Countries, Sir Thomas Gresham. Nor did the 'Remembrance' fail to recognize the sensitivity of the assignment, for an afterthought cautioned that 'this matter is verie weightie & would be well wayed before it be enterprized, I meane concerning this second commission'.

The substance of the 'Remembrance' was adopted by the Queen: the first part virtually to the letter, and the second somewhat more loosely. The first commission was established on June 19th, 1561.[30] True even to the suggestions for personnel, Winchester, Mildmay and Sackville were included, but – another hint of his authorship – Bacon was added at the head of the group, and Arundel, Pembroke and Cecil were also named. Judging by the weighty evidence of its activity over the next few years, the committee took its duties every bit as seriously as the 'Remembrance' had intended, and there is every indication that the Lord Keeper played a leading role in gathering the required data.[31]

As if the final cautionary note of its author had been taken to heart, the second committee proposed by the 'Remembrance' was not formed as intended, i.e. as a single committee, but several of the individual assignments which were to have pertained to this committee were carried out at the Queen's command by *ad hoc* groups. Thus, for example, Clinton, Knollys, Cecil and Mildmay, only two of them members of the first committee, were empowered to audit Gresham's accounts on June 30th, and their obligation to do so was renewed at regular intervals for several years. Several other audits of office in this second category also appear in Bacon's papers, and thus he may well have played some role in carrying out both halves of his recommendation.[32]

At about the same time that the 'Remembrance' was being compiled and presented, Elizabeth had begun to come to grips with the serious problem of devalued coinage which had plagued the realm ever since her father had tinkered with the monetary works.[33] In a series of measures designed to squeeze more money out of a fixed amount of specie, Henry had diluted the fine content of gold and silver coins by the addition of small amounts of base metal. Not only did this effectively devalue the coinage of the realm, but as he had diluted gold and silver coins with different amounts of base metal, he had also destroyed the traditional bimetallic ratio. The results had been sharply felt. 'Good coins' of the old issue were hoarded, and when merchants raised their prices in compensation for the lower values of the new coinage, serious economic dislocation ensued. These problems had been recognized under Edward and Mary, but only half a solution was forthcoming in their reigns. Coins with a higher fine content were issued in 1552 and again under Mary, thus restoring 'good' coinage which was nearly equivalent to the original Henrician standard. But the later Henrician coins were not recalled, and an even more pronounced duality in monetary values ensued.

As Elizabeth came to the throne the effects of the unsound coinage were widely experienced, and many of the economic woes of the realm were attributed to that problem. At first she ordered the mint to strike coins at Marian values, but this was merely an interim measure until a more enduring solution could be worked out.[34] Before long it became evident that all base coinage would have to be removed from circulation so that the dual standard could be eliminated. It was also recognized that a completely new issue of both gold and silver coins would have to be struck simultaneously, so as to restore a single, sound and bimetallic standard. Such an enormous task was without precedent in recent English experience, and entailed many risks. Obviously the planned recoinage would have to be kept strictly secret if massive speculation were to be prevented, and yet extensive consultations, well beyond the perimeter of the privy council, proved necessary as well.

In this context, William Cecil and a few others were given the chief responsibility in February 1559 for gathering advice and formulating a comprehensive scheme to accomplish the re-coinage.[35] During the months that followed, Cecil solicited advice from experts in various fields, and received numerous reports on all aspects of the problem: the nature and value of the new coinage, the problems of minting such a large amount of currency in a short time, the means of exchanging the old for the new coinage, the effects on foreign trade, and the impact of the whole venture on Ireland and Wales.[36] Throughout this entire process the secret was guarded as closely as possible, and not until Elizabeth made her first announcement of the recoinage at the end of September 1560 was the whole privy council apprised of the project.[37]

During these months of planning, Bacon acted as an unofficial but effective assistant to Cecil in gathering and evaluating the solicited opinions from which the final plans were formulated. A number of contingency plans for the modification of the Irish coinage survive among Bacon's Redgrave Hall Papers, and are endorsed in the Lord Keeper's unmistakable hand.[38] Although Bacon does not seem to have submitted any plan of his own, Cecil clearly relied upon his judgement regarding the recoinage up to and beyond the Queen's promulgation of September 1560. Much remained indeterminate following that proclamation, and in the ensuing weeks Bacon offered his advice on such matters as the desirable standard of the new issue, the means of indenting and delivering the new coins, and of assuring a true minting from Thomas Stanley, the Master of the Mint.[39] Although Bacon was not appointed to the committee which saw to the operation of the mint during the actual recoinage, his corre-spondence, and the meetings with Cecil to which it alludes, indicates that he kept well informed of the issue. His later participation on similar commissions, especially that of 1578 which recommended adjustments in the standard issue of coin-age, further bears out his expertise and interest in problems relating to coinage.[40]

Other aspects of the government's domestic policy which figure prominently in Professor Bindoff's argument concern the administration of law throughout the realm, and here again Bacon's role seems crucial. He did indeed work out with Cecil a plan for reducing the number of J.P.s[41] and, as has been noted, regularly exhorted the justices of the assize towards more professional conduct in the discharge of their responsibilities.[42] The latter theme, it must be noted, also ran through many of Bacon's reforms in the Chancery.[43] In addition, Bacon was very much attuned to the idea of codifying the common law. This may be seen not only in the two instances which Professor Bindoff observes – in the distribution of a digest of statutes throughout the shires in 1561 and 1562, and in his remarks to the joint Houses of Parliament in the opening session of 1563[44] – but also in his later proposal in the form of a 'Devise how the statutes of this realm are to be ordered and printed ... '[45]

In view of Bacon's commanding role in formulating the government's economic and social measures between 1558 and 1563, it is indeed appropriate to suggest his active and perhaps even dominant participation in the making of the Statute of Artificers. Although it, too, was conservative and repressive as a document of social legislation, it did not deal with most of the issues which Bacon would probably have found objectionable in the 'Considerations' of 1559. The observation that Thomas Seckford and William Cordell are known to have played a decisive role in steering the basic principles of the ultimate statute through parliamentary committees is of considerable significance in this respect.[46] As regular members of the lower House they had the freedom to participate in such debates which Bacon did not have, and which Cecil and other privy councillors often could not exercise to the same effect. Cordell, who was possibly the author of the final bill, was a Marian rather than an Elizabethan appointment in the Chancery, and was Master of the Rolls when Bacon came to that Court, but he was close enough to the Lord Keeper to have worked in harmony with him for several years, and would later help in the 1572 election of Bacon's son as Knight of the Shire for Suffolk.[47] Seckford, a Suffolk man like Bacon and Cordell, had been a fellow bencher to Bacon at Gray's Inn for over a decade, and was also a likely choice to assist Bacon in getting the statute through.[48]

In sum, the suggestion of Bacon's role in the making of the Statute of Artificers seems on the whole well-founded, considering the circumstantial evidence at hand. But its validity appears to rest upon the Lord Keeper's record in the inter-parliamentary years rather than upon his alleged connection with the 'Considerations' of 1559. Beyond that specific piece of legislation, however important, Bacon's participation in exhorting the justices to diligent discharge of government policy, in planning the great recoinage, in assessing the state of the royal finances, and in seeking to bring about a codification of the statutes, establishes him as one of the architects of early Elizabethan social and economic policy.

VIII

Disgrace and Recovery, 1563-5

By the conclusion of the Parliament of 1563 Nicholas Bacon had established himself as an integral part of the privy council, and all who were familiar with his activities knew him as one of the most diligent and industrious of its members. Yet many times in the past the vicissitudes of Tudor politics had demonstrated the thin line between personal triumph and disgrace in the service of the crown, and within the year Bacon's fortunes would plummet from one extreme to the other. Unlike such victims as Wolsey or Cromwell, it cannot be said of Bacon that pride went before his fall. Nor did his disgrace prove terminal. Almost anyone who attained high office in that age had to reckon with the harsh infighting which came with it. In the Elizabethan era, Bacon was one of the first to experience those perils. In his case as in most, the stakes were higher than his own future: at the least they involved the political hegemony on the council, and at the most, the determination of the royal succession.

The earliest indication of the intense factionalism which was to dominate the Elizabethan privy council throughout the reign came in the spring of 1559, when Robert Dudley, not yet a member of that body, emerged as the royal favourite. With his youth, charm and skills in the courtly arts, Dudley was the courtier *par excellence*, and his rise in the royal esteem was little short of meteoric. Although for some time he demurred from speaking out on political issues, he rapidly became known as a rich source of patronage and influence. In that capacity he ministered to all parties: Catholics and protestants, clerics and laymen, peers and fortune-seekers alike sought him out for the influence which, thanks to the Queen's bounty, lay at his command. By 1560 Dudley had grown high enough in Elizabeth's favour for it to be rumoured that he meant to do away with his wife and press for the royal hand in marriage. Such widespread rumours gained sudden credibility in September of that year when his unfortunate spouse was discovered at the foot of her staircase with a broken neck.[1]

The rapidity of Dudley's rise and the suddenness of his availability as the Queen's suitor inspired a mixture of awe, hostility and dismay among most of the privy councillors. His open and fervent pursuit of Elizabeth's hand did little to allay those emotions. Cecil in particular, for he had the most to lose by the new rivalry, led the rest in despair, and upon one occasion came close to resigning his office.[2] At last the court and privy council had a *casus belli* in their midst, and the sides were quickly drawn. The Earl of Bedford and Marquis of Winchester among the peers, and Throckmorton, Mildmay and Francis Knollys among the commoners, supported Cecil from the start.[3] Although Bacon had already shown that he could be independent of Cecil in the question of sending troops into Scotland, there can be little doubt that he also supported his brother-in-law without reservation against this new threat. It is in no sense valid to suggest, as has recently been done, that Bacon had his own designs on the leadership of the privy council.[4]

Dudley's own supporters are more difficult to isolate. They included Sir Thomas Parry, the Earl of Pembroke and Sir Henry Killigrew, but even in 1566, when Cecil compiled a list of his adversary's forces, there were few others of prominence among them.[5] Parry, who had not long to live, seems to have been anxious to cling to the comet's tail, while Pembroke's loyalty is more difficult to account for. Killigrew, an old friend of the Cecils, had fallen out with William, and even in 1564 the Secretary would disapprove of Sir Henry's marriage to Catherine Cooke, another of Sir Anthony's prodigious brood of daughters.[6] Although Killigrew later renewed his friendship with Cecil, he would always be considered a Dudley follower. Of greatest importance, Dudley seemed to have the support of the Queen, and that threatened to make all the difference in the balance of power at court.

What may have been the point of no return in the Cecil–Dudley rivalry came in October 1562, when Elizabeth fell gravely ill with smallpox. At her peak of her illness she slipped from consciousness, and her death appeared so certain that the court hastily prepared for mourning while the councillors met hurriedly to consider the succession. Almost miraculously, she regained consciousness and drew her advisers to her bedside. In an unsteady whisper she told them that if she should not survive she would have them name Robert Dudley as Lord Protector of the kingdom. He was not even a member of the privy council at the time.[7]

Shortly thereafter, Elizabeth began a slow recovery, and thus obviated the council's compliance with her wish. But once uttered it could not be forgotten, nor could the political and personal relations among her advisers ever again assume the same amity and openness which had characterized the first months of the reign. As if to fling the apple of discord further into their midst, Elizabeth shortly afterwards made Dudley a member of the council.[8] He now had not only a ready source of patronage, but a platform from which to speak out on issues of policy.

Given the close call of the previous October, it was only to be expected that the Parliament of 1563 would dwell at greater length on the issue of the royal marriage and succession – an issue which had easily been shelved at the first Parliament. This time the debate was pointed and prolonged, and the members demanded more than Elizabeth's previous promise to remain a virgin. The petition urging her to marry, which Bacon dutifully conveyed from the House of Lords, had no greater effect than the debates themselves,[9] but at the same time there were other moves afoot regarding the royal marriage and succession which were not openly discussed.

Some time before this Parliament convened, a former government official and Marian exile named John Hales, who would take his seat as a member for Lancashire, wrote a 'book' favouring Lady Catherine Grey's claim to the throne. It opposed the rival claims of Lady Margaret Lennox and – of greater consequence – Mary Stuart.[10] Hales had intended to circulate the tract among sympathetic M.P.s in order to gain their support in urging Elizabeth to acknowledge the Grey claim. Although the tract made no reference to Dudley, it could well have been used as an effective thrust at his pretensions. As Hales went about this plan, Elizabeth was working to bring about a marriage between Dudley and Mary Stuart, and would soon name him the Earl of Leicester to make the match seem more attractive.[11] If Elizabeth could be made to recognize the Grey claim, the favourite might be thwarted in his presumed ambition to gain a crown by marrying her; for even if Elizabeth gave in to Leicester's earnest suit, such recognition could facilitate a marriage such as Mary Tudor arranged with Philip of Spain, whereby the bridegroom was king in name only and without hereditary rights to the throne. To say the least, Hales had set to work at a crucial time.

In order to establish his case for Lady Catherine's claim, Hales had to prove two points. He first had to show that her initially clandestine marriage to the Earl of Hertford some four years before was in fact quite legal. In her rage at discovering the match as a *fait accompli*, Elizabeth had empowered a commission to investigate the marriage and, to no one's surprise, it had been declared illegal. To allow it to remain so would not only weaken Lady Catherine's chances of gaining Elizabeth's recognition, but would effectively debar from the succession any children of the match: already there were two such heirs. Secondly, he had to show that the will of Henry VIII, of which the original had been lost, explicitly precluded the Lennox and Stuart claims from succession after the demise of his direct line. Hales worked hard to build his case, gathering a learned consensus favouring the validity of the marriage, and even sending an aide to sample the opinion of various Continental divines. The tract had then been circulated surreptitiously in the months after its completion, and came accidentally to the attention of the Queen in the early spring of 1564.[12]

It could hardly have done so at a less auspicious time, and Elizabeth's furious and indignant reaction created waves which lapped at the highest reaches of her government for months to come. Catherine's unacceptable marriage to Hertford, and the birth of two children to that match – males, no less – despite the unpropitious circumstances of the couple's imprisonment, had already predisposed Elizabeth to look with considerable disfavour on any claims from the Grey camp.[13] Those feelings alone, widely known at court, should have dissuaded Hales from his plan, but his puritan zeal had long since got the better of his judgement in the matter. On a broader level, Elizabeth was only then beginning to recover from the blow to her prestige represented by the loss of Newhaven a few months before.[14] At the same time, her delicate negotiations for Mary's hand in marriage to Leicester could be utterly destroyed by the appearance of the tract. Finally, the clandestine and well-organized manner in which Hales had gone about his scheme made her fear that her very tenure of the throne, not by any means secure, was under siege from unknown forces operating at the heart of Westminster.[15]

All things considered, there were many questions on the Queen's mind in the early spring of 1564. Who had suggested the device of appealing the findings of her commission regarding the legitimacy of the Grey–Hertford marriage? Who had funded the fact-finding mission to the Continent? Finally, had Hales acted alone, or had he merely been the expendable front man of a conspiracy? To obtain the answers to these questions, she commissioned Cecil, himself not entirely above suspicion, to launch an investigation.[16] Before long, her wrath found an object in Bacon.

Assuming, as Elizabeth seems to have done, that Hales had not acted alone in the design or implementation of his scheme, the Lord Keeper was certainly conspicuous among those who might have helped. Although he had proved his ability to prosper and endure in office under a Catholic monarch, he had always been identified as an ardent protestant, and had long felt threatened by the prospect of a Stuart succession. It was that fear which had led him to speak out against the meeting of Elizabeth and Mary Stuart that had been planned for 1562 – a meeting which pointed towards a rapprochement between the Queens and a possible recognition of Mary's claim to the succession.[17] He could hardly have been unaware that a blow struck for Catherine was a blow against Leicester, and in Bacon's view Catherine herself, a trustworthy protestant, was an attractive prospect for the succession, the advancement of whose cause would augur well for his own future. Finally, only someone with Bacon's legal expertise was thought capable of having provided either the professional advice necessary to several points of the scheme or the whereabouts of the Chancery enrolment of Henry's will.[18]

But the most incriminating factor, and one which came to light only in the course of Cecil's investigation, was Bacon's interview with Francis Newdigate some time in mid-1563. Newdigate was Hertford's step-father, and an admitted party to the scheme. According to Newdigate's testimony of May 2nd, 1564,[19] only he, Hales, and Lord John Grey of Pyrgo, Lady Catherine's uncle, had been in on the planning of the scheme at the beginning. But when Hales became unsure of the best way to launch an appeal against the marriage ruling, he sent Newdigate to consult some of the privy councillors about the problem. Having first been brushed off by Cecil himself, Newdigate then went to the Lord Keeper. Bacon refused to aid any appeal through the courts, but allegedly agreed to help bring an appeal directly to the Queen. If he ever acted on that presumed offer, no record of it has survived. Finally, Newdigate recalled that he 'left no copie of any [of] theise books [i.e. copies of the tract] with any of the privy councell onlie yt were with my L Kep wch as I sayd I do not perfectly remember'. This was the strongest indication of Bacon's contact with Hales's plan, and was sufficient to connect him with it in the eyes of the Queen.

In view of the later course of events, it is odd that Bacon seems not to have experienced the Queen's wrath immediately after Newdigate's disclosure. He is not mentioned in Cecil's accounts of the Hales affair and its aftermath sent to Sir Thomas Smith in April and May,[20] and the surviving records of the Star Chamber show him present and drawing his diet through the last sitting of that court for the Trinity Term, on June 16th.[21] Not until July did Bacon seek clemency from the Queen, and he did not attend the special Star Chamber sessions of the 3rd or 10th of that month.[22] Two weeks later the Spanish Ambassador de Silva reported that, at Leicester's urging, Sir Anthony Browne would soon replace Bacon at the Chancery.[23] Yet Bacon was still present at the council in August, and was there again when the Star Chamber opened its Michaelmas session in October.[24] Not until mid-November, a full six months after the first signs of Elizabeth's displeasure, was Bacon finally denied access to the court and privy council.[25] He last appeared at the Star Chamber on November 10th,[26] and wrote seeking Cecil's advice on his dilemma on the 27th.[27]

Such a lengthy delay seems strange indeed, and can only be accounted for in one of three ways. Either Mason and Cecil were able to keep Newdigate's incriminating testimony from the Queen until November, or more evidence regarding Bacon came to light after the end of the investigation in May, or something other than Bacon's alleged complicity in the Hales affair was the conclusive reason for his banishment.

The first possibility seems remote. To begin with, Elizabeth's ardent desire to get to the truth made it too difficult and perilous for Cecil and Mason to shield Bacon in such a manner. In addition, Cecil, Thomas Norton and Leicester had commanded Mason to interrogate Newdigate, and none of them can have remained ignorant of the ensuing testimony. Of the three, moreover, Leicester at least could hardly be expected to shield the Lord Keeper.[28] The second possibility seems equally remote, and there appears to be no evidence to support it. Could it be that Bacon was toppled for another reason, for which his alleged part in the Hales fiasco served as a pretext? Although some measure of truth may linger in the traditional acceptance of Bacon's guilt, close scrutiny discounts much of the circumstantial evidence which had been accepted as proof.[29] On the other hand, this and other evidence, some of which has not generally been discussed in this context, indicates that there was more at stake in Bacon's disgrace than has met the eye.

Despite the fact that he may well have welcomed the succession of Lady Catherine Grey, which hardly made him unique even among the privy councillors, there is no evidence to suggest that he preferred her claim actively. We know, however, that Bacon did work actively on behalf of other arrangements for the royal marriage and succession both before and after the Hales episode. Prior to 1564 he had worked secretly to promote the project of a marriage with the Archduke Charles, and he would return to that task early in 1566. Later still he would support the idea of a match with the Duke of Anjou.[30]

While Bacon's ability to deliver a legal opinion regarding various aspects of Hales's scheme is undeniable, he was again hardly unique in that respect, and the same might be said for his presumed access to whatever repository held the enrolment of Henry VIII's will. Hales himself was no stranger to the law or to the keeping of legal records in the environs of Westminster. A protégé of his uncle Sir Christopher Hales – Master of the Rolls, Solicitor General, and then Attorney General under Henry[31] – and the career bureaucrat Sir Ralph Sadler, he himself had served as Keeper of the King's Writs in the Court of King's Bench, Keeper of the First Fruits and Tenths, and Keeper of the

Hanaper in Chancery.[32] If this background were not sufficient to obtain for Hales the information he required, and there is nothing to indicate that it was not sufficient, he also had recourse to the offices of his cousin Edward Hales; since 1549 the latter had held the post of Keeper of the Records in the Tower, the most likely place for the missing will to turn up.[33] So far as we know, Bacon had no personal access to that office at all, and it was even disputed at the time whether records in the Tower pertained to the Master of the Rolls, the only Chancery official including Bacon who could conceivably have enjoyed ready access to them.[34]

There is a contradiction in the assumption of Bacon's accusers that Newdigate left a copy of Hales's tract with the Lord Keeper at their meeting. This would hardly have been necessary had Bacon been in on the plan from the beginning.

It is also important to note that the contemporary accusations of Bacon's role in the Hales scheme seem in most cases to have derived from sources hostile to Bacon. The Earl of Leicester was credited by more than one observer with implicating Bacon beyond the evidently harmless testimony offered by Newdigate, and rumour of that involvement seems to have been picked up from Leicester by the Spanish Ambassador; from there it seems to have made its way into the literature of Jesuit polemics.[35]

Finally, events following the Hales case, and not immediately related to it, further support Bacon's innocence of anything beyond his interview with Newdigate. If Bacon had truly been an accomplice in furthering the tract, Hales had done him a very good turn in shielding him of any suspicion during the protracted course of the investigations, for there is no evidence that Bacon's name came up in any testimony save that of Newdigate on May 2nd. It would certainly have been in Bacon's best interests to maintain amicable relations with Hales as far as possible without showing any overt display of friendship. Yet, far from acting in that manner, Bacon seemed almost to go out of his way to vex the schemer *both before and after* his tract had come to light.

Several months after the investigations of April and May Bacon had not the slightest hesitation in intervening against Hales in a dispute regarding the rightful possession of the keepership of the Hanaper in Chancery. Hales and his erstwhile patron Ralph Sadler had received a joint patent for that office in 1545, and had held it until after Hales went into exile on the Continent in 1551. Three years later, and still abroad, Hales quit-claimed his share of the patent to Sadler, and in 1557 Sadler took on Francis Kempe as his new co-holder of the patent.[36] Upon his return from exile Hales claimed that he was still the rightful holder of the office, and in January 1566 he enlisted Cecil's aid in his suit to regain it.[37] Yet by that time Hales's suit for the office had rested for several years without success before Bacon at the Chancery, and the Lord Keeper had steadfastly refused to support it. Bacon acknowledged as much in a letter to the council written in January 1565, when he was still very much in disgrace and thus presumably vulnerable to accusations from Hales.[38] A full year later Hales complained again to Cecil of Bacon's intransigence.[39] This is hardly the behaviour of a shielded conspirator towards his protector, and clearly indicates that Bacon had nothing to hide in his dealings with Hales. In all probability, therefore, Bacon's complicity in the whole affair was limited to his foolish interview with Newdigate, and must be considered a lapse, however consequential, on his part. Others had done as much and escaped punishment entirely. William Fleetwood, for instance, was thought to be even more deeply implicated than Bacon and, as Recorder of London, was a conspicuous member of the government circle, yet he escaped without censure. Professor Levine has attributed this to Fleetwood's ties with Cecil, but this argument seems unconvincing. Bacon's ties to the Secretary were as strong as anyone else's, and in any case, Fleetwood was more of a follower of Leicester than of Cecil, and was even known to many at court as 'Leicester's Mad Recorder'.[40]

If nothing but the meeting with Newdigate could be held against him, one may well wonder what led Elizabeth to banish Bacon from court, a full six months after the fact became known. Whatever or whoever led her to that step must have had a prodigious influence, for even Cecil could not stay her course of action. Such factors, however circumstantial, point only to one conclusion; it is the conclusion which William Camden reached much closer in time to the events.[41] Only Leicester could have brought about Bacon's disgrace, for few held his sway over Elizabeth, and none had stronger motives. Opposed on the one hand by a formidable and often dominant section of the privy council in nearly all that he hoped to accomplish, and harried on the other by serious negotiations for a Stuart marriage which he did not want,[42] Leicester sought to strike out against those whom he saw as his chief antagonists: Cecil and – both in his own right and as the most prominent and vulnerable supporter of the former – Bacon. Thus the Earl had confided in early October that he considered the whole marriage scheme a ruse on the part of Cecil,[43] who no doubt would have enjoyed removing Leicester from the court. Whether or not Leicester's allegations were well founded – and there is much to indicate Cecil's ardent approval of the marriage plan[44] – the crucial point is that Leicester considered them so.

For several months after Sir James Melville's mission to Westminster on Mary's behalf early in October, the match appeared to have an excellent chance of coming to pass.[45] Those months were extremely difficult for Leicester, and permitted him a very limited scope of action. Even he found it virtually impossible to balk outright at a plan which Elizabeth had adopted with such zeal, but marriage to Mary was a still more disturbing prospect. There were but two reasonable courses of action which he might adopt, and he seems to have pursued them both as far as he was able under the circumstances. He could work with great circumspection towards cooling Mary's ardour for the plan. He did this not only by humbling himself before Melville in their October meeting, but also by clandestine support for the young Lord Darnley, for whom Mary had already taken a liking.[46] Beyond that, he could work with equal circumspection to regain the political initiative at Westminster, so as to place his opponents on the defensive. Only then might he be able to dissuade Elizabeth from her design.

It was just at this crucial period, hardly a month after Melville's mission, that Bacon, already in royal displeasure for a full six months, was banished altogether. The intersection of timing and circumstances is too vivid for coincidence. There is every reason to believe that Bacon's ultimate disgrace came not primarily through his insignificant role in the Hales scheme, but because that pretext made him the most vulnerable target for a dramatic riposte by Leicester, who used his chance to thrust at Cecil and his followers. Thus the blow fell on Bacon's shoulders in November, when Leicester had recovered sufficiently to turn Elizabeth against his foes for the time being, and not in May when the alleged wrong-doing had come to light.

When Cecil first reported the Lord Keeper's banishment in his letter to Sir Thomas Smith, he also noted the strain which the affair had placed upon Bacon: ' ... he hym selfe is not voyde of peryll by heaviness of mynd.'[47] Indeed those months had taken their toll, first removing Bacon's dignity and security at court, and then imperilling his health. On the same day that Cecil wrote to Smith, Bacon had written to the Secretary to tell him what he had already learned.[48] The Queen would no longer suffer him at court unless he could establish his innocence, which he knew not how to do. He would welcome a trial, but saw little hope of securing one. In the meantime, he would rather not live at all than live on in the Queen's disfavour. Perhaps Bacon had intended the letter for the eyes of the Queen as well as Cecil, for he went on to describe his perilous state of health as well as his disquietude of mind. Finally, he asked Cecil to intercede with the Queen if he could, and to speak with Leicester as well, to secure his restoration. If we can take Camden's word for it, Cecil tried his best, though there was little he could do.[49] Bacon knowingly turned his pleas to Leicester directly, and played the thoroughly defeated and contrite adversary in his touching appeals.[50] But try as he might, the Lord Keeper did not fully regain his position at court until April 1565, and then only slowly did he make his way back into his old routine.[51]

The episode of the Hales tract and its aftermath had three enduring effects on Bacon, each of which played some part in his future activities. By reminding him once again how much he relied for his fortunes on the support of the Queen, the affair gave him much pause in openly espousing views which were controversial in nature, and increased the usual circumspection with which he treated such issues. Despite a superficial appearance of political amity in the year or two after the episode, the affair probably served to harden the lines of cleavage in the privy council, and led Bacon to an even closer alignment with Cecil and his followers. Finally, his complaints of illness were not entirely contrived for dramatic effect. Bacon in his mid-fifties was not in sound health. In the year following his return to the Queen's grace, he was reported to be 'at this tyme so visited with

sicknes that he is not able to travel to the upp. howse of ...
parliament', and was consequently replaced for the time by
Robert Catelyn, Chief Justice of the Queen's Bench.[52] He had
been troubled on and off for decades by sundry ills, including
gout and the stone, but with middle age came the excessive
poundage so evident in the familiar portrait in the National
Portrait Gallery (see Plate 3). His stoutness may have been a
source of mild amusement to his Chancery retinue, who waited
chuckling in their collars along the staircase to the Court while
he paused for breath at the top,[53] but it also took its toll of his
accustomed vigour. In addition to those burdens he seems to
have suffered at least some of the time from ' ... decay of his
memory [although this is not evident in his subsequent actions]
and hearing, griefes accompanyinge hoary hairs and old age,
and ... slowe amendment'.[54]

IX

The Years of Intrigue, I:
1565-70

In the weeks following his restoration to the privy council in the spring of 1565, Bacon found most of his colleagues in an emotional trough. Resigned by January to the match between Mary Stuart and the young Lord Darnley, many minds had slumped to a profound dismay after the event itself was celebrated in March. Fears of a Catholic fifth column in England became more vivid than at any previous time in the reign, and many saw the Scottish match as a direct threat to an English protestant succession.[1] Even in that pervading atmosphere of pessimism, however, it is doubtful if the gloomiest observer could have foreseen the difficulties which would befall both England and Scotland in the half-dozen years to come.

For that matter, Mary's marriage would not by any means form the entire context of those coming troubles. Shifts in the political alignment of the European nations would play their part, as would political juxtapositions among the members of the privy council. On the Continent, the continuing strife in France perpetuated the erratic and unstable political climate which had already pertained for a decade. The Habsburgs of Spain had begun to face the imminent threat of revolt in the Netherland provinces. Although the troubles of both regimes appeared internal in nature, the implications of the French religious wars and the Dutch revolt were not restricted to the boundaries of those states. Not even the English Channel could isolate their impact.

In the privy council the lines of cleavage which had been apparent during the first half of the decade, and which were so clearly at work in Bacon's disgrace, still applied, but a new factor had crept into the council's factional divisions with the appointment in 1562 of Thomas Howard, Fourth Duke of Norfolk. He initially came as a protégé of Cecil, but his outspoken manner caused the Secretary to regret his sponsorship, and the duke quickly became his own man.[2] Though young and inexperienced, he was the rightful standard-bearer of the still powerful Howard clan, and was England's only duke. From his palace at Kenninghall he ruled over his domain as a virtual monarch and served as a natural focal point for the interests of the older, largely Northern, and often Catholic, aristocracy.[3] When early in 1564 his second wife died in her twenty-fourth year, Norfolk, like Leicester, became one of the most eligible widowers in England.[4] Considering the pre-eminence of his position, that unresolved state could hardly be taken lightly.

But through all these events ran the constant theme of Mary Stuart's proximity to the succession, and English politics of the late 'sixties and early 'seventies were to be dominated more than ever before by that factor. The most immediate consequence of Mary's marriage for English politics was the increased determination on the part of nearly everyone for Elizabeth to follow suit. Only a royal marriage could save England, or so it appeared, from an ultimate Catholic succession. However, the probable candidates remained the same. Leicester still loomed as the most likely choice if she decided to marry at all, and his adversaries at court were once more compelled to propose suitable alternatives to his ever-ardent suit. Cecil looked again towards the Habsburgs, and Bacon helped him in the effort to encourage the young Archduke Charles.[5] Leicester countered Cecil's ploy by introducing the red herring of the French King, Charles IX: a proposal which he knew would detract from Cecil's effort but which ran small risk of gaining Elizabeth's acquiescence.[6]

This situation endured through 1566, when the Parliament added its concern in the form of strong pleas for Elizabeth to declare her choice.[7] In that session Bacon's continuing ill-health compelled him to contribute no more than the opening and closing addresses,[8] and he could hardly speak his own mind in such a formal arena. He might have done so in a guarded way in past sessions, but this Parliament heard a contrite Lord Keeper, who could but echo the Queen's wishes for a short debate and no deviation from the agenda.[9] When the lower House ignored his admonition and debated the succession issue at length, he could

Psalmi latine & Saxonice alternis lineis.

MEDIOCRIA ★ FIRMA ·

N. Bacon eques auratus & magni sigilli Angliae Custos librum hunc bibliothecae Cantabrig. dicauit.

1574.

I Bacon's commemorative bookplate, designed for his gift of books to Cambridge University Library, 1574

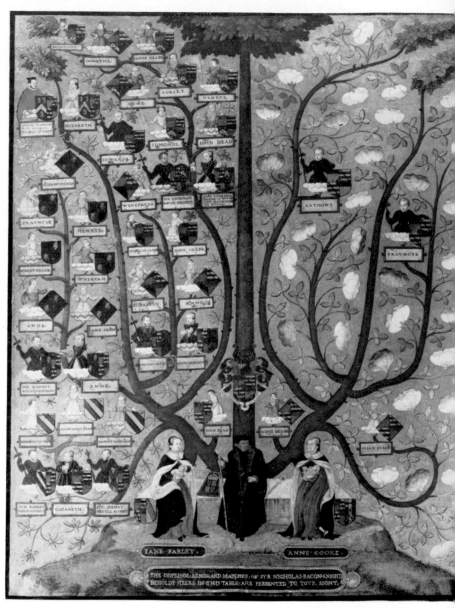

2   Sir Nicholas Bacon's family tree, 1578 (anon.). This unusual
    work is our only source for several Bacon children who failed
    to survive to adulthood

only chastise them in his closing address for their untoward meddling. Even then he spoke from notes written out by the Queen, and Elizabeth was still not content until she had added her own words to what the Lord Keeper had said.[10]

Once again the blandness of Bacon's official pronouncement need not mask for us his deep concern over the burning issue of the royal marriage. He persisted in his hopes for a Habsburg match until Elizabeth issued her flat denial of the suit and thus put the matter to rest in the following year.[11]

By then, events in Scotland demanded the attention of the privy council, and removed the sense of urgency for such a suit. In a rapid sequence of ill-considered moves, Mary had done much to discredit herself both as the potential successor to the English throne and as the ruler of Scotland. In February Lord Darnley's mutilated body was discovered amidst the rubble of the old provost's lodge at Kirk o' Field, outside Edinburgh, and Mary's likely complicity in the grisly murder and her sordid alliance with the Earl of Bothwell brought swift retribution from the Calvinist lords. By early summer, Scotland was torn by civil war.[12]

Elizabeth and her councillors watched this anti-heroic epic with close attention, and shortly after hostilities erupted she dispatched Sir Nicholas Throckmorton to inquire about Mary's situation and intentions.[13] Unfortunately for Throckmorton, she failed to describe with sufficient precision her terms of reference, and left that pre-eminent diplomat somewhat puzzled regarding the nature of his mission. In search of clarification he conferred with Cecil and then, perhaps at the Secretary's suggestion, he stopped at Gorhambury to seek counsel from the Lord Keeper.[14] Bacon did not fail him, and offered a suggestion which, as endorsed by Cecil, proved to be an integral part of the English bargaining position with Mary for a decade to come. He pressed upon Throckmorton the importance of English custody for the infant James – Mary's son by Darnley – as a fundamental condition for any aid promised to Mary. Not only would such a course shield James from the perils of warfare, but it would assure him of an English protestant, rather than Scottish or even French Catholic, upbringing. Recalling Bacon's counsel a few days later, Throckmorton wrote to Cecil that the Lord Keeper 'dothe in thys as he dothe yn all other matters, consyder depely

& advysydly and therefore yt shall be well don how soeuer his health do not serve him to be amongst you, lett not hys opinion be from amongst you.'[15]

Throckmorton's mission accomplished little beyond the general gathering of news, and subsequent English attempts to bring both sides in the Scottish conflict to an agreement proved largely fruitless. In May 1568, events took a startling turn. In despair of a just hearing or a military victory in her own kingdom, Mary fled across the border into England.[16] Once again Elizabeth had lost the initiative in dealing with her cousin, and now had to face a major and wholly unanticipated dilemma.

The foreseeable consequences of allowing Mary to remain in England were as complex as the motives which had led her to come. Prolonging her stay would keep her from France or from the righteous wrath of her own nobles. On the other hand, it would also imply approval of her recent actions, and thus gravely impede the chances of concord between England and the Scottish lords. What could not be foreseen was the extent to which Mary's talent for discord would follow her nearly all her life.

As part of her ensuing deliberations, Elizabeth sought to assess Mary's complicity in the murder of her late husband, and the nature of her strange dealings with Bothwell. In this respect she sent off three of her councillors, Norfolk, Sadler and Sussex, to meet with Mary at York. When the 'casket letters' came to light in the York meetings, and with them the more pronounced indication of Mary's guilt, Elizabeth evidently decided to discredit Mary by the subtle disclosure of her alleged role. So that Mary's part might be more widely known, the Queen's first step was to move the meetings to the more prestigious surroundings of Westminster. Except for surface appearances, which were scrupulously maintained, all attempts at impartiality in the hearings had been abandoned.

When Cecil had drawn up a list of candidates suitable to be sent to York in September, the Lord Keeper's name had been conspicuously missing.[17] As long as the Secretary had been able to secure the support of Leicester, through the appointment of Sadler, and both Norfolk and Sussex by their own participation, there had been no need to include one of his own followers in the York delegation. It was important to Cecil that his antagonists on the council saw for themselves what charges could be laid at Mary's feet, lest they accuse him of outright partisanship in such a sensitive confrontation. Furthermore, Bacon's precarious health may not have allowed such a journey. But when the meeting shifted to Westminster the English strategy had changed considerably, and Bacon's presence became necessary to create the desired impressions of gravity and impartiality. Along with the addition of several peers to the English delegation, a means of assuring the proper prestige, Elizabeth gave over the direction of the proceedings to the Lord Keeper.[18] In effect, Bacon was thus installed as chief judge in what rapidly assumed the trappings of a state trial.

The Westminster Conference met every few days from November 23rd until it petered out unceremoniously by mid-December.[19] Bacon moderated at the presentation of both Scottish parties – the Earl of Moray for the protestant lords, and the Bishop of Ross for the Marians – and also served as Elizabeth's spokesman, thus effectively performing a dual role. In contrast to an earlier disputation which he had conducted at Westminster, Bacon now moderated with a mask of impartiality that was admirably maintained, and which perfectly fulfilled the government's design.[20]

To the surprise of virtually no one, the results of the Westminster Conference were utterly inconclusive. Mary had skilfully been made to appear unco-operative, so that in the end it was her own refusal to continue which effectively terminated the talks. It remained for Elizabeth only to express surprise and disappointment that her cousin had failed to render a better account of her activities. To further dignify Elizabeth's summary pronouncements, many of the Northern earls were invited to Hampton Court at the end of the second week in December, but those pronouncements themselves were grossly anti-climactic. Only by implication did they deal with the question of Mary's guilt, and only in the same manner did they exonerate the Scottish lords from allegations of an unjust revolt. Elizabeth, however, had determined that Mary was to remain in England, and the co-operative Earl of Moray would return as Regent of Scotland.[21] Clarifying the government's intentions a week later, Cecil adopted the idea stressed in Bacon's counsel to Throckmorton: that it was crucial that an English upbringing should be secured for the young James Stuart, and that Mary should be retained in England for as long as possible.[22]

Mary's trial had been a highly successful exercise in the politics of deception, carried out with consummate skill and finesse by all concerned, and with the accord of all the factions on the privy council. Yet even as it ended, the conclusion of this era of good feelings at the council board was already in sight. Mary's flight and the ensuing Westminster Conference were but the first steps in the events leading to the Northern Rising of the following year.

One other episode which served as a prelude to that rising unfolded at about the same time, when a late November storm scattered a small fleet of Spanish ships and blew them ashore in several south coast ports. By 1568 Elizabeth and her council had become concerned over the Spanish effort to crush the rising in the Low Countries. Although Philip had been on relatively friendly terms with Elizabeth and had shielded her from excommunication for over a decade, his patience had recently begun to wear thin. The Spanish military presence on the North Sea coast was not primarily intended as a threat to England; nevertheless, it pressed hard against a traditional sore point in England's sense of security, and gave hope of deliverance to unknown numbers of English Catholics. In short, it could hardly be ignored. Elizabeth had wisely resisted the temptation of open intervention on behalf of the Dutch rebels, but all the while she turned a blind eye to English privateers preying on bullion shipments on the Spanish main. When Philip's ships were unexpectedly blown ashore in November 1568, they offered a unique opportunity to vex the Spanish. The flotilla's rich cargo had come from the bankers of Genoa and was bound for Antwerp, to pay the Duke of Alva's troops.[23]

When Elizabeth promised the Spanish Ambassador de Spes to protect the money for Philip she was probably sincere, but that was before she had learned much about it. Further news moved her to a rapid about-face: the gold did not belong to Philip until its delivery, and the Genoese were as willing to extend the loan to her as to him. When on December 28th she informed de Spes of her decision to transfer the money to Westminster for her own use, he was understandably aroused but hardly surprised. Having anticipated her move several days before, he had already alerted Alva and urged him to seize all English shipping within his reach. Alva had followed up on this suggestion by the 29th – before Elizabeth had effectively carried out her own confiscations, and also before the duke knew for certain that she intended to do so. Elizabeth could now take ironic satisfaction in appearing to perform a retaliatory act, but the fear of what Alva might do next somewhat abated her triumph.[24]

Cecil fully shared the Queen's apprehensions, and readily found in the matter his own cause for concern. His openly anti-Marian and anti-Spanish stance, enhanced by his compliance with Elizabeth's seizures of the payships, had laid him open to constant sniping from his adversaries at the council board. In addition to threatening English security, further retaliatory steps by Alva might vindicate the policy of those foes and seriously undermine Cecil's own precarious position. Norfolk, Pembroke, Arundel and others who had built up a deep resentment of Cecil's pretensions were well aware of the stakes at hand, and hoped to exploit the issue to their own advantage.[25]

Ever since the conclusion of the Westminster Conference, Bacon had been at Gorhambury for a long Christmas vacation. But Cecil needed assurance from his own supporters in the impending crisis, and wrote to the Lord Keeper accordingly in the first few days of January. Much to the Secretary's relief, Bacon's prompt note of January 5th showed the anticipated degree of concern, and offered a sound, dispassionate analysis despite both his relative ignorance of events and his troublesome gout, which caused him pain even as he wrote.[26] Judging from Bacon's reply, for we have no record of Cecil's initial communic-ation, the latter had specifically requested Bacon's interpretation of Alva's motives. To Bacon, all hinged not upon what Alva might do next, but on what had prompted him to act in the first place. He reasoned, correctly, as we now know, that Alva could not have acted on Philip's command, 'for tyme saith so', and therefore he pointed to de Spes as the motivating factor behind the seizure of English shipping. If the Ambassador rather than the King had been the culprit, there was less to fear. As to the breach of diplomatic form represented by de Spes's disservice, he suggested 'the ambassador of spay wold be spoken with to know whether he avow yt, for avowing yt [i.e., *if* he avows it] I see no cawse of hys tarrying here except he can speke good reason why'. On a more personal note Bacon promised to journey to court – for Cecil had obviously requested his personal support – when the discomfort of his gout permitted, and he asked to be excused to the Queen in the meantime.

Once again the chance survival of crucial documentation allows us to observe the manner in which Bacon's advice was received. Three days after he wrote to Cecil, the latter echoed many of Bacon's thoughts in his memorandum on the problem:[27]

> The Spain: ambassador wold be admonished of the stra[n]g procedy[ng]es of the Duke of Alva and request to know wyther he taketh this act to be doone by the Kyng of Spay or no.
>
> ... the severite of the [proceedings] in Antwp and other plaices wold be sett furth to hym, and thereuppon lett to understand that hir Maty can doo no other, but both for hir honor, and for satisfaction of hir subjects make arrest of the Kyng his Ms subiects, and Lykewise to appoynt some gentillmen to attend uppon hym in his howse, until she may here what shall become of hir subiects being in Custody of men of warr ...

It soon became apparent that Bacon had correctly assessed the situation, for Alva had indeed acted on the advice of de Spes rather than Philip, and in consequence the latter began seriously to question de Spes's value as a judge of English policy.[28] Nevertheless, the move against English shipping had already been made, and whatever regrets he may have felt about becoming entangled in such a way with the English, Alva now found himself engaged in an unofficial trade war which lasted for several months. This turn of events was equally unwelcome to Elizabeth, Cecil and Bacon, and made the policy of those councillors eminently vulnerable to attack from reactionaries on the privy council. No doubt Cecil remained the chief target for those who hoped to use the issue as a pretext for their own political ascendancy,[29] but his supporters – particularly those who had endorsed the policy of securing the payships – were also fair game, and none of them stood out so prominently as Bacon.

In the eventful year from mid-1568 to mid-1569, the Lord

Keeper had conspicuously adhered to Cecil's policies on nearly every issue of consequence. He had supported both the policy of retaining Mary Stuart in England, with the custody of her son if possible, and the decision to seize Alva's payships. On still other issues he had long indicated his determined Protestantism and his readiness to badger both Catholics and conservative Anglicans whenever the chance arose.

In 1566 he had joined Cecil in refusing to help Matthew Parker enforce the statutes prescribing proper clerical vestments, and thus gave a fillip to the puritan antagonists in the vestments controversy of the mid-1560s.[30] Two years later Bacon again ran afoul of his old friend Parker by a similar transgression. When in the spring of 1568 the Archbishop led a visitation to Norwich Cathedral to investigate the administration of Bishop Parkhurst, he found that two of the six prebendaries of the Cathedral were personal appointees of the Lord Keeper and were unlicensed to preach. To his greater dismay he found that one of them, Thomas Fowle, had for some time organized weekly prophesyings at Bacon's parish church in Redgrave. Instead of feigning embarrassment or contrition, Bacon stubbornly and openly refused to co-operate with the inquiry, and for some months broke off relations with the Archbishop.[31]

Such incidents had nothing directly to do with Spain or Mary Stuart, but they maintained Bacon's reputation for radical Protestantism among the Catholics and conservatives at court. Although he was merely defending the letter of the law against Catholic recusants when he uncovered a subscription list of supporters for English Catholics in exile, he was painted as 'one of the most pernicious heretics in Europe' by the Spanish Ambassador.[32] It is therefore no wonder that when the reactionaries began to gather forces against Cecil and his unabashedly protestant policies, Bacon also was one of their prime targets.

As we now know, and as Cecil suspected by the spring of 1569, the events of these months pointed to the imminent likelihood of an open revolt. With Mary Stuart already in England, Alva and his army just across the Channel, Elizabeth adamant against Mary's release or a Spanish alliance, and the apparent direction of English policy in the hands of Cecil and his followers, it was only a matter of time before something would have to give way. On a more personal level, Cecil and Bacon must have realized that they themselves would be foremost among the objects of such a reaction.

The hopes of the various malcontents – disaffected Catholics, jealous peers, and political reactionaries of varying stripe – soon came to focus on the prospect of a marriage between Mary Stuart and the Duke of Norfolk. From that point, visions diverged considerably. The more extreme saw such a marriage as the immediate departure point for a *coup d'état* which would bring Alva's troops across the Channel, purge the protestants from power at Westminster, and depose Elizabeth in Mary's favour. The more moderate merely hoped to use such a match as a means of securing Elizabeth's recognition of Mary's claim to the succession. Either plan would necessitate the overthrow of Cecil and Bacon.[33]

The ensuing course of events is well known. Gathering about him Arundel, Pembroke, Throckmorton, Lumley and – at the start – Leicester, and bolstered by the support of de Spes, some of the Scottish lords, and the mysterious Roberto Ridolfi, Norfolk secured Mary's consent to the scheme and so informed the Northern earls. By midsummer 1569 the marriage plan was well known to Cecil. When the Queen found out about it shortly afterwards, the denouement was close at hand. Panicking at Elizabeth's expressed disapproval, Norfolk left the court without her permission on about September 21st, hesitated for a few days, and then turned towards his palace at Kenninghall where he lay in feverish indecision. By the time he determined to obey Elizabeth's summons in October, the fat was in the fire.[34] Even without him the Northern earls rose in November 1569: they were crushed by the following March.

When a contrite Norfolk arrived at Westminster in the first week of October, he was placed under guard in the Tower at the insistence of Cecil and Bacon. A few days later Elizabeth appointed the Secretary and the Lord Keeper, along with most of their followers – Northampton, Bedford, Knollys, Sadler and Mildmay – to investigate the duke's precipitate actions.[35] He was not released until the following August.[36] Throughout the early months of 1570 this group continued its broad investigation, and pressed home its political advantage against the hopes of Mary Stuart and her erstwhile suitor. Bacon and Cecil dominated these events to an extent which led the Spanish

Ambassador to declare that 'those who usually oppose Cecil in the council are now prisoners, whilst he is free and can, with the help of his brother-in-law, the Lord Keeper, do absolutely as he pleases'.[37]

De Spes's report contained little exaggeration. Together, Bacon and Cecil received much of the news of the negotiations with the Marian earls regarding their part in the rising across the border.[38] They dominated discussions with de Spes at Windsor,[39] bore the brunt of Catholic allegations of intended treachery against Thomas Howard,[40] and, in recognition of their role, would again be the most prominent targets of the abortive autumn rising in Norfolk.[41] In mid-March they were largely responsible for the Queen's decision to send the Earl of Sussex on a punitive expedition into Scotland against the Marian earls,[42] and when Elizabeth wavered in that policy in early April, they reaffirmed to her their counsel.[43]

Even in these early months of 1570, however, Elizabeth's wrath against the erstwhile rebels began to subside, and such Norfolkites as Arundel and his son-in-law, Lord Lumley, were restored to favour.[44] Ironically, talk of a Norfolk marriage to Mary could once again be heard at Westminster, and two unexpected events of the new year launched the captured Queen once more into the centre of attention. The short-lived tranquillity of Scotland had been shattered by the assassination of the Regent Moray in January, and the civil hostilities in France had drawn to a close at about the same time, freeing Charles IX to support demands that Elizabeth restore Mary to her kingdom without delay. These events, coupled with Scottish hostility towards Sussex's bloody incursion in April, placed a great deal of pressure on Elizabeth to consider Mary's restoration. Norfolk's liberated followers joined the Earl of Leicester in urging her on, and in the crucial weeks of that spring only the determination of Cecil and Bacon seemed to stand in their way.[45]

Five years had elapsed since Bacon's restoration to the Queen's favour, and by 1571 he had fully regained his former position. Yet what lay before him once again was a battle for nothing less than his political future. Elizabeth had relied upon him and Cecil both during and immediately after the Northern Rising, but if she let them down now by giving in to the Marians, both his position and Cecil's would be seriously and perhaps permanently undermined. Yet if the months ahead would bring the second and final challenge of his political career, Bacon could at least enjoy the full freedom of action which had in the first instance been denied him.

X

The Years of Intrigue, II:
1570-72

Bowing to the weighty diplomatic pressures of the early spring, Elizabeth took what appeared to be an important step in Mary's favour by freeing John Leslie, the Bishop of Ross, in May. Ross, Mary's confidant and spokesman, had been implicated in the events of the previous fall, but was now to represent Mary in negotiations for her release. As usual, Elizabeth remained chary of committing herself, and in order to forestall the resolution of the matter, she appointed Cecil and Bacon to the English delegation as counter-weights against Leicester's sympathetic stance. Finally, she consented to have the meetings open at the Lord Keeper's York House residence: hardly neutral ground.[1]

Bent on protecting his own interests and preventing Mary's release by stultifying the negotiations, Bacon opened the first session, on May 5th, with a lengthy and somewhat belligerent harangue. He reminded Ross of the recent allegations against him arising out of the events of the previous autumn, and of his presumed authorship of a treatise libelling Elizabeth. Only then did he acknowledge his mandate to discuss terms for Mary's release.

For his part, Ross returned Bacon's compliment by informing his listeners that he would rather have spoken with the Queen directly. He slyly parried Bacon's allegations of his wrong-doing, and defended the treatise of which Bacon had spoken. Turning to the matter at hand, he entreated the English delegation to approve Mary's return to Scotland as a matter of justice, and offered sureties for his mistress's good conduct. Taking his cue from Ross, Cecil expressed grave doubts that sufficient guarantees could be devised for Mary's behaviour, and he then thrust forward the persistent question of James's custody. With that issue the two sides reached the very impasse which Cecil and Bacon had hoped to achieve.

No sooner did the meeting end on that note than two tracts appeared in defence of Mary Stuart; their timing suggests that their anonymous author may in fact have been no friend of the Scottish Queen. In any event, Bacon brought them to Elizabeth's attention, and did so with telling effect. Elizabeth was sufficiently disturbed to send Sussex's troops once again across the border.[2]

Towards the end of May, however, the Queen's intentions seemed to swing once again to a position of sympathy with Mary's cause. The French Ambassador Fénélon worked out a settlement with her to effect Anglo-French co-operation in bringing peace to Scotland, and Elizabeth promised to resume negotiations for Mary's release. Not content with this coup Fénélon flaunted his triumph before the anti-Marians at the council board, who took great umbrage at the news.[3] Bacon, now more than ever the *'chef de la partie contraire'* in Fénélon's words, poured forth his anger to the Queen. In what was described as a 'marvellously insolent speech', he warned Elizabeth that she was being misled by the French Ambassador, who was nothing but an agent of the Guises, and that even members of her own council – and here he gestured at Leicester – had betrayed her trust. To consider granting Mary's liberty was a craven course, unworthy of bold King Henry's daughter. It would encourage the French to sense and take advantage of England's weakness.[4] When Elizabeth replied in kind by telling Bacon bluntly to refrain from such immoderate language and allegations, he stalked from the court in anger, and retired a day or two later to Gorhambury.[5]

However bold Bacon's actions, they did little to resolve the isues at hand, and the discovery at about the same time of a papal bull of excommunication against Elizabeth, which had been nailed to the door of the Bishop of London's house, further unsettled the Queen's mind.[6] Although the bull had long been anticipated, its sudden appearance just at that time caught everyone off guard, and created new pressures for Elizabeth to strike a workable agreement with Mary. She shortly recalled her council to consider this turn of events and its implications for her policy, but Bacon refused to heed her summons. Instead he continued to pout at home and let it be known that participation at the council board was useless, for the Queen refused to accept good advice when she received it.[7] If we are to believe Fénélon, Bacon had not come to this pose without prior consultation with his allies, and so it was not entirely an act of sustained anguish. No doubt he was still frustrated by Elizabeth's vacillation, but he also hoped to cause her to reconsider the position he had so forcefully represented a week or so before. At the very least he hoped to delay what threatened to be a headlong rush into Mary's embrace. Nor was his pout entirely without its effects. His absence was conspicuous, and the Earl of Arundel, whose erratic nature made him capable of any position but who was not usually in sympathy with Bacon's causes, sought out the Lord Keeper at his home and convinced him to return.[8]

Even when Elizabeth had convened her advisers, little came from their deliberations. She now decided to hold back Sussex's army, and went through the motions of negotiating for Mary's release to satisfy her agreement with Fénélon, but these meetings went on intermittently throughout the summer and into the winter without conclusion.[9] In mid-January 1571, Elizabeth sought to prolong her pretence of determination by naming Bacon, Cecil, Sussex, Mildmay, Knollys and Lord Howard of Effingham – none of them committed to Mary's release – to a delegation empowered to revive negotiations, and the Regent of Scotland, the Earl of Morton, came down on February 21st to represent his protestant allies.[10] Bacon's memorandum of that date outlined the strategy for the meetings, but admitted of no advance for Mary's cause.[11] By March the talks had halted once more, this time on the pretence of allowing Morton to consult with the Scottish Parliament.[12] Throughout it all Burghley* and Bacon continued to drag their heels at the first signs of progress, and often resorted to the sticky problem of sureties for Mary's behaviour when a breakthrough appeared at hand.[13] In this manner, as we now know, Elizabeth continued to fulfil her promise for negotiation, while retaining the anti-Marians in the best position to block progress. Burghley and Bacon had no certainty of her intentions in this regard, but readily exercised whatever choice of action remained open to them in their un-

* William Cecil became Lord Burghley in February 1571.

flagging effort to thwart any rapprochement with Mary.[14]

When a change in this impasse did come it came gradually, and from an unexpected quarter. The French, who had created such pressure on Elizabeth in the spring of 1570, adopted a softer tone with the coming of summer, and by late autumn Westminster gossips speculated openly about a match between Elizabeth and Anjou. Their chatter had some foundation: Burghley, Walsingham, and Thomas Sackville, now Lord Buckhurst – the latter two through their diplomatic roles – had indeed been engaged in negotiations towards that end. This protestant enthusiasm took for its base what later appeared a vain hope at best, but after the struggle against a Stuart rapprochement, the possibility was most welcome.[15]

Bacon must have known about this scheme by early winter, and thereafter worked hard to put the match across, both at the council board and to the Queen herself. In Burghley's succinct phrase, 'My Lord Keeper hath dealt earnestly in it ... '[16] One of the primary tasks to which Bacon set himself in this regard was the composition and distribution of a brief extolling the advantages of the match. His 'Discourse of the Queenes Marriage with the Duke of Anjoye' is a lengthy and well-reasoned tract which states the case in characteristically clear and pragmatic terms.[17]

In the opening sections of the 'Discourse' Bacon explained that a royal marriage would diminish the chance of a *coup d'état* and would, he blithely assumed, reduce dissension by producing an heir. He then summarized the ways in which such a match would assure the tranquillity of the realm, and laconically acknowledged that it would undermine the likelihood and desirability of a match between Mary and the Duke of Norfolk. These were his basic premises. He went on from there to outline the 'discommodities' of such a match, and then answered those objections. Fundamentally, the tenor of the piece was realistic and compromising. Bacon supported a Catholic suitor, about whose person he found little to discuss, as simply the best way out of a potentially calamitous situation.

Most likely, the 'Discourse' was neither intended for Elizabeth's eyes nor seen by her, for the terms used to discuss the Norfolk/Mary match seem overly candid, and might well have angered the Queen. Having had his fingers badly burned in the Hales episode only a half-dozen years before, it is most likely that

Bacon tempered the earnestness of his message with discretion in its distribution. It seems rather to have been circulated among those at court who could be expected to receive it with sympathy. One of the extant copies is endorsed in the hand of Sir Walter Mildmay, who seems not to have been converted to the project in the end, but who would at least not betray Bacon's part.[18]

Negotiations for the Anjou marriage made good progress during the spring and summer. By June, the actual talks were being carried on chiefly by Walsingham and Buckhurst in Paris, and Leicester and Burghley at home.[19] By July, Sussex and Bacon had joined in,[20] and in mid-August we find Howard of Effingham joining Leicester, Burghley and Bacon for an interview with the French Ambassador.[21] But by the end of that month the general optimism which had prevailed among the negotiators at last began to fade. Bacon, Burghley and Sussex were left to defend the idea against those who had come round to the idea of an Anglo-French alliance without a marriage. Leicester, Knollys and Clinton seem to have been in the forefront of the latter group.[22] Negotiations dragged on until 1572, but even after Catherine de Medici substituted the Duke of Alençon for his elder brother, no one could have expected the plan to succeed by that time.[23]

The project of the Anjou marriage had, however, served its function. At the time of its inception many thought Elizabeth well disposed to Mary's restoration, and the anti-Marians had not known where to turn. To Bacon and others of a similar mind, even a French Catholic match seemed preferable to the continuing prospect of Mary Stuart. Furthermore, by the time the ardour for the match had cooled, other factors had emerged which would, in the end, undermine Mary's claims even more completely than a royal marriage could have done. These new factors included the growing Anglo-French rapprochement of 1571-2, which ended in the Treaty of Blois and proceeded without recognizing the principle of Mary's restoration,[24] and the anti-Marian hostility in the Parliament of 1571. Yet all of these together counted not half so much as the Ridolfi Plot, which Burghley and his aides began to unravel in the summer of 1571.[25]

The discovery of the Ridolfi Plot, in which Bacon played no discernible role, set off an anti-Marian reaction at Westminster which was unrivalled in its intensity by any similar outcry in recent decades. Fortunately for those who continued to see Mary as a threat, the Queen felt obliged to call a parliament late in the spring of 1572. It opened well after the final details of the Plot had been exposed, and after the Duke of Norfolk's trial and condemnation, but not late enough for the emotions of the assembled members to have subsided.[26]

Mary's antagonists on the council had worked too long and hard against her, and against the pretensions of Thomas Howard in her regard, to let the opportunity of this Parliament slip by quietly. Although at the opening session Bacon was compelled to convey the Queen's earnest admonitions that the members avoid 'trifling digressions from matters proponed [and] idle and long discourses' so that the session might close before the heat of summer,[27] his own intentions, and those of his allies, were nothing of the sort. Nor could he avoid some gesture that would allude to those thoughts despite the constraints of his official position. In consequence, he embarked upon a lengthy peroration about the laxity in ecclesiastical discipline which plagued the realm; it took up a far larger portion of his remarks than any other issue. Such a detailed oration seems out of place. Elizabeth did not call Parliament for a discussion of ecclesiastical discipline, she did sincerely want a short and businesslike session, and that same issue had been dealt with at considerable length in the Parliament of the previous year. In its proper context, however, Bacon's intention becomes quite clear. It was meant as a call to arms for the puritan members and others likely to attack Mary and the forces which had supported her. Further, it could well have been a pretence for prolonging the session and allowing time for the desired reaction to occur. Finally, it was intended to remind his listeners that they would indeed find friends at the council board for whatever anti-Marian pressure they might bring to bear.

Such sympathy was immediately evident when, at the undoubted urging of Burghley and others, the radical lawyer from Norfolk, Robert Bell, was chosen speaker.[28] In Bell's capable hands the full-voiced puritan chorus would find sure direction for its liturgy of recrimination against Mary and Norfolk. Led by Arthur Hall, Thomas Wilbraham and Bacon's friend Thomas Norton,[29] the outcry was almost instantaneous. Yet while the parliamentary radicals needed no prompting when it came to dealing with Mary, not everyone shared Thomas Norton's stout heart in attacking the duke. When many wavered on Norfolk's fate, it was Burghley's cousin Thomas Dannett and Bacon's protégé Thomas Digges who reaffirmed Norton's indignation and pressed the issue.[30] Thus from the very opening days of the session Elizabeth could hardly have been unaware of the strident demands for the attainder of Mary and the immediate execution of the duke.[31] Shortly thereafter, and perhaps as a concession to protect Mary, Elizabeth gave in and signed Howard's death warrant. Not even his gestures to Burghley and Bacon – leaving his children to the benevolence of the former and a jewelled crystal cup to the latter – could save him, and he met the executioner's summons with calm resolve on the second day of June.[32] Although Elizabeth refused early in the session to agree to Mary's attainder, and in the end never actually committed herself on the bill removing her claims to the succession, she gave at least some hope that she would ultimately bow to the latter.[33] With the arrival of the closing ceremonies the determination of Parliament had clearly been felt and, despite some chagrin at the Queen's irresolution, Bacon could mouth his message of thanks with a feigned dispassion that could not quite mask his own satisfaction.[34]

The unfolding of the Ridolfi Plot and the retributive acts which followed in its wake inaugurated a new era in the relations among the privy councillors. Not only had the threat of Mary's succession been greatly deflated, and the pretensions of the late duke been removed altogether, but the heat of Leicester's enduring suit for Elizabeth's hand also abated.[35] *Pro forma* talks for the hand of the Duke of Anjou and others in marriage to Elizabeth would still be held from time to time after 1572,[36] but the entire issue of the royal marriage and succession found itself relegated for the time to idle gossip. With its departure went also many of the personal tensions which had long prevailed at the council board. From Bacon's point of view, once Leicester and Mary had been removed as threats to the succession, he could somewhat relax his vigilance. Others seem to have experienced a similar reaction, and the next few years marked a distinct lull in the political infighting which had long characterized Tudor government. One might also have observed that Burghley was now generally acknowledged as the pre-eminent figure on the council,[37] and Bacon, who had stood shoulder to shoulder with him from the beginning of the reign, had also come to the summit of his influence. With Cecil's apparent acquiescence, he had virtually assumed leadership of the anti-Marian forces in the summer months of 1570. His standing was apparent in his forceful representation to Elizabeth during May, and even more so in his dramatic departure from the court which followed. That exit proved a stark contrast indeed with his forced retirement from Westminster five years before, when he had been obliged to humble himself before both Elizabeth and Leicester in order to return. Now he could engage in a blunt exchange with the Queen, slap back at Leicester, and stalk angrily away without so much as the Queen's leave. The day was rapidly approaching when his ill-health would more frequently curtail his participation at the council board, but by 1572 Bacon had earned the role of elder statesman. Not only was he older, at sixty-two, than nearly any other councillor,[38] and senior in years of service, but the general regard which now came his way from Elizabeth and his colleagues secured him that position in its fullest sense.

Although its timing was perhaps coincidental, nothing symbolizes this emergence so appropriately as the Queen's first visit to Bacon's home, which took place in the month following Thomas Howard's execution and the prorogation of Parliament. Elizabeth had never visited Redgrave and, although it had been substantially complete since 1568, neither had she journeyed to Gorhambury. Now she intended to surprise him with a visit during the course of her summer's progress. When word of that impending honour reached him on short notice and 'by common speech', Bacon was quite beside himself with pride and apprehension at what must have been the realization of a long-cherished dream. By the time Elizabeth arrived at Theobalds for her stay with Burghley, Bacon's hasty preparations must have been largely complete. Yet his nerves got the better of his poise, and he dispatched a messenger to ride the thirty miles or so to Theobalds and express to his more genteel and experienced brother-in-law his state of anxiety:

Understanding ... that the Queen's Majesty means to come to my house, and knowing no certainty of her time of coming, nor of her abode, I have thought good to pray you that this bearer my servant might understand what you know therein ... and if it be true, then that I might understand your advice what you think to be the best way for me to deal in this matter, for in very deed, no man is more raw in such a matter as myself.[39]

Precisely when she arrived and how long she stayed is not recorded, but it was evidently upon this occasion that Elizabeth remarked to Bacon about what a little house he had built, to which he replied that his house was fine enough, but 'it is you that have made me too great for my house'.[40] Coming from the gross-bodied Sir Nicholas, this was somewhat of a *double entente*, but – notwithstanding his girth and the fact that he proceeded to build a gallery of 120 feet for the next royal visit – it also suggests his understanding of the position he had gained in the royal esteem. He would continue to enjoy that status throughout his remaining years.

XI

The Home Front:
Bacon and the Politics
of Norfolk and Suffolk

One of the ways in which the tumultuous events of these years
placed Bacon's career on a more secure footing was not immediately evident to observers of the Westminster scene. The
demise of Thomas Howard in 1572 threw into flux the traditional patterns of political hegemony in his home territory of
Norfolk and Suffolk. The vacuum which followed in the wake of
the duke's fall permitted various non-traditional political forces
to enter into competition for power at all levels of the regional
political structure. Foremost among such forces was an active
and theologically inspired coterie of young puritan gentry revolving round the Bacon family. Close scrutiny of the Lord
Keeper's activities in these two shires indicates that his own
political and social resources, built up over three decades, contributed more than any other single factor – save of course
Norfolk's execution — to the emergence of that group. In large
part, the markedly new distribution of power which characterized these two shires in the 1570s and after is a measure of
Bacon's success, and the few years remaining to him saw him
emerge a full blown magnate in regional political life.

In constructing the foundations for his political influence in
Norfolk and Suffolk Bacon utilized several basic resources. These
included the obvious prestige and concomitant influence attached
to his career at Westminster, his widespread landed holdings, his
marital ties stemming from the extensive relations of the
Ferneleys, the further ties engendered by the marriage of his six
children by Jane Ferneley, and the substantial amount of ecclesiastical patronage which in one way or another fell to his

presentation.

From the time he first acquired an office at the Court of Augmentations until after he became Lord Keeper, Bacon could always count on his Westminster offices to support his quest for status in shire and regional affairs. In the earlier stages of his career this may have entailed nothing more than the execution of a kinsman's will or the purchase of an orphaned relative's wardship,[1] but as his position grew, so did the opportunities which came his way from local and regional interests. Major or minor, nearly all instances of Bacon's advice or intervention helped to secure his standing.

In 1563, for example, he helped the town fathers of Ipswich unravel the complications arising from the charitable bequest left by Henry Tooley.[2] Three years later they called upon him to settle a dispute among officials of the town, and noted, after he had resolved the matter, that ' ... the Lord Keeper in this matter hathe shewed himselfe an especiall friend to this Towne'.[3] In return, the officials of Ipswich honoured Bacon's request to provide aid for an indigent relative,[4] and voted him a full Burgess of the town 'wthoute othe taken'.[5] Finally, several of the leading citizens of Ipswich helped to elect his son Nicholas as First Knight of the Shire in 1572.[6]

On a more personal level, Bacon performed similar favours for individuals who might prove useful to him in the future. In one instance, and only after ascertaining the justice of the cause, he effected the release from prison of one of Sir Ambrose Jermin's followers; Jermin was high on the list of influential Suffolk gentry, and his influence could well have proved of value.[7] On another occasion, he performed the same service for Nicholas Farmer, a friend of his son Nathaniel; Farmer went on to serve Bacon and his allies in future years. In 1576 we find the Lord Keeper writing to have Farmer appointed Undersheriff of Norfolk and Suffolk.[8] Although there is little reason to believe that Bacon indulged in such patronage more than anyone else of his status, these instances, multiplied several times over, did much to secure his standing in regional affairs. At the same time, moreover, such practices constituted a time-honoured means of affecting the processes of local government.

His presence as a landowner, so amply described by Dr Alan Simpson, created for Bacon an interest in eight shires, but was of particular importance in Suffolk and Norfolk.[9] When Bacon resided at Redgrave Hall he naturally made that the centre of his interests, but even after he moved to Gorhambury in the late 1560s and left Redgrave to his son Nicholas, it continued to occupy his thoughts. The manor of Stiffkey, Norfolk, which Bacon purchased and upon which he built a fine home, was intended for his son Nathaniel, and the Lord Keeper himself never resided there.[10] Yet in his characteristically industrious manner he maintained an intense interest in the construction of these homes as well as in the remainder of his extensive properties.[11]

Aside from the traditional emoluments, rights of patronage, jurisdiction and dependents which accompanied such land ownership, Bacon shared in the sundry offices and honours which came with that station. Though individually often of modest account, these offices assured him of a firm foothold in the various echelons of regional politics and society. Such posts included election to the stewardships of the Honour of Clare, Suffolk, and the town of St Albans in Hertfordshire, as well as the ownership of the Liberty of Bury St Edmunds.[12] His ownership of the Liberty of Bury, together with his personal associations with the area, placed upon his shoulders considerable responsibility for the town's dignity and welfare. This led him to seek the award of a royal charter for the Borough in 1562.[13] Stewardships implied similar powers and responsibilities, and particularly the duty of lobbyist at Westminster, without land ownership. In the case of St Albans, however, the post brought with it the privilege of naming the burgesses to parliament, and this was no small matter. The members for 1563, 1571 and 1572 are attributed to Bacon's choice.[14] At least two other boroughs, Sudbury and Eye, both in Suffolk, allowed Bacon considerable influence in naming their M.P.s, but it is not clear that Bacon did this in the capacity of steward.[15]

Along with his land, office-holding and status at Westminster, Bacon's extensive network of family ties in Norfolk and Suffolk were extremely important resources for his career in regional affairs. Although the significance of the alliances facilitated by Bacon's marriage into the Cooke circle is immediately apparent, the more obscure connections wrought by his first marriage probably did as much for his career. These relationships may

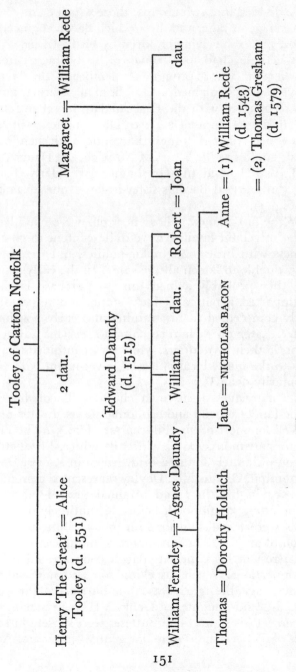

Figure 4 The Ferneley Relations

151

properly be divided into two groups: those which came directly from his marriage to Jane, and those which Bacon engineered in marrying off his six surviving children by his first wife.

William Ferneley had spent much of his business career in London, where he was a prominent member of the Mercers' Company;[16] but he remained a Suffolk man at heart, and his children intermarried with the East Anglian merchant elite of which he considered himself a part. The complex web of relationships which resulted brought Bacon ties with such leading commercial families as the Redes of Norwich, the Daundys and Tooleys of Ipswich, and the Greshams, particularly Thomas Gresham, who married Bacon's sister-in-law Anne Ferneley in 1544 (see Fig. 4).

Save for the last named, whose horizons were considerably wider, these merchant families were quite content to go about their business with little thought for politics, but they proved extremely valuable to Bacon all the same. In the early stages of his career they probably helped him to purchase land, and certainly imparted a patina of local status and respectability which aptly complemented his training and early positions at Westminster. Later on their turn came to seek his advice and intervention in their own affairs, while they continued to afford him access to the many local offices of government with which they customarily dealt.[17]

With the marriages of his own children, Bacon hoped to enhance the family's social and economic status. In this respect he chose well for most of his children (see Fig. 5). The first to contemplate matrimony was his eldest daughter, Elizabeth, for whom Bacon ultimately found a bridegroom in Robert Doyley, of Chislehampton, Oxfordshire. Doyley represented a prominent line of gentry in his shire and attained several offices and honours, including knighthood, before his untimely death, but his interests were too distant for him to contribute to Bacon's construction of an East Anglian sphere of influence.[18]

With the rest of his children, Bacon concentrated on East Anglian connections. When his eldest son and namesake approached marriageable age, it was Anne Buttes, daughter of Sir Edmund and grand-daughter of Henry VIII's physician, upon whom Bacon set his sights. The Butteses were closely linked to the Bureses of Acton – another major gentry clan – and Anne's

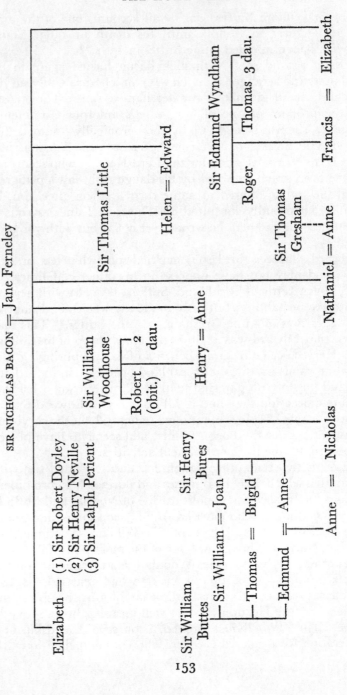

Figure 5 Relations of the Bacon–Ferneley Children

uncle, Sir William Buttes, was by all accounts one of the most powerful figures in Suffolk until his death in 1583. Young Nicholas Bacon married Anne Buttes in 1561.[19]

For his second son, Nathaniel, Bacon turned again to the Greshams, and arranged a match with Sir Thomas's only surviving child, an illegitimate daughter named Anne. Though she was the product of one of her father's amorous Continental escapades, she was brought up by and – ironically – named after his own wife, Sir Nicholas's former sister-in-law.[20] The marriage was a great source of pride for the Lord Keeper, who seems not to have been much troubled by his daughter-in-law's pedigree. When the couple offered to name their first son after him, he tactfully but proudly consulted Sir Thomas: 'I am desyrous to have it beare my name,' he wrote, 'yet not so but with yor good liking.'[21]

Edward, Bacon's third son, married somewhat less prestigiously, and may not have done so in his father's lifetime. His bride, Helen Little of Shrubland, Suffolk, brought with her undoubted respectability, but only moderate wealth and none of the connections of Anne Gresham or Anne Buttes.[22] This may suggest that Edward was at times the black sheep of his father's flock. He received the same benefits of early upbringing and education as his brothers, but less land or money in his father's will, and possibly no paternal help at all in securing a bride.[23] Upon one occasion they had a falling out over Edward's plans for foreign travel.[24] He is mentioned only rarely in the surviving correspondence of the Bacon family, and seems to have played a subordinate role in their political activities.

With his two remaining daughters, Bacon welded ties with two families which, like the Butteses and Bureses, held prominent positions in the social and political life of Norfolk and Suffolk. Henry Woodhouse, who married Anne Bacon some time before 1568, was the son and heir of Sir William Woodhouse of Hycklyn, Norfolk. Though not one of the more powerful Woodhouses of Kimberly, the elder Woodhouse sat frequently on the Norfolk commission of the peace. He had married his two daughters to scions of other leading families in the shire: the Sheltons and the Heydons.[25] The well-meaning but not overly shrewd Henry Woodhouse proved a source of friendship and exasperation for the Lord Keeper, who felt compelled to extricate his 'sonne Woodhouse' from the quagmire of debt, and to obtain for him offices which might keep him from succumbing again. In the first instance, the paterfamilias had to emphasize the value of good book-keeping.[26] In the second, he secured for Woodhouse the Vice-Admiralty of Norfolk and Suffolk for £310 in 1578, helped effect his appointment to the Norfolk commission of the peace eight times between 1569 and 1578, and probably had much to do with his attainment of knighthood in the latter year.[27] In return, young Woodhouse fulfilled a good many social and political missions on Bacon's behalf.[28]

In Francis Wyndham, married to his youngest daughter, Bacon had the most capable and independent of his sons-in-law, and again he did a great deal to further a fledgeling career. A graduate of Cambridge and Lincoln's Inn, Wyndham proved a worthy recipient of the knighthood of the shire for Norfolk in 1572, the coif of a queen's serjeant in 1577, and the robes of a chief justice of the common pleas in 1579, all of which Bacon almost certainly helped him to obtain.[29]

As was the case with most marriages of that day, the negotiations beforehand bore the distinct ring of commercial transactions. In contrast, the post-marital relations of the extended Bacon clan were characterized by a genuine warmth and intimacy. No doubt this tendency stemmed from the non-traditional attitudes towards the family exhibited by both humanists and puritans, which were then making inroads against the harsher and more formal domestic conventions of English family life.[30]

Notwithstanding his occasional coolness towards Edward, no one better exemplifies this familial concern and even tenderness than the paterfamilias himself. Throughout the surviving family correspondence we can observe Bacon's care not only in securing offices and opportunities for his sons and sons-in-law, but also his genuine concern for the happiness and well-being of his wife, children and grandchildren. Bacon rarely omitted greetings and blessings to all in his family letters. The following conclusion to a letter for Nathaniel is typical: 'Thus with my hartie comendacons to my daughter [in-law] and to my sonne Woodhowse, and his wief, with God's blessinge to all the children … '[31] On another occasion his concern was mildly anxious in tone: 'You writt nothinge unto me howe my daughter your wief doeth, nor her mother wherin you do not well. Commend me to them bothe, and tell them if they want any thing this Christmas the fault is theirs and not myn, for they might have had it by a word of their mouth or by writting.'[32] In still another instance he urged Nicholas that ' ... you shall doo well to cause soome care to be taken of yor systr that she spend the day well & vertuisly ... whylst she seekes hur healthe ... '[33]

With that tone set from the top, the children followed suit, and seem to have been a particularly close-knit clan. As we can see from the Lord Keeper's greetings to Woodhouse in the first of these excerpts, as well as in a wealth of correspondence among other members of the family, Henry frequently saw Nathaniel and young Nicholas, and remained closely associated with them in personal as well as in official affairs. When Woodhouse had financial difficulties, which seems to have been much of the time, it was a matter of grave concern for Francis Wyndham and Nathaniel as well as the Lord Keeper.[34] When his debt to a Mr Townshend fell due, the family bailed him out with a guarantee of repayment, and the names of all three of the Bacon brothers were affixed to the document.[35] Wyndham, more frequently in London than the others because of his duties at Lincoln's Inn and later as Queen's Serjeant and Judge, dined often with the Lord Keeper and served as his messenger upon his return home after term time.[36] When Francis's wife anticipated a difficult lying-in, Woodhouse's wife came and 'never left my wyfe after she came to her ... wch was to her great comfort'.[37]

Nor was this family intimacy confined to the immediate circle of Bacon's first set of children and their spouses. When Nathaniel found his bride lacking in domestic accomplishment he sent her for finishing to his step-mother. When she returned home some time later, she exemplified her new training by writing a warm note of thanks to Lady Anne Bacon, and included regards for 'my brother Anthony and my good brother Frank'.[38] By the same token, we find Wyndham and Nathaniel interceding on behalf of their 'cosin Daundy' – presumably one of Jane Ferneley's maternal relations, and certainly far removed from Wyndham, who brought the matter to Nathaniel's attention.[39] Finally, the Lord Keeper himself frequently conveyed regards to his son Nicholas's mother-in-law, Anne Buttes, who often stayed at Redgrave.[40]

Aside from the interest which these relations may hold for students of social attitudes – who might find here an interesting contrast with the more formal and even harsh relations of the Paston family a century earlier – this intimacy serves as an important indication of how these individuals, alike in both their level of educational attainment and in their humanist and puritan outlook, came to form a tight-knit political faction under the paternal gaze of the Lord Keeper.

It is also important to note here that such men as Woodhouse and Wyndham, who came from families of far greater prominence than the Bacons, still relied upon their connection to the Lord Keeper for their political sustenance. This is abundantly clear in the surviving correspondence, and has best been accounted for by Dr Smith, who has found that by the second half of the sixteenth century the combination of an old family and a successful father no longer guaranteed a place of leadership for the son in shire affairs.[41] New links to effective patronage were always needed, and Bacon's willingness to perform the service of good lordship was a virtual necessity for the advancement of these younger figures.

As a further consequence of both his offices at Westminster and of his presence as a landowner in Norfolk and Suffolk, Bacon held a vast number of advowsons in those shires. It fell to the Lord Keeper, *ex officio*, to make presentations to all crown-owned livings whose value did not exceed £20 per annum, and Bacon made far more clerical presentations between 1558 and 1579 than any other patron in the realm. According to a recent reckoning, this averaged out at no less than 113 a year![42] Yet if such presentations are to be considered in the context of Bacon's standing in East Anglia, it is helpful to distinguish between those made on behalf of the crown, and those made to livings which he personally controlled on his own lands. With the former and much larger group, Bacon made a practice of screening out undesirable candidates, but was more likely to adopt a latitudinarian position on the matter of doctrine: benefices had to be filled with a minimum of delay, and the general shortage of clergymen throughout this period made it difficult to pick and choose according to a particular bias. With the latter category, in which Bacon appointed roughly two dozen clerics to livings under his personal control in Norfolk and Suffolk, we may assume that he chose with far greater discretion. In consequence, at least six are known to have been among the leading puritans in those shires.[43]

Thomas Fowle was Bacon's chaplain at Redgrave, as we have already noted, but he was also a prebendary of Norwich Cathedral at Bacon's presentation, and one of the earliest organizers of the puritan classical movement in Suffolk.[44] Robert Johnson served as the household chaplain at Gorhambury and organized prophesyings around Ely, but was also possessed of a Norwich prebend at Bacon's presentation. He greatly embarrassed the Lord Keeper when his notoriously puritan activities reached the ears of the privy council.[45] Thomas Smyth, the subject of Bacon's falling out with Matthew Parker, was an unlicensed and nonconforming preacher; he was also one of Bacon's protégés at Norwich Cathedral.[46] Finally, a Dutch Calvinist by the name of John Thomas, also known as Hylocomus, was appointed by Sir Nicholas as Master of the Bury St Edmunds Grammar School.[47] Even in the lesser advowsons which lay at his disposal as lord of various manors, Bacon seems to have been concerned to appoint one of the 'right religion', but most of these presentations went to figures sufficiently obscure to preclude their identification as puritans. Not only did such appointments bolster the puritan forces in Norfolk and Suffolk, and thus reinforce the temporal activities of the Bacon sons, but young Nicholas and Nathaniel were often consulted before the Lord Keeper made them.[48]

The basis for Bacon's standing in the society of Suffolk and Norfolk was thus a complex matter, composed of his position at court, his land ownership, his office-holding at the local level, his rights of patronage and jurisdiction, and both the nature and extent of his family ties. These factors served to identify him as a figure of some account even prior to the duke's demise. He utilized his parliamentary patronage in Eye, Suffolk, and perhaps Sudbury, in 1563.[49] He was asked and often tried to use his influence in securing local offices for aspiring officials,[50] he must have had some share in eliminating many of the more vocal Catholics from the commission of the peace after 1558,[51] and he served as Deputy Lord Lieutenant of both shires, all prior to 1572.[52]

His protégés and allies who would form a puritan stronghold in northern Norfolk, especially his son Nathaniel, Francis Wyndham and Henry Woodhouse, were already settled in that area, while those resources which provided a similarly strong puritan stronghold in west Suffolk were equally in evidence by 1572.[53] In regard to the latter it should be noted that in addition to Bacon's own established position in Bury St Edmunds – including his patronage of the grammar school, lordship of the Liberty of Bury, good offices in the attempt to gain a charter for the town, and personal ties going back to his childhood[54] – several of his relatives and retainers resided in the area. His brothers-in-law Robert Blackman and Robert Sharp,[55] and his retainers Thomas Andrews[56] and Francis Baldero,[57] all made Bury their home; his personal treasurer, Bartholomew Kemp, lived in nearby Pakenham;[58] and of course his son Nicholas was at Redgrave. Although not all of them were puritans, and Andrews for one seems to have been somewhat antagonistic towards the puritan outlook,[59] they were all well regarded and loyal to Bacon, and did much to secure his position in west Suffolk. However, despite the abundant evidence of Bacon's resources in Norfolk and Suffolk prior to 1572, the nature of the political structure in those shires prevented Bacon's emergence as a regional magnate until the death of the duke.

In addition to the important gentry families such as those to which Bacon had linked his children in marriage, at least two other groups figured actively in regional politics: the Howards' following, whose influence was seriously challenged only after the duke's fall, and the several families from the ranks of the lesser gentry who had begun to encroach on the places of the more established clans.[60] Underlying all the activities of these contending groups, the issue of religious rivalry was never far from the surface of regional politics.

The Duke of Norfolk was not yet twenty years of age when Elizabeth came to the throne, and would not be sworn a privy councillor for almost four years. Without a shadow of doubt, however, he was the single most important political force in Norfolk and Suffolk until his execution in 1572. 'My contry mene', he wrote to Cecil, 'schall have harde cawse to have [to justify] that enye matter concernyng the quenes maiestyes sarvys in norfolk or suffolke should rather have bene comytted off first to others than to me.'[61] This was no idle boast, but a laconic matter of fact. In Norfolk alone it is possible to attribute to his preference at least twelve out of twenty-five M.P.s known to have served between 1559 and 1571, and seventeen out of thirty-two J.P.s during the same period.[62]

We may suppose that a similar pattern would emerge in Suffolk if there were more complete documentation for that shire, for in many ways both political structure and personalities freely transcended the boundary between the two shires. They shared several key officials: in the secular realm, the sheriff and undersheriff (until 1575), the lord lieutenant and the vice-admiral, and in the clerical, the bishop and his administration (for both Norfolk and Suffolk were in the diocese of Norwich). As he had boasted to Cecil, Howard, like the Bacons and others of lesser position, certainly included both shires in his sphere of influence. We know that the duke personally controlled an impressive number of advowsons in Suffolk as well as in Norfolk, he himself served as Lord Lieutenant, and several of his followers presided as sheriffs of both shires between 1558 and 1572.[63]

The final significant element in the power structure of the region was also the most recent and in many ways the most dynamic: the lesser gentry. It is now clear that by the last third of the sixteenth century a significant number of families of lesser stature, sometimes only recently settled in Norfolk or Suffolk, had made deep inroads into the traditionally dominant position of the older county families.[64] The Bacons and the Farmers typified this newer element, and – except for his standing at Westminster – the Lord Keeper's base of power is roughly typical of the resources which such families could bring into play in their striving for recognition.

Until 1572 neither Bacon nor any other potential aspirant to influence in this region could compete on equal terms with the Duke of Norfolk. Yet when the executioner concluded his work on Tower Hill, the traditional structure of politics and society in Norfolk and Suffolk could be laid to rest with the duke's remains. The extensive Howard following, his relatives, tenants and other dependents, largely Catholic and loyal to the old order, were suddenly leaderless. Into the ensuing void rushed several forces which had never enjoyed true hegemony.[65] Prominent among these proved to be the coterie of young puritan gentry, most of them with legal training, surrounding the Bacon family. Aside from Francis Wyndham, Henry Woodhouse and the Bacon sons

3   The Lord Keeper, in the last months of his life (anon.)

4   Bacon's funerary monument, St Paul's Cathedral

– particularly Nathaniel and Nicholas – the group included several of their associates, like Ralph Shelton, Drue Drury, and – of lesser stature – Thomas and Nicholas Farmer. These individuals, some of whom also had other connections of political value, figured prominently in nearly all the major disputes which constituted the norm of political life in Norfolk and Suffolk for the next several decades. Throughout these skirmishes they remained loyal to each other, and to the principles embodied in Puritanism and the common law.[66]

The Lord Keeper was not a participating member of this group in the literal sense. In fact, he spent little time in Suffolk and perhaps none at all in Norfolk during these years. But a strong case may be made for the suggestion that, built upon the groundwork of three decades of involvement, Bacon's political activities regarding these shires after 1572 established his followers as major contenders for political hegemony. He appears to have performed this role in several ways: he used his influence to secure key offices in regional government, swayed the course of some important parliamentary elections and, in his characteristically unobtrusive manner, used his position at court to place the activities of those followers in a rosy light.

Appointment to the commission of the peace and election to parliament were perhaps the two most coveted political attainments at the shire level: the former because of its potential for wielding magisterial power in the shire itself, and the latter for the inherent prestige of representing the borough, or preferably the shire, before the realm. Preponderance of political power in any shire can nearly always be measured by reference to these two offices.

The fact that it was Bacon's duty as Lord Keeper to appoint the J.P.s was not alone sufficient to secure a county bench of his own choosing, for he was advised and heavily influenced in his choice by the predominant political interests of the shire. It is, however, evident that during his years in office the constitution of the Norfolk commission of the peace – the returns for Suffolk are too sketchy to permit analysis – underwent two perceptible changes in character which significantly reflect his participation. In the decade after 1558 a considerable number of papists were purged, leaving a combination of moderate Catholic and crypto-Catholic followers of Thomas Howard on the one hand, and a large representation of the traditionally important gentry families who were not Howard followers on the other. Some members of the lesser gentry were also in evidence, and appeared on the bench with increasing frequency.[67] Between 1569 and 1572 this balance shifted even more to bring in a large number of puritans, drawn both from the older and newer gentry. Furthermore, their emergence at this time came at the expense of some of the traditionally Catholic families who had followed the duke.[68] It is in this second shift that members of Bacon's coterie began to appear with regularity. Nathaniel and Nicholas sat regularly from 1574 and 1579 respectively – the latter having sat in Suffolk since 1575 – Wyndham from 1569, and Woodhouse from 1570.[69] Throughout the next several decades these figures and their associates utilized their place on the commissions of the peace as a base from which to bring their puritan values to bear on the political and social life of the shire. This activity included not only engagement in political issues, but also attempts at passing judgement on the social and moral life of their milieu.

In terms of his influence on the parliamentary elections in Norfolk and Suffolk, the context for Bacon's role can be stated no more succinctly than in Sir John Neale's observation that ' ... a county election furnished an opportunity unique in the life of a community, of testing the social standing of an individual or the strength of rival groups and parties'.[70] This maxim had certainly applied through the elections of 1571, in which the standing of the duke had virtually assured his privilege of selection, or at least of approval, of the knights of the shire and a large number of burgesses in the two shires. Even in 1571, when the duke's position was already considerably compromised, it is probable that he secured the election of six followers from Norfolk: John Blennerhasset (Norwich), William Barker (Yarmouth), Philip Appleyard and Thomas Hugge (Thetford), George Dacres and Nicholas Lestrange (Castle Rising); and at least two from Suffolk: William Humberston (Dunwich) and Robert Higforde (Aldeburgh).[71] After the duke's influence was eliminated, we might expect subsequent parliamentary elections to reflect new patterns of strength. Such expectations are well met, for Bacon's following emerges more clearly in the election of 1572. Although he had never before launched a conscious challenge to the traditional distribution of parliamentary representation in either shire, Bacon now effectively engineered the election of both knights of the shire for Norfolk, and the first knight of the shire for Suffolk. He did so, moreover, at the Queen's command. The Parliament of 1572 is one of the very few in which Elizabeth attempted to use her influence in assuring the election of co-operative members. She sent a letter to prominent individuals in each shire requesting their aid in that regard. Bacon's name was listed alone for Norfolk, and with that of Lord Wentworth for Suffolk.[72] When it is considered that none of his three candidates, Henry Woodhouse and Francis Wyndham for Norfolk, and Nathaniel Bacon for Suffolk, had ever before sat in parliament, this display of Bacon's dominance is all the more impressive. Both elections are worth examining in greater detail.

Norfolk had been even more strongly controlled by the Howards than Suffolk, and was characterized by even greater polarization of Catholic and puritan factions. Such polarization was less evident before Thomas Howard's fall because his strength had been sufficient to forestall any real challenge by other interests. With the end of his dominance came the willing and potent challenge which had for so long lain dormant. With the Lord Keeper's royally inspired support, Woodhouse and Wyndham sat firmly in the puritan corner and the Catholics, still stunned by the loss of their leader, were anxious to contest the election. The Lord Keeper had evidently made his choice known shortly after the writs for election had been sent out, and Sir Edward Clere, a prominent Catholic follower of the late duke who had sat for Thetford in 1563, emerged some time after as the Catholic champion. His campaign consisted of a barrage of letters to the leading Catholic families of the shire, but in the end he proved no match for the young puritans, whose own electioneering seems to have been carried out on a far more modest scale.[73]

The Suffolk election provides us with a clearer glimpse of the Lord Keeper in action as the manipulator of regional political forces. Of the two recipients of the Queen's letter for Suffolk, Bacon was patently the more powerful, and Nathaniel's candidacy met with no apparent opposition from Lord Wentworth. Shortly after the announcement was made Bacon carefully outlined to his son the strategy for the campaign. In a letter which characteristically combined personal concern with more serious political considerations, he opened by warning his son not to enter into debt for more than £100 in campaign expenses, and offered to underwrite any costs in excess of that figure.[74] He then made it clear that, although he would help in any way he could, he thought it best to keep his name from entering too directly into Nathaniel's efforts. Acting in precisely that spirit, Bacon had been at work behind the scenes. By April 24th he had lined up the support of his Chancery associate William Cordell, a native and the Steward of Ipswich. Cordell arranged for the support of his tenants, led by a Mr Walme, behind Nathaniel's efforts. Bacon then wrote his assessment:[75]

> The diffycultes that you shall fynd will rest in thys, that yf sr R wyngfield [who had sat for the Shire in 1563] and the mr of the requestes [Thomas Seckford, who had sat for the Town of Ipswich in 1563 and for the Shire in 1571] doo Ioyne to gether ageynst you & no other Ioyne with you, then perchance the matter wyll be the harder but yet yt may be you shall doo well ...

Nathaniel did indeed do well, and was launched on a long career in Parliament. Wingfield followed in the poll for the second seat, and Seckford had to settle once again for a seat at Ipswich.[76]

Still another means by which Bacon used his resources to bolster the fortunes of this coterie was by his subtle but direct intervention on their behalf at Westminster. This is demonstrated in several instances, both of minor and major importance to his followers and to the ideology which they held in common. His intercession on behalf of Nicholas Farmer as cited above fits into this category. Farmer was an associate of young Nicholas and Nathaniel Bacon, and had been found guilty by the Catholic magistrate William Heydon of counterfeiting the coin of the realm. The Lord Keeper's willingness to effect Farmer's release may be seen as a counter-thrust against the Catholic faction on the Norfolk commission of the peace. Farmer remained a Bacon follower for a long time to come.[77]

The same principle may be seen in the appointment of *ad hoc* commissions by the privy council to deal with specific problems which arose in Norfolk and Suffolk. Whether the commission was to enforce the regulations governing the sale of wool[78] or to investigate a dispute between the new Bishop and his Chancellor,[79] some of the Bacon sons or their allies seem almost always to have been named in the years following the upheavals of 1569–72.

This kind of good lordship which Bacon performed for his followers through his place on the privy council or at the Chancery is particularly well illustrated by what may be called the Hubbart Pirate Episode. In August 1576, Nathaniel Bacon wrote to tell his father that a series of successful pirate raids had been disrupting the trade of Dutch protestant shipping out of Flushing.[80] The pirates were known to be led by one Henry Carey or Carew and Thomas Hubbart. Carew was the brother-in-law of Sir Christopher Heydon, one of the most prominent of the Norfolk gentry and at that time favourable towards Catholicism, who had evidently used his standing to shield Carew from discovery. Hubbart was a member of the notoriously Catholic Hales family of Hales Hall, Norfolk, and had been described earlier in the same year as ' … a gentleman of great worship in England who is ready … to send 8 or 9 thousand soldiers and eight hundred mariners [to the King of Spain for an invasion of England]'. Although the report is obviously exaggerated, the smoke of its rhetoric suggests at least some fire at the source. Ironically, Hubbart had earlier purchased one of the Queen's ships, the *Mary Ross*, to spearhead his pirate flotilla.[81]

Pirate activity was common enough in English waters not to excite much attention, but this particular series of raids had obvious implications for local and even national politics. Nathaniel Bacon saw in the case a chance to expose his fellow J.P., Heydon, for the papist he had become, while any blow struck against the Hubbarts and their allies, who openly aided the pirates with supplies and a market for their booty in the small coastal towns of Blakeney and Cley, was a blow for the 'true religion'. As Nathaniel put it in his letter to the Lord Keeper, 'I wold not have written to yr Ld: againe in this matter, but I heare sundry complaine and are grieved at yt, that these mene being enemies unto God … shold in this manner be suffered.'[82]

The Lord Keeper's experience and acumen allowed him to see in this report a potential political windfall. Firstly, as he wrote to Nathaniel in reply, 'This matter being wyselie and discretelie handled may brede yore credite amongst my Lord [presumably, in this context, the Lord Admiral] and the rest of the Counsell, and so may it in the countrie also ... '[83] Secondly, Bacon could hardly have remained unaware of the effect that a full privy council hearing of the matter would have on the papists of Norfolk, or on those people at Westminster – including the Queen herself – who tended towards a pro-Spanish, anti-Dutch policy at that time.[84] In short, he welcomed this opportunity wholeheartedly, and exerted all the powers at his command to ensure that the affair was squeezed for every drop of its worth.

After carefully explaining to Nathaniel the best and surest method for apprehending the pirate leaders and their crews,[85] he went to work from Gorhambury to enlist the help of some of the sympathetic members of the council. The Lord Admiral was notified and his support gained for the device of bringing the case before the council. Then Bacon persuaded the council itself to appoint an *ad hoc* committee to see the pirates brought to trial and to investigate the extent of their activities. Nathaniel Bacon, Henry Woodhouse, Ralph Shelton and Sir William Buttes, along with a very red-faced Sir Christopher Heydon, were appointed to fill that office.[86] As a result of Bacon's careful instructions from Gorhambury and their diligent execution by members of the commission, the pirate leaders were duly captured, brought to Westminster for trial, and sentenced to the Marshalsea by the privy council.[87]

Although the Queen's pro-Spanish inclinations at that time led her to overrule the council and set the pirates at liberty, Bacon had attained his immediate goals. Heydon had been properly exposed, allowing the Bacon group to win a point in their factional rivalry, and everything possible had been done to place the Spanish and their English adherents in a bad light at court. The Lord Admiral had been particularly impressed by the younger Bacon's efforts, and in his opinion, 'Maister bacon deserveth greate thankes for his advertizements the which I will declare unto my lordes of the councell.'[88] Shortly thereafter the council followed suit in a commendation to the entire committee,[89] and Walsingham for one expressed his chagrin to the Lord Keeper at the Queen's pardon.[90]

Despite the significant amount of influence which Bacon had

acquired prior to the collapse of the Howard empire, the full potential of his regional political presence was only attained in the wake of that event. Even then he chose not to use his position for himself. In the most immediate sense, he used it to further the interests and careers of his sons and their colleagues, and in this he played an invaluable role in the establishment of a strong and enduring party of puritan gentry whose force would be long felt at Westminster as well as in East Anglia. In a broader sense he fulfilled the civic responsibility of his puritan calling and humanist background by attempting to bring the ideal of godly rule to the secular state. Finally, Bacon's role in regard to the politics and society of Norfolk and Suffolk adds an individual dimension to the much-heralded crisis of the aristocracy. In using his self-made resources to foster a successor party to the Howards', he effected a replacement of the traditional attitudes of the old order with the newer factors of merit and training, social mobility, and the rule of law through the agents of central government.

XII

The Conscience of a *Politique*: Religion and Foreign Affairs, 1572-8

The 1569–72 era marked a turning-point in Elizabeth's reign. The events of those years settled, at least for a time, the distribution of influence among the Queen's chief advisers, removed the urgency of a royal marriage, and effectively curtailed the hopes of Mary Stuart. In other ways as well, the concerns of the government and the preoccupations of political life had been redirected and redefined. For one thing, the emergence of a viable puritan group in Norfolk and Suffolk by 1572 was not an isolated phenomenon: it coincided with a short-lived but vigorous era of puritan assertiveness throughout the realm and at Westminster.[1] For another, the government could now regard its relations abroad with a somewhat greater detachment and broader perspective than had been possible in the perilous years of the Northern Rising and the Ridolfi Plot. Whereas the Queen's council had then found it necessary to assume a posture of armed preparedness against imminent invasion, it could now enjoy for at least a few years the relative luxury of mere vigilance and the possibility of its own intervention in the affairs of other states.

That era also had an impact on the political outlook of Nicholas Bacon. Whereas, prior to 1569, one of the most immediate motivates for his circumspection in support of radical or controversial causes was his legitimate fear of falling out of the Queen's favour, his loyalty and staunch support in that year largely obviated that anxiety. Thereafter, Bacon was tempted to follow a more openly radical course at court and, especially in regard to religious matters, to join forces with such zealots as

Leicester, Knollys, Killigrew and, from 1573, Walsingham. But with the removal of one restraint, others – which had always been present but which had previously remained subordinate – now came to the fore. While he continued to support puritan radicals in his private life, in the regional politics of East Anglia, and even in matters of secondary importance at Westminster, his deep concern for the viability of the Elizabethan nation led him to subordinate theological and other personal preferences to reasons of state. Now more than ever he assumed the mantle of a statesman. These priorities are particularly evident in the issues of religion and foreign affairs which, between them, more or less dominated the politics of the mid-1570s.

In the context of his private life, Bacon's support of radical protestants is more apparent in the last decade of his life than at any previous time. His home at Gorhambury sheltered a great many more religious dissidents in the 1570s than Redgrave had ever done. These included such figures as Robert Johnson, Humphrey Wiblood, Percival Wiburn, Thomas Wilcox and John Field.[2] Gorhambury was of course more commodious than Redgrave, and Bacon probably spent more time there than he had at the earlier residence. Much credit must also go to the lady of the house, for Anne Bacon – who had resided at Redgrave only briefly – was extremely forthright in her support of puritans. Without detracting from Lady Anne's role in this respect, however, the master of the house did more than acquiesce in the preferences of a demanding wife. Acting with the spirit that had earned him lavish praise from no less a Calvinist than Theodore Beza,[3] Bacon diligently found livings for several of these house guests,[4] and pointedly continued his support of at least one such protégé long after it became a political burden to do so.

The saga of Robert Johnson, like that of Thomas Fowle a few years earlier, is one of the most prominent illustrations of Bacon's wrestling with the conflicting pressures of official duty and personal conviction. Johnson had been the first of the family chaplains to serve at Gorhambury, and he had used it as his base for organizing prophesyings in the diocese of Ely and at the nearby Abbey Church – now Cathedral – of St Albans. Later on, Bacon secured for Johnson a prebendary's stall at Norwich which lay at his disposal.[5]

In 1571 Johnson's blatant nonconformity was uncovered by

Archbishop Parker, and when he refused to subscribe he was duly suspended.[6] When Parker initiated proceedings against him, Johnson took refuge at Gorhambury, and was not at all reluctant to invoke Bacon's name in his defence. 'My Lord and his family', wrote Johnson to Parker,

> have wanted, longer than accustomed manner hath been, those most necessary, comfortable, and Christian helps and exercises of religion, especially regarding the number of their youthful retinue ... My duty herein to his Lordship's household particularly considered ... moves me with all due humility and submission to beseech you to restore me to my former liberty.[7]

He then promised to resign his prebend ' ... that I have, by his Lord, the Lord Keeper, Sir Nicholas,' within six months – which in fact he never actually did – and ended by signing the submission proffered by Parker. The whole was endorsed 'from the Lord Keeper's House at Gorhambury, beside St Albans'. Although Bacon himself seems not to have intervened directly in any of this, his role could hardly be denied, and would soon cause him some embarrassment.

Just two years after Johnson was reinstated, Parker secured the co-operation of the privy council in punishing those who had disseminated some of the radical diatribes of Thomas Cartwright. In July 1571, Parker and Archbishop Sandys of York came before the council with four zealots who had been accused of disseminating Cartwright's later work: Edward Dering, Percival Wiburn, John Browne, and the same Robert Johnson. Bacon was doubtless chagrined by the presumably unexpected appearance of his chaplain, and all the more so because it had fallen to his lot to chair the meeting. Here was Bacon's dilemma once more ensnaring him, but in a more open and significant arena.

As the meeting progressed, Bacon and other members of the council evidently displayed great reluctance to proceed with Parker's intended admonitions. When Parker's turn to speak came at last, he rapidly gave full vent to his exasperation. Soundly chastising his listeners for their dilatory proceedings, he warned that the Queen could not accept such half-hearted enforcement of the ecclesiastical laws. When the councillors replied that they were loath to comply in that 'popish tyme',

Parker proposed the administration of an oath whereby no private person could criticize the letter of the Settlement without prior permission from the Queen. The puritans, realizing that a petition for such royal permission would be in itself a form of criticism, were willing to take the oath. As they discovered this loophole, however, Bacon emerged from his silent quandary and made his position clear. The decision cannot have been easy, but his legalistic mind had allowed him to see the reason for the puritans' compliance, and he now proposed a device to counter their move. Any such petition, he stipulated, would have to be signed by its author's name, and thus no mere anonymous tract or protest could be interpreted as a petition to the Queen. The council could only follow the Lord Keeper's example of being *plus royal que le roi*, and Parker was allowed to prevail.[8] The hapless puritans, including Bacon's own protégé, had fallen prey to the Lord Keeper's ultimate defence of Parker's position.

Three years following this session Bacon met yet another case of clerical nonconformity which similarly pitted his puritan sympathies against his political conscience. This concerned Edmund Grindal. Although Grindal had been one of the few who could reasonably have succeeded Matthew Parker as Archbishop of Canterbury, and was appointed with little hesitation on Elizabeth's part, he was a puritan. Within months of his elevation he antagonized the Queen by refusing to prohibit prophesyings. He then further assured his own disgrace by tactlessly lecturing her on the limits of royal authority in ecclesiastical affairs.[9] When Elizabeth asked the privy council to convene in the Star Chamber and consider depriving the new Archbishop of his office, Bacon became, *ex officio*, the chairman of the meeting.

In addition to Bacon's personal sympathy for the value of prophesyings, he and Grindal had long been friends. They may have met as early as 1551, when Grindal began to serve as chaplain to the boy King Edward.[10] They worked together on a committee to restore the lightning-damaged steeple of St Paul's after 1563,[11] and saw each other socially from at least 1568.[12] Yet when compelled to take charge of Grindal's hearing, Bacon could hardly refuse.

By the time of the meeting, in November 1577, Edmund Grindal was no longer a well man. He had six more years to live, not a short time for a man of his age in those years, but he was already losing his sight and experiencing a good many other bodily ills. When the appointed day came for his appearance he was too ill to attend and, although he seems to have had his statement already prepared,[13] he was compelled to send his apologies instead.[14] Bacon had also prepared himself for that meeting with a speech, and although it was never delivered, it has come down to us in its intended form. As the occasion demanded, it set out clearly the conflict between the Queen and her Archbishop, and is noteworthy in that Bacon implied no sympathy for his friend. It was obvious, he reminded those present,

> ... how hee was accused of greate and waightie causes neither in secret nor by anie privat person, but by magistrates, judges, and [men] of good caulinge & bisshops, and that both by letters and messages as hereafter should be manefested ... so as that theie woulde bothe marveile at the heinous matters so committed by him, and also not disalowe nor mislike of hir Majestes proceedings againste the same.[15]

When word of Grindal's indisposition came to the councillors, the hearing was put off until his recovery,[16] and in the end the illness lingered long enough for Elizabeth to cancel it altogether. Thus Bacon was spared the unpleasant task of presiding at the figurative defrocking of a friend, but the tenor of his initial speech leaves little doubt that he viewed this as a matter of state, and would not have tried to intervene on Grindal's behalf.

In sum, Bacon's attempts to support puritan practice and practitioners in his last half-decade may be abundantly demonstrated with reference to the advowsons under his control, the entourage at Gorhambury and his role in the politics of East Anglia, but none of these activities could be considered crucial to the national interest. In matters of greater political consequence he seems to have consistently placed a higher priority on the preservation of law, order and due process of government than on other loyalties. Whereas the tenor of his actions in this phase of his career does not appreciably differ from that of a decade earlier, Bacon's motivations were no longer quite the same. Whereas he would formerly have acted in large part out of an immediate concern for his status at court, he now felt sufficiently secure to exercise freedom of choice. Although his decisions were not thereby rendered easier to make, he now seems to have chosen the path of the *politique* out of personal conviction rather than mere obedience. That transition not only serves as a yardstick for Bacon's security in the royal favour, but also in his emergence as an independent and statesmanlike councillor.

The quandaries of foreign affairs provided a second arena in which Bacon's personal preferences did battle with his sense of political principle, for the temptation to base his counsel primarily on personal convictions, as did Walsingham and other zealots, lay ever before him in these last years.

In the pre-Elizabethan stages of his career we have no indication that Bacon ever thought at length about foreign affairs, nor did he have any particular cause to do so. When he was first called to tender such advice as a privy councillor under Elizabeth he seems understandably not to have been at ease. As we have noted, his early statements on such matters as the French intervention in Scotland and the projected English marriage alliance with France were often well reasoned, but seldom demonstrated more than an awareness of immediate circumstances. In addition to the question of national security, such circumstances often included the financial situation of the realm, with which he was usually quite familiar, politics at court, and of course the matter of religious loyalties. Based on these factors, Bacon's advice was often astute in its judgement, and admirably pragmatic in its substance, but an overall sense of direction emerged only in the very broadest terms.

When faced with similar issues in the last several years of his life, however, Bacon's maturation in outlook becomes evident. One may finally discern true policy in his pronouncements. Still concerned with such matters as England's preparedness, the plight of protestants at home and abroad, and – most fundamentally – the preservation of the Elizabethan state, he has now some clear ideas regarding the priorities of those goals and the means by which to attain them. In general, he accepted the dictum that England's security lay in the confusion of her enemies. In concrete terms he took that to mean that the internal difficulties of France and Spain had to be sustained, even though it might involve clandestine English intervention. At the same time, it is clear that he would not have extended open aid in support of protestant rebels on the Continent where English security could be jeopardized in the effort, nor, on the other hand, would he have objected to negotiated settlements – such as the projected Anjou marriage – where such co-operation could work to English advantage. Thus, although he did not always agree with the means by which Elizabeth, Burghley, or other moderates hoped to effect their policies, and was not afraid to say so, Bacon was not willing to go so far as to support the designs of the council's ardently puritan wing. This outlook of the 1570s becomes particularly evident in the intricacies of English policy towards the Dutch revolt.

Although the imminent threat to England from foreign invasion had largely subsided after 1572, and would not again be a factor during Bacon's lifetime, both the French civil wars, which neutralized the French threat only as long as they continued, and the Dutch revolt, in which control of the crucial North Sea coast was at stake, bore the close scrutiny of the Westminster strategists. The two struggles, moreover, were not unrelated.

The Dutch situation had become particularly complex.[17] Despite superior numbers, training, leadership and ordnance, the Duke of Alva's forces had been unable to dislodge the tenacious rebels from their strongholds. In 1572 Alva even lost the strategically important port of The Brill [Brielle], and faced more determined opposition than ever in the wake of that impossibly daring rebel triumph.[18] By autumn 1573 Alva retired from the battle a frustrated man, and was replaced by Don Luis de Zúñigay Requeséns.[19] In the campaign to recover his Dutch patrimony, Philip ardently desired England's benevolent neutrality. He enticed Elizabeth with his proffered friendship throughout much of the 1570s;[20] considering the relative strength of the two nations, this was a substantial allurement.

Elizabeth and Philip had little in common that would sustain mutual amity, but one of the few factors that served such a purpose was fear of France: in that regard, it might seem as though little had changed in several decades. The course of the recent French troubles had been so erratic that she might at any time set her house in order and embark once again on expansionist policies. The French might turn against the Spanish in alliance with William of Orange, or they might try to knock once more on the gates of England's northern border, but in either possibility lay good cause for maintaining amicable relations between England and Spain. Beyond that, however, it was not easy for many at Westminster to like a Spanish alliance. Past transgressions aside, a Spanish victory in the Netherlands would place a potentially hostile and extremely potent military presence on the North Sea shore. It would also strike a direct blow to the hopes of English protestants. In consequence, the English puritans lobbied tirelessly for English support to their co-religionists.

While Elizabeth and her advisers were content to observe rather than engage in the Continental frays of the early 1570s, they well knew how tenuous that luxury might prove. In retrospect, it has been possible to cite evidence of a generally consistent policy on Elizabeth's part[21] and, on the whole, the hypothesis of such a policy has withstood recent attempts to discredit it.[22] Save for short-range digressions, it is evident that Elizabeth would not jeopardize her peaceful relations with Spain by openly aiding the Dutch, but that, at the same time, she did not intend either side to enjoy a decisive victory. The best that she could hope for in keeping the North Sea coast from the total control of any independent power was a prolonged deadlock between the combatants, either by treaty or by pressure of circumstance, which would leave such hegemony unresolved. At the same time, of course, she hoped to keep the French at bay, and her own resources as uncommitted as possible. She thus set herself a difficult task, and the fact of her success for well over a decade should not obscure for us the diplomatic and political skulduggery which sustained that success.

While the Dutch more or less held their own in the early years of the decade, Elizabeth's policy seemed valid and logical, and Bacon found little difficulty in accepting it in full. When William of Orange suffered several major reverses in 1575, however, uncertainty began to creep in at the highest reaches of Westminster. Elizabeth could extend to the rebels the sort of clandestine aid which she had offered the Scottish Lords of the Congregation and the Huguenots in past years, but that policy was not without its risks. In addition, it was not even certain that the modest amounts of aid which could be proffered in that manner would suffice to keep Orange's battered forces in contention. When the Prince implied towards the end of 1575 that he would have to look to France if Elizabeth continued to temporize on his requests for support, the luxury of procrastination at Westminster began to fade.[23] It was recognized that Orange's threat was not an empty gesture, for he had good reason to fear French dominance, and his pleas could only be seen in the light of his desperation. The Queen put the matter fully before her councillors.[24]

The length of the ensuing debate – it went on for over two weeks – is some indication of both the complexity of the issue and the diversity of opinion it engendered at the council board. Nor did the councillors carry on their deliberations in a vacuum: they earnestly consulted envoys recently returned from Spain and the Low Countries,[25] and on January 9th, Bacon, Burghley, Leicester and Walsingham met with Orange's envoys to consider his appeal at first hand.[26] Although little more than snippets of the actual debate have come down to us, it is clear that the ideological differences between puritans and moderates which would dominate the discussions at the council board for a decade to come were already discernible on this issue of foreign policy.[27]

In the scant two years since being sworn a privy councillor, Francis Walsingham had rapidly overtaken the Earl of Leicester as the chief puritan spokesman on the council. A generation younger than Bacon, Sadler, Mildmay and others of the old guard, he had not entered politics until the relatively tranquil Elizabethan era. Perhaps for that reason he lacked the reserve and moderation which characterized those veterans of the 'forties and 'fifties. Walsingham viewed policy largely in religious terms, and had for some time envisioned Europe as neatly divided between protestants and Catholics. England, in his vision, was destined to lead the forces of the former, and the thrust of his efforts at the council board had consistently been directed towards that end.[28] Now he spoke in forthright terms in favour of open support for the Dutch rebels and the severance of all links with the hated Spanish.[29]

Bacon studied these and other arguments as they unfolded before him, but much as he may have favoured the cause of the Dutch protestants at heart, Walsingham's impassioned plea on their behalf proved unacceptable to his sense of moderation. When his turn came he spoke on the issue in the rational tones of the *politique*. To begin with, he was too greatly impressed by the might of Spain to hazard Walsingham's course of action. He felt that England's own naval forces and financial ability were grossly inadequate to meet the demands of the Anglo-Spanish war which would surely result from support of the Dutch, and thus he could not condone an open break. Nor, he considered, could England count on aid from any other foreign power as Walsingham had implied. The French were not to be trusted in a matter of such importance, and the protestant forces on the Continent had proved weak, divided, and largely unreliable. Whatever the outcome might be, Bacon could not condone open aid to Orange at that time. On the other hand, he could hardly stand idly by and witness Orange's defeat. England must be more liberal with secret shipments of money and supplies; the Queen might even support in a suitably discreet manner some sizeable force of mercenaries to forestall a Spanish victory.[30]

In many ways, this was sound policy. Burghley endorsed its observations and recommendations in subsequent memoranda,[31] and when it fell to his lot to summarize the weight of the council's opinion on January 16th, Bacon's stance proved close to the consensus.[32] Because of the perils of a Spanish victory in the Netherlands, which were rehearsed in full and stark detail, the Dutch had to be maintained in their autonomy and in the enjoyment of their ancient liberties. Yet they had also to accept the Habsburg overlordship if peace were to be obtained. To extend open aid was, as Bacon had emphasized, entirely too risky, but two viable alternatives remained: negotiation towards a compromise settlement, or secret English aid to the Dutch which – it was hoped – would obtain a military stalemate. Towards the first alternative, Elizabeth was advised to send her envoys back to Orange and Requeséns – Alva's successor – to sound out both sides on the plausibility of a negotiated settlement. If such a device proved fruitless, Elizabeth was to sustain the rebels by secret aid and even countenance limited French involvement with no loss of honour to herself.

Although the policy of encouraging both sides to negotiate had proved unsuccessful the previous autumn, it was the part of the council's recommendations that Elizabeth seized upon most readily.[33] Again, however, it proved fruitless, and by spring the relations between England and the Dutch were becoming increasingly strained by a series of piratical seizures of English shipping in the Baltic and North Seas. Although Orange disavowed any control over the Sea Beggars, and probably did so with considerable sincerity, Elizabeth held him accountable; in consequence, she turned a much friendlier face towards Spain as the summer wore on.[34]

This pro-Spanish stance caused great chagrin among members of the council, and not only with such zealots as Walsingham and Leicester; Bacon and Burghley now joined them in an earnest attempt to reverse it. Each went about that common intent according to his temperature and influence: Walsingham by direct appeals to Orange – which were ultimately successful[35] – and Bacon by a characteristically more subtle means. Fortunately for him, the news of the Hubbart pirate raids, sponsored by the Spanish against protestant shipping, reached him from his son at just this point, and Bacon seized his chance to present Elizabeth with what he saw as an essentially opportunistic and hostile Spanish attitude towards England.[36] As we have seen, Elizabeth was not much moved, and in fact she freed the imprisoned pirates. Perhaps hoping to welcome a new ally to his cause, Walsingham quickly wrote a note of commiseration to Bacon after the Queen's partisan act of clemency.[37] The Lord Keeper accepted Walsingham's sympathy, but not the policy which, by implication, came with it.

Towards the end of 1576 it began to look as though Elizabeth's hopes of a compromise settlement were about to be realized after all. Faced with widespread mutinies of Spanish troops in late October, and greatly encouraged by Orange, the hitherto loyal Estates General joined with the rebellious States of Holland and Zealand on November 8th in signing the Pacification of Ghent.[38] They then insisted that the newly appointed Spanish governor, Don John of Austria, who was then only *en route* to assume his new command, agree to it. He did so in the following February by the so-called Perpetual Edict.[39] According to this settlement, all parties joined together in acknowledging loyalty to Philip as Duke of Burgundy, and also reaffirmed their ancient liberties and their allegiance to William as Stadtholder.[40] At about the same time, moreover, Elizabeth and William came to terms over what had virtually amounted to an undeclared war at sea.[41] Thus, by the end of the year, Elizabeth and her councillors felt much more at ease in regard to the Dutch question than they had for some time.

Unfortunately, the vision of a permanent settlement along the lines of the Pacification of Ghent proved ephemeral, and within a few months English vigilance was again in order. In retrospect, it is clear that without the consent of the Prince of Orange to the Perpetual Edict, and with only the reluctant co-operation of Don John – who had had little choice in signing the proffered document – the settlement was not fated to endure. The two leaders soon began a war of nerves in which the loyalties of the Estates General and the several uncommitted provinces were at stake. On the whole, Orange had gained the upper hand in diplomatic terms by midsummer.[42] When Don John recognized this loss of ground, he had little hesitation in violating the Pacification to stem the tide. He did so in July by storming the fortress of Namur.[43] It was rumoured that he meant to gain a firm enough grip on the provinces to use them as a staging area for an invasion of England. In any event, Don John's two Dutch antagonists, Orange's forces and the Estates, were again hard pressed for relief, and at least for a time found unwonted receptivity at Westminster. Elizabeth dispatched William Davison to consult with Orange about his needs,[44] and Bacon now joined Walsingham and most other councillors in favour of open aid to forestall what appeared a certain calamity.[45]

Incapable of tendering his advice in person, 'not of an unwilling heart and mind, but of an unable and unwieldy body', Bacon wrote from Gorhambury his analysis not only of the Dutch situation, but also of France, who could yet prove a grave menace through Scotland once she set her own house in order, and of the general lack of preparedness at home, which the fearful Lord Keeper saw as an invitation to open invasion. The timing of the letter, however, made the problem of the Low Countries its chief preoccupation, and here Bacon had some interesting suggestions:

> I knowe no way soe suer as to kepe the prynce of Orenge in harte and lief as I think till he be eyther wonne from them or overthrowen out of those partes will growe no greate

perill to yor majestie. The States there are so divided as I here amongs themselves that yt may be dowbted whether any trust may be reposed in them where one trustethe not another, mary and it might be brought to pass by good councell from hence, that the Duke of Ascot and the rest of States might governe the countrey according to their auncient liberties and to Receave the prynce to have the rule of all their marsyall matters and soe to ioyne their forces ...

Although the scheme agreed in most respects with the general tenor of feeling at Westminster, Bacon's suggested recourse to the Duke of Aerschot ('Ascot') was a novel and perceptive approach. Philippe de Croy, Duke of Aerschot, was one of the most prominent of the ancient Walloon nobility, and had remained loyal to the government right from the first uprisings of the mid-1560s. But when the Spanish troops mutinied in the autumn of 1576, and the anti-Spanish pressure from the populace grew to mammoth proportions in consequence of this and other factors, Aerschot had utilized his status, as Knight of the Fleece and Councillor of State, to reconvene the Estates General. Almost immediately voted Chief of the Council of State, he had then been largely responsible for engineering the Pacification of Ghent.[46] Whereas Orange had come to lead the first revolt of the previous decade, it was now Aerschot who emerged to lead this second revolt, that of the Estates, a decade later. If, as Bacon reasoned, the two leaders and their respective forces could be joined together, a viable bulwark might be formed against a complete Spanish victory. At the same time, as Bacon no doubt also recognized, such an agreement would only be acceptable to Aerschot's Estates if allegiance to Philip were maintained along with the 'auncient liberties' of which he wrote. In this manner, he hoped that a *status quo ante bellum* might yet be obtained.

Unfortunately for Bacon's plan and for the hopes of most of the councillors, Elizabeth's resolve to aid the Dutch was as short-lived as it had been dramatic, but her retreat came in legitimate response to a surprising chain of events rather than as a personal whim. Formerly ardent in seeking English help, the Estates General faced the new crisis by turning instead to the Empire, and shortly secured the aid of the young Archduke Matthias.[47]

Although it was no doubt justified in view of Elizabeth's previous reluctance to commit herself, this Dutch *volte-face* was a sharp rebuke for English policy. Walsingham was most upset,[48] Elizabeth had been made to look foolish, and the implementation of Bacon's plan of September now rested in foreign hands. By the time the envoys from the Estates had reluctantly accepted Elizabeth's proffered benevolence, she had already decided to save face by withdrawing the offer.[49]

Just after the Estates chose to accept her help, but before he knew of her retraction of that offer, Bacon took up his pen to express once again his sentiments on the knotty problems of foreign affairs.[50] He re-emphasized the importance of securing Scotland against the French, who were then at peace, and the urgent need to prepare at home, but he then turned to the subject of the Low Countries. Bacon found the situation very confusing, not because he lacked the news from court, but because that news itself was riddled with uncertainties. He would have Elizabeth dispatch some trusty envoy to the Prince of Orange – whom Bacon, like Elizabeth, found in the end more reliable than the slippery leaders of the Estates – to seek his opinion about the current crisis.

Although not at all averse to gathering additional information before taking decisive action, Elizabeth in the meantime found refuge in her familiar hope for negotiation. She thus let it be known that she would again try to move the Spanish to conciliate. Until the situation became clearer there was little else to be done, and she followed through in short order. Envoys were sent to Philip and the Estates in January,[51] but the Spanish were unwilling to wait for the arrival of Matthias. On the last day of January, Don John surprised a large army of the Estates and won an overwhelming victory at Gembloux.[52]

In deep consternation, Elizabeth convened the privy council at once to consider the implications of this further blow. Hastily arriving from Hampton Court, the councillors met at Bacon's York House residence on February 5th.[53] With hardly any opposition, they determined to forget the recent effrontery of the Estates and to commit English aid at once.[54] Before they could convince Elizabeth of that course, however, she hit upon a plan of her own which appeared to her a more viable alternative. This sudden inspiration came in the form of a suggestion that

Duke Casimir of the Palatinate could be persuaded to lead a substantial force of protestant mercenaries against Don John.[55] By encouraging that mission and by supplying its fiscal and military requirements, Elizabeth could effect substantial relief in a covert manner which need not endanger her ties with Philip. This was not a new idea. She had previously sent Casimir £20,000 to supply his forces to the Huguenots,[56] and the possibility of his intercession in the Low Countries on his own had been a matter for speculation since the previous autumn.[57] Bacon had considered him worthy of Elizabeth's friendship and support in September 1577, both for his leadership of Central European Calvinists and for his adventures on behalf of the protestant rebellion in France.[58] When considered as an alternative to direct English aid to the Estates after the fall of Gembloux, however, Casimir's aid seemed unreliable and insufficient to most of the councillors.

When Elizabeth gave the duke his head, he readily proved the sceptics correct. Although he seemed willing enough, he was slow to come to terms with the Dutch, and slower still to muster his troops once the agreement had been made. When he finally arrived, his efforts proved more of a hindrance than a help, for he could not keep his undisciplined troops from ravaging the Dutch countryside.[59] For their parts, neither Orange nor the Estates seem to have thought much of the prospect of his services in the first place.[60]

By March, the Estates felt compelled to look more kindly on the persistent offers of help from the Duke of Alençon.[61] Although she herself had done much to drive Orange to a similar course by her dilatory proceedings, Elizabeth now came to regret the rebels' plight: Alençon, virtually evicted from the French court by his brother the King, was an aggressive and wily adventurer with uncertain motives. Did he sincerely want to help roll back the Spanish advance out of sympathy for the protestant cause, or would he proceed to take the Low Countries for himself? Beyond that, if Orange tried to back out of his tentative arrangement with the impetuous duke, or sought to block his ambitions once the alliance had been set in motion, would Alençon then join with Don John in a common front against Dutch resistance? None of these alarming possibilities seemed remote at Westminster, and once again Elizabeth turned to her council.[62]

Burghley seems to have feared the worst from Alençon, and in the ensuing debate took the position that the French adventurer meant nothing less than to make himself master of the Low Countries.[63] In his estimation Elizabeth had left herself but two cards, and she would have to play both of them to come out ahead. He insisted that Elizabeth send over envoys of good account to dissuade the Dutch from their French flirtation, and then he urged her once again to attempt mediation. If her envoys successfully overcame the problem of Elizabeth's credibility and managed to wean the Dutch from their French suitors, Elizabeth would then have to be ready to supply Orange's wants in full, for Alençon would surely attach himself to Don John if Orange abandoned him. So concerned was Burghley over the prospect of French involvement that he was willing to have Elizabeth threaten Orange with an Anglo-Spanish alliance if he persisted in dealing with the French.

Although the lack of a date for Burghley's opinion makes it impossible to tell who stated his position first, Bacon's advice on the matter, in the form of a letter of May 6th, differed from that of his brother-in-law.[64] In contrast to his earlier letters on the subject, Bacon now allowed himself an air of self-righteousness and pessimism:

> Most gratious soveraigne, By my former letteres thre things that ... I with all humbleness did advise Your Majestie to doe as the beste of your suretie to my understanding. The first was to assiste the Prince of Orenge; the second to assure Scotland; the third to make all safe and redie at home. Now seeinge it hath not pleased God to move Your Majestie's harte to give that assistance to the Prynce in tyme as was wished and desired, which I cannot remember but greatly to my griefe, ye best counsell I can give is that care be taken for the other two ...

After reiterating his former counsel regarding domestic preparedness and the danger of invasion through Scotland, Bacon returned to the plight of the Low Countries. It looked to him as though Orange had been left high and dry; the Prince could not withstand Don John on his own, and yet any help he might receive from England – if Elizabeth decided to grant it – could not arrive in time. 'Thes thinges considered', he went on,

> yt is best for the States to receave Mounser [i.e., Alençon] with such conditions as they can gette, so they be not over dangerous. For, yf Don John and Mounsier joyne than they are to look for no conditiones, but such as the conquerores geve to the conquered; and as soe to doe is least harmful to them, Soe yt ys to Your Majestie also, for soe shall the amitye of Ffraunce and Spayne be broken by all lyklihood … Albeyt I thinke as I have before written yet yt were best to be advertised from the prynce and States whom the matter chiefly concernethe and next know what ys best for them [and] what they thinke best to be done in this matter.

Like Burghley, Bacon had made his judgement as a *politique*, subordinating religious to political considerations; but he was more willing than the former to take a chance on Alençon. In addition, he was not at all reluctant to disagree openly with his friend and ally by speaking his mind on that issue. Walsingham, in contrast to both, continued to see the problem in the black and white tones with which he viewed nearly all political issues: the same hands that had dealt in the St Bartholomew's Day Massacre, he warned, now dealt with Orange, and if the latter came to terms with them it would be tantamount to signing over control of his territory to the French.[65]

It is interesting to note here that, although they may have disagreed sharply in their approach to political questions, Bacon and Walsingham seem to have remained on good terms, and there is little indication that Bacon shared Burghley's apparent resentment of the younger man's growing influence at court.[66] This may be seen not so much as a desertion of Bacon's principles or allies, but rather as a sign of his advanced years; rounding out his seventh decade, the Lord Keeper was simply no longer as interested or as involved in the inter-personal rivalries at court as he had been a decade earlier, and thus had less occasion to feel threatened by Walsingham and other younger lights than had Burghley. In these last years, Bacon found it much easier than ever before to select his friends without regard for their political views. In consequence, he found it possible to maintain useful dialogue on matters of policy even with those whom we should expect to be his opponents.

Thus, when Elizabeth resolved to send Walsingham abroad in a final attempt at fostering negotiations, he and Bacon kept up what was evidently a steady and even warm correspondence. As the futility of the Secretary's mission became apparent, Bacon wrote him his mind in confidence, as a friend.[67] He had been away from court since Walsingham's departure, and was out of touch with the opinions current at Westminster. From what the Secretary had already written, however, the possibility of peace seemed remote. If this impression proved accurate, he could see but two courses: either the Dutch could prolong the war by a stubborn defence of their towns, or they could break up an impending Franco-Spanish alliance by placing their trust in Alençon. Even if 'Monsieur' turned on the Estates and wrested control for himself, French hegemony seemed to Bacon preferable to Spanish. Yet he could conceive of a scheme whereby even Alençon's domination might be rendered temporary:

> ... the best way that I can thinke of to bringe it to passe ys for the States to adventure somewhat largely with Mounser to the offence of Spayne, and fraunce to continewe which to my understandinge muste in tyme turne to their [i.e., the French] overthrowe for that Spayne will enduer that Monsieur shall possesse any parte of his Dominion ys harde to beleve.

The result, he continued, would be a deadlock between the French and the Spanish over the possession of the Low Countries. This might in the end lead to a *status quo ante bellum* settlement in which no one would win a decisive victory, but which would in the meantime assure peace of mind for England, which was clearly Bacon's highest priority. It is hard to imagine that Bacon expected Orange to receive such a suggestion with enthusiasm, much less Walsingham, but as Alençon was at that time virtually allied with the Dutch cause the possibility of such a course of events was not at all remote.

With that statement, so far as we know, Bacon expressed his last thoughts on the quandaries of foreign policy. Half a year later he would lie dying in London, and in the interim he seems increasingly to have withdrawn from the meetings of the privy council.

To the last, Bacon's counsel in these knotty problems of policy kept in view the fundamental recognition shared by nearly all at Westminster: English security could best be served by a stalemate settlement of the Dutch revolt, and England's logical role was to bring about such a settlement in any way she could. In seeking measures to achieve that goal, however, Bacon proved quite capable of finding his own path as the circumstances demanded. He was neither lured by the protestant zeal of the Walsingham faction, nor – although he often sided with them – did he feel compelled to agree with Burghley and the other moderates. Whereas in the past he had sometimes been swayed from an opposing view to Burghley's course – as in the December 1559 debate on Scotland – or risked the Secretary's censure for his patent independence – as in the Newhaven question of 1563 – he had now gained sufficient prestige and standing to advocate a course of his own. He accepted that latitude for what it was, and tendered his advice as well as he was able in those years of declining health and somewhat abated activity.

In sum, Bacon's approach to foreign affairs appears wholly consistent with his attitude towards religion and other issues. His first concern was always for the preservation of the Elizabethan state: the survival of the Queen upon her throne, the forms and institutions of Tudor government, and the fundamental structure of the Anglican Settlement. In these respects, at any rate, he was far from unique, but his counsel was nearly always sound and was well regarded by his colleagues at court.

These last years thus saw Bacon attain the ultimate stage of his political growth. He had begun his career as a talented bureaucrat, acquired considerable sophistication in the arts and letters and gained a foothold in the upper reaches of Elizabeth's government, yet not until the crisis years of 1569–72 fully tried his mettle could he cast off the shell of insecurity which had defined and somewhat constrained his activities at court. Only in these last years did he fully enjoy the confidence of the Queen and her court and the consequent freedom of action which allowed him to attain the full potential of his political career.

XIII

Epilogue

During most of his years of service to Elizabeth, Bacon suffered from sundry ailments ranging from gout and the stone to insomnia and hardness of hearing. Some, no doubt, were compounded by the corpulence of his later years. At best, these discomforts proved a constant source of irritation, while at worst, they sapped his energy and curtailed his activities. The ceremonies of his own office-taking in 1558 had probably been postponed by his suffering from the 'quartain',[1] and diverse ailments caused his replacement at the Chancery or in parliament on several occasions throughout the two decades which followed.[2] In September 1575, when he was too 'pained with the stone' to attend the Chancery,[3] it was rumoured that he would be offered the less strenuous post of Lord Privy Seal.[4] He attended the meetings of the privy council less frequently during the 1570s,[5] and in the latter years of that decade he showed less of his old spark: he made fewer proposals to the Queen, initiated fewer reforms in the Chancery, and seemed more willing to allow younger men their day at court. Yet at no time can we speak of total retirement or waning mental faculties. In his very last year he performed dutifully at the Chancery and, if he did attend the meetings of the privy council less frequently, he at least let his pen speak for him on issues of major importance. He still managed to fulfil a commission to investigate the workings of the mint in the spring of 1578,[6] and within weeks of his death in the following February, we find him bustling about to settle the accommodations of the cursitors in Chancery[7] and the construction of a chapel at his old Cambridge college.[8]

While Bacon increasingly endured the ravages of old age, he also reaped more than ever the rewards of a lifetime of hard work. The high regard of his colleagues, dedications of poetry and prose,[9] and New Year's greetings from suitor and sovereign

187

alike, marked the passage of his last years.[10] In the spring of 1577 Elizabeth extended to him one of those gestures of respect which compensated in many ways for her parsimony in granting titles and rewards. She made Gorhambury a pre-announced stop on her summer's progress, and paid her Lord Keeper the compliment of a lengthy and memorable visit.[11]

Unlike her first visit, announced on short notice and equally brief in duration, this was to last a full five days: from May 18th, a Saturday, until 'Wednesday afterdinner following'.[12] It was, to Bacon, a state occasion. With his debut as a host to royalty now behind him, and a great deal more time to prepare than had previously been the case, the Lord Keeper spared no pains or expense to fête the Queen in proper style and to revel in her approbation. He employed upholsterers to repair the furnishings, and workmen to manicure the grounds. Special cooks were fetched from London in hired carriages, and nearly every food and beverage in fashionable use was stocked in ample supply for their artistry. With the hiring and rehearsal of a band of revellers and the purchase of gifts for the Queen and the officers of her household, his preparations were at last complete. From all indications he did himself proud in entertaining a monarch used to lavish display. Excluding his gift to the Queen, the entire visit cost Bacon no less than £577 6s. 7d.

Amid the varied ills and comforts of old age it is also to be expected that Bacon's thoughts turned to death. As befits one whose life was successful and chaste, he faced the prospect with confidence and characteristic forethought. His preparations were as methodical as his speeches in parliament, and his chosen accoutrements as reflective of the proud – but not ostentatious – parvenu as his home at Gorhambury.

Symbolically enough, Bacon chose to be buried at St Paul's, near the seat of government, rather than at his Gorhambury residence. By August 1576, we find Alexander Nowell, Bacon's friend and the Dean of St Paul's, instructing the Cathedral verger to allow Bacon and his workmen access at all times to the future site of the Lord Keeper's tomb: between two pillars near the door on the south side of the Cathedral choir. They were also given leave to remove such stonework as was necessary for the tomb 'there to be sett upp'.[13] Less than a year later, with the edifice apparently complete, Bacon arranged for its perpetual care by representatives of the Cathedral.[14] Were Bacon a lesser man, such a grand gesture as a funerary monument in the choir of St Paul's might have engendered resentment from those of nobler birth, but his reputation and achievements were sufficient to overcome his mean origins. When the Earl of Pembroke came to erect a monument for his late father in 1581, he instructed the masons to take care that 'the sayde Tombe doe not exceade the breadth of the late L. Keprs'.[15] In an age when noblemen and members of the gentry were still far apart in their social perquisites, such a request from the Second Earl of Pembroke reveals the magnitude of Bacon's reputation.

All that remains of the Lord Keeper's monument after the Great Fire of London and other molestations of time is an alabaster representation of Bacon himself, complete except for the lower legs and some minor damage to the rest. It lies in the Cathedral vault, all but lost amongst the funerary memorabilia of more recent worthies. Fortunately, we have both a description and a detailed drawing of the original edifice.[16] (see Plate 4). Here Bacon lies, slightly larger than life, his hands clasped in an attitude of submission and his body clothed in a simple suit of armour. He rests on the uppermost of two stone slabs, both of which are sheltered by an open-sided and canopied edifice. On the lower slab rest the effigies of his two wives, side by side, and much more cramped than he for lack of space. At the base of the whole lies the inscribed sarcophagus, on a two-step pedestal. Three Corinthian columns in the front and a Roman arch on either side support the triangular, unadorned, classical pediment which serves as a façade for the canopy. Bacon's arms dominate the apex of the pediment, and a death's head rests at each corner. Its size alone would have made this an impressive monument: it was roughly eight feet long at the base, at least twelve high, and five deep. Although not austere in the manner of other, mostly later, funerary monuments, Bacon's is marked by a classical restraint and economy of design which is wholly in keeping with his own stoic outlook. In this, it is interesting to note, it contrasts markedly with the ornamental bombast of other monuments of that and later decades. The memorial of Sir Christopher Hatton (d. 1591), a figure comparable to Bacon in his reputation and attainments, is entirely more ornate and elaborate. All attempt at restraint or simplicity has been abandoned, and the effect comes close to gaudiness.[17] Even the 1576 monument of Bacon's father-in-law, austere puritan though he may have been, appears busy and cluttered in contrast to the restrained elegance of the Lord Keeper's edifice.[18]

When the end came, therefore, Bacon was prepared, and yet his death itself, if we accept family tradition, came not through any of the maladies which had so long plagued his days but rather through the carelessness of a servant. The winter of 1578–9 was one of the coldest in memory and London experienced intense frosts, which inspired the young to strap on their shin-bone skates and head for the frozen Thames, while the elderly were left to crowd their hearths. As Stow tells us:

> The fourth of Februarie, and in the night following fel such an abundance of Snowe, that on the fifth in the morning, the same was founde at London to lye two foote deepe in the shallowest ... it snowed till the eight daye, and freezed till the tenth ... the twentieth of February, deceased Sir Nicholas Bacon ... [19]

Bacon, it seems, had remained in London following the conclusion of Hilary Term, evidently unwilling or unable to hazard the trip to Gorhambury in view of the weather. In expectation of the thaw which would allow his journey, or perhaps just out of boredom in those quiet winter days, he had, as his son Francis later recalled,

> ... his barber rubbing and combing his head. Because it was very hot, the window was opened to let in a fresh wind. The Lord Keeper fell asleep and awakened all distempered and in great sweat. Saith he to his barber, 'why did you let me sleep?' 'Why, my Lord', saith he, 'I durst not wake your Lordship.' 'Why then,' saith my Lord, 'You have killed me with kindness.' So [he] removed into his bed chamber and within a few days died.[20]

For over two weeks after his terminal bout of what appears to have been pneumonia, Bacon's body lay at York House. Notices of his passing and tributes to his person filled the news and gossip sheets of the day, as they would for some time to come. They ranged in style from Burghley's terse diary entry to the flowery commissioned verse of George Whetstone, who seems to have been put to the task by Bacon's old Gray's Inn colleague and longtime friend Gilbert Gerrard.[21] Amid this laudatory out-pouring were two commentaries which Bacon would have found especially pleasing. One was the verse which came to adorn his tomb, the work of the Scottish humanist and royal tutor George Buchanan, and the other was a letter from Bacon's puritan friend Thomas Norton to the young Anthony Bacon.

Buchanan's tribute, which may or may not have been known to Bacon before he died, would have pleased the Lord Keeper for its learned exposition, its concise summary of his accomplishments, and especially for its observation that

> Not the Wheel of Fortune or blind error
> Prefer'd [him] by Chance, but Solid Justice, Truth,
> Religion, Learning th'Inmates of his Youth.[22]

Modest though he may have been by the standards of the day, Bacon could not have denied considerable satisfaction in knowing that those were the traits by which he would be remembered.

Norton's sentiments were altogether more intimate and spontaneous in nature. He had known Bacon personally rather than by reputation and could appreciate the nature of the man himself without the need to appraise the formal accomplishments of his career. Writing in a mood of genuine remorse on the very day of Bacon's passing, Norton was particularly moved by his friend's attainments as a Christian and a father:

> ... my Lord your father lived in honor, lived in favor of his Soveraigne, in love of all good menne, lived in Knowledge of the Gospell, of his Salvation, lived to a blessed age, lived out a time to see you all brought up in the fear of God, & in hopefull likelyhood of worldly blessings, he died in all these ioyes, & in dyeing he hath overlived all mixture of disease, paines, sorrowes, & feare, Lastly, you may not forgett that your father liveth, and hath left you well instructed & well furnished, & soe much the more deeply bound to serve and comforte your mother ... [23]

Norton's emphasis on Bacon's parental legacy is not what one finds in most assessments of his career, and yet it provides an acute insight into the nature of the man. The Lord Keeper had indeed, with the aid of his helpmate, left his children 'brought up in the fear of God, & in hopefull likelyhood of worldly blessings', and certainly 'well instructed & well furnished . . . ' All five sons were educated by tutors and at institutions of their father's choice, and his intellectual stamp – a love of learning, a respect for the gospel, and a firm grounding in the classics – marked them all. Although Francis and Anthony set out on a more politically ambitious path than their three half-brothers, whose political activities were perhaps more ethically pursued but also more local in extent, all bore their father's keen devotion to the world of law and politics. All but Anthony would taste success and satisfaction in those terms.

The myth that Bacon left little to the material comfort of his wife and children – assailed even in the closing of Norton's remarks – has extended into relatively modern times,[24] but nothing could be further from the case. Although his was not one of the great fortunes of the age, Bacon had planted shrewdly and reaped well from his landed holdings, offices, and few scattered commercial investments.[25] He also spent modestly. Besides size-able expenditures for his building projects – some on behalf of his sons – he travelled little, rarely entertained in the grand manner, and had few of the courtier's tastes which habitually plunged so many of his contemporaries into debt. Thus his worth in ready cash and plate alone at the time of his death amounted to the considerable sum of £4,450 – roughly equal to his gross annual income by 1579 – while his lands were worth several times that amount. Perhaps equally indicative of his financial state were his total debts which, at a mere £860, were relatively modest.[26] The fullness of Bacon's coffers at the time of his death may, as Dr Simpson has suggested, have been a temporary state, preparatory to the intended purchase of an estate for the young Francis, the only one of the Bacon sons not provided for in that way. This suggestion, which seems entirely reasonable, tends further to discount the tradition of parsimonious behaviour.[27]

The final draft of Bacon's will, drawn up in December 1578, listed bequests of land, property, cash, and assorted gifts and personal effects to an impressively large number of individuals and institutions.[28] Aside from the bequests to his immediate family, among whose members nearly all of his lands were distributed, some four hundred marks went to institutions of charity and no less than sixty specific individuals received bequests.

Among them were twenty-five of the Lord Keeper's associates at court, nine retainers (with sums also allocated to lesser ranks of serving men and women by office), seventeen relatives, and nine friends and colleagues who do not fit any of these categories.

Nor did Bacon forget to provide for a proper funeral: when the coffin of the Lord Keeper was borne through the streets of London on March 9th, the populace witnessed one of the largest and most ceremonious funeral processions in recent years.[29] Over three hundred marchers accompanied Bacon's remains, all provided with black mourning cloth at the prior request of the deceased, and at a total cost of nearly £700. The bells of St Martin's-in-the-Fields, just across from York House in the Strand, were paid to toll throughout the day. The entire display cost upwards of £900, and must have been a memorable spectacle for the hundreds who lined the way to witness the stately procession.[30]

Four centuries after his death, with all but a few of his political papers lost to modern scholarship in the ruins of Gorhambury and the paeans of his mourners no less stilled by time, what may one conclude of Nicholas Bacon? The relative paucity of documentation renders it impossible to know Bacon as we have come to know many of his contemporaries: some of them far lesser men. It relegates to the realm of speculation many conclusions which one would hope to draw with greater certainty. Yet when these caveats have been issued, it is still apparent that those who have written of this era have not often given Bacon his due. The evidence that has survived allows a fuller portrait, and one at variance in many details with the traditional image.

Bacon's career makes both a paradigmatic and a particular contribution to our understanding of his age. Much of the former aspect has been recognized by recent scholarship, and is perhaps most fully presented in the work of Professor Simpson. Bacon's progress from the Suffolk yeomanry, through Cambridge and Gray's Inn, and finally to a successful career at court on the one hand, and his acquisition and shrewd management of considerable landed holdings on the other, exemplify the 'rise of the gentry' or the path of the representative 'new man' in the fullest economic, social, and political connotations normally attached to those terms.

At the same time, the example of Bacon's life suggests an

additional and related phenomenon of social change which pertains no less appropriately to his age. His layman's interest in the more genteel pursuits, including the appreciation of classical languages and literature, the composition of poetry, the perfection of oratorical style and the planning of educational curricula, indicates the extent to which the values and concerns of the Renaissance had reached into the consciousness of the English gentleman by Bacon's time. It also suggests that the 'new man' of whom so much has been written was frequently something other than a more enterprising version of the generally boorish and provincial aristocrat of medieval England. Bacon's example portrays the ascendancy of a broader concept of aristocracy: one based on gentility as well as birth, and training as well as power. We may recognize Bacon's aspiration to this image of aristocracy in his own career, and we may also conclude that he himself was quite conscious of that ideal. He clearly held it in mind while designing the curriculum for his proposed academy for the wards of the crown, for he expressed at that time his chagrin that 'gentlemen' habitually spent more time and money training their dogs and horses than educating their children. If Bacon had been nothing more than a mere time-server in his various offices, these accomplishments would still constitute a worthy paradigm for a most important and dynamic group in Tudor society.

In actuality, Bacon was a great deal more than a time-server in his official career; beyond the paradigmatic virtues of his life lie particular contributions of considerable significance in the three broad fields of his endeavour: the politics of his home region, the law and the Court of Chancery, and the court and privy council.

Bacon's ascendancy to a position of prominence in the shires of Norfolk and Suffolk, achieved by the skilful manipulation of family ties, land ownership and court connections, typifies the replacement of the traditional, feudal-based structure of shire politics with the dynamic and court-oriented newer gentry. In a more particular sense, Bacon's rise to regional prominence at the expense of the Howards and their Catholic followers fostered the establishment of a viable political force with strong protestant convictions in East Anglia. Largely through Bacon's support and guidance, that group secured a fair share of the chief shire offices, from J.P. and sheriff to burgess and knight of the shire, which had in the past been dominated overwhelmingly by the Howards. So well did Bacon build that these individuals continued to flourish in regional political life long after his own death.

In his proper *métier* of the law, it is now apparent that Bacon did more than vindicate his reputation for sagacity and honesty. He set out to accomplish a broad range of reforms to facilitate the due process of his own Court of Chancery, and earned the gratitude of his many successors who relied upon those precedents. Beyond the confines of the Chancery, he demonstrated interest and initiative in addressing himself to such important judicial issues as the nature of equity law, the severity of contemporary judicial punishment, and the enforcement of the statutes. Finally, his scholarship and integrity established for the Elizabethan bench a mark of professionalism well above previous Tudor standards.

On the privy council, Bacon was neither the cipher of William Cecil nor the mere administrator of policies devised by others. He most frequently sought the middle path between the factions of openly puritan or openly Anglo-Catholic sympathies, and that predilection tended to unite him with Cecil and other moderates on most issues. But despite his affinity for policies of moderation, and the relatively insecure nature of his position at court – where little beside the Queen's favour kept him from utter ruin and obscurity – he was on various occasions sufficiently bold and independent to register his dissent from Cecil and the Queen herself. Although his participation in the council's deliberations extended to all areas of policy formation, he felt most at ease dealing with domestic issues. Social and economic policy, and the administration and enforcement of such policy, were his recognized areas of expertise. When he proffered advice on such foreign policy issues as the confrontation with France over Scotland in 1559–60 or over Newhaven in 1563, or the intrigues emanating from the Dutch revolt, his words were seriously considered by his fellow councillors; but in the formulation of domestic policy on such issues as the recoinage, the Statute of Artificers and the Northern Rising, his word carried far greater weight, and his role seems to have been of signal importance. During his two decades of membership on the

Elizabethan privy council one may now consider Bacon's position subordinate only to a few great councillors of state – Cecil, Leicester, Norfolk (for a brief period), and perhaps Walsingham, who was just coming into his own – and credit him with his rightful share in the establishment of several fundamental principles of Elizabethan domestic policy.

Just as the precise nature of Bacon's accomplishments have often remained obscure to the student of Tudor England, so have his motivations and outlook. The attempt to reconstruct these less tangible elements of his life proves a far more speculative task, but here again some factors appear with clarity. His emergence from the obscurity of the Suffolk yeomanry, signalled initially by his striking success at Cambridge and Gray's Inn, seems largely to have been founded on a good measure of ambition, considerable natural ability and a boundless capacity for hard work. These qualities, along with the Protestantism which he also acquired early on, served as the hallmarks of his early career. Thus fortified, he embarked upon a political apprenticeship at the Courts of Augmentations and Wards and Liveries during two of the most turbulent decades of the Tudor Age. His appointment after those troubled years as the chief legal officer of the realm under Elizabeth was, as Buchanon recognized, neither a product of chance nor, as others have suggested, of having the right friends in high places. It came about in large measure because Bacon formulated a distinct and perceptive political creed in response to the lessons of the 1540s and 1550s, and because he kept that creed ever before him.

Drawing upon his experiences and observations of those formative years, and recalling the writings of the later Stoics, whose work he so admired – particularly 'my Senecke', as Bacon called him – he grasped two maxims of political thought which aptly fitted his own situation: the imperative of obtaining royal favour, and the value of moderation in its pursuit. Seneca's classic plea for the favour and clemency of the Emperor Nero[31] had a profound relevance for Bacon throughout his career, for neither he nor his Roman counterpart had any resources to fall back upon in the failure of such continuous bounty. That imperative sustained Bacon the bureaucrat in his continued service under Mary Tudor. It led Bacon the jurist to understand that the law must be administered as an agency of clemency as well as with the force of righteousness. Finally, it spurred his deep awareness that the preservation of a society ruled by law, and of his own place in such a society, depended upon the preservation of legitimate monarchy.

Perhaps an even more valid lesson drawn from those years of apprenticeship was the value of moderation in word and deed. From all too close at hand, Bacon had witnessed the dangers of extremist policies and the perils of political lust. He would never lose sight of the need to avoid these snares in his own career. In this regard his chosen motto, *Mediocria Firma*, and the stoic tenor of much of his poetry, were not mere vacuous accoutrements of his acquired life-style; they were succinct expressions of the very outlook which had allowed him to attain that status. In this commemoration of the mean estate he was not unique among the political elite of his generations. It has wisely been observed that the unwritten rules of political behaviour which character-ized the first part of the Elizabethan era were founded on the common acceptance of that principle.[32]

Having gained his ultimate position of authority in the reign of Elizabeth, Bacon's characteristic attitudes reflected the impact of contemporary humanist thought and aspects of puritan doctrine as well as the lessons of his own experience. His evident confidence in the intrinsic worth of man, surely taken from the humanist rather than the Calvinist fount, and his apparent sense of vocation in the effort to bring about a godly society, now became common themes. His tenderness towards his family, his concern for at least the rudimentary education of the poor as well as the wealthy, his preference for seeing a man 'twice whipped' rather than 'once hanged', and his profound concern for the due process of law bespeak those foundations with little ambiguity.

One seeking to fault Bacon's achievements would do well to consider three factors: his capacity for political leadership, the scope of his competence, and the extent of his political vision. Partly because of his time-consuming duties at the Chancery, and partly because of the cautionary restraints upon his ambi-tion, Bacon never engaged in the contest for leadership on the privy council as did Cecil, Leicester and Walsingham. If to our minds that failure of nerve so close to the summit may be counted a mark against him, Bacon himself seemed quite content with that somewhat subordinate position. Secondly, as one trained formally in the law and apprenticed less formally in the ranks of legal administration, Bacon sometimes found it difficult to cope effectively or to sustain an active participation in such issues as foreign affairs, diplomacy and commercial relations. This, too, kept him from rivalling those few greater lights on the council, but, again, Bacon seemed satisfied to concentrate his energies upon domestic concerns in so far as his heavy work load at the Chancery permitted.

Finally, at a perspective of four hundred years, Bacon seems to have suffered a visionary myopia which is common to most statesmen in any age. Whereas he found it relatively easy to perceive faults in the existing systems of government finance, local administration, and even his own Court of Chancery, and although he readily proposed specific reforms to amend many of these flaws, he lacked the foresight to evaluate those institutions in the context of a rapidly changing society. While his abilities as a reformer made him an illustrious participant in the Tudor political system, his ultimate failure to achieve a broader vision, a fault shared by nearly all his contemporaries, kept that system from coping effectively with the new and severe economic and social pressures placed upon it. Therein lay not only the failure of Nicholas Bacon, but the tragedy of Tudor government.

Abbreviations

B.L.	British Library (British Museum)
C.P.R.	*Calendar of Patent Rolls*
C.S.P.	*Calendar of State Papers*
D.N.B.	*Dictionary of National Biography*
L. and P.	*Calendar of Letters and Papers, Henry VIII*
P.R.O.	Public Record Office
S.P.	State Papers
S.T.C.	Pollard and Redgrave, editors, *Short-Title Catalogue, 1475–1640*
Wing	Donald Wing, editor, *Short-Title Catalogue, 1641–1700*
B.I.H.R.	*Bulletin of the Institute of Historical Research*
T.R.H.S.	*Transactions of the Royal Historical Society*

Notes

Unless otherwise stated, all books referred to are published in London.

Preface

1 From 'Timber, or Discoveries', in J. E. Spingarn (ed.), *Critical Essays of the Seventeenth Century*, Vol. I, 1605–1650 (1908), 26.
2 William Camden, *The History of the Most Renowned and Victorious Princess Elizabeth, late Queen of England*, ed. Wallace T. MacCaffrey (Chicago, 1970), 18.
3 Cf. below, especially Ch. VI, VII, IX, X and XII.
4 From Elizabeth's speech to Egerton upon his accession to office, May 6, 1596; Bodleian Library, Oxford, Tanner MS. 82, f 92.
5 John Campbell, *The Lives of the Lord Chancellors and the Keepers of the Great Seal of England* ... (5th edn, 10 vols., 1868), Ch. XLIII.
6 J. Payne Collier, 'On Sir Nicholas Bacon, Lord Keeper, with Extracts from some of his Unprinted Papers and Speeches', *Archaeologia* (1855), XXXVI, 339–48.
7 *Proc. Suffolk Inst. Arch.* (1951), XXV, ii, 149ff.
8 Virgil Jack Barnard, 'The Political Career of Sir Nicholas Bacon' (unpublished M.A. thesis, University of Chicago, 1957); Ernest R. Sandeen, 'The Correspondence of Sir Nicholas Bacon' (unpublished M.A. thesis, University of Chicago, 1955); K. M. Dodd, 'A History of the Manor of Redgrave in the County of Suffolk, 1538–1700' (unpublished Ph.D. dissertation, University of Chicago, 1959); Alan Simpson, *The Wealth of the Gentry, 1540–1660* (Chicago, 1961).

Chapter I

1 Will of John Bacon (d. 1513), Consistory Court of Norwich, 119–125 Johnson, Norfolk and Norwich Record Office.
2 Will of John Bacon (d. 1500), Consistory Court of Norwich, 26–27 Cage, Norfolk and Norwich Record Office.
3 Will of Robert Bacon (d. 1548), P.R.O., Prob. 11/32/19.
4 Robert had not yet married Isabel by 1500, the date of his father's death, but their first child must have been born by 1509. Will of Robert Bacon, op. cit.

5 Charles Welch (ed.), *Register of Freemen of the City of London in the reigns of Henry VIII and Edward VI* (1908), 72.

6 *L. and P.*, xx, i, 668; Alfred B. Beaven, *The Aldermen of the City of London* (2 vols., 1908–13), I, 274.

7 J. Steven Watson, *A History of the Salters' Company* (1963), 51; A. W. Hughes Clarke (ed.), *The Register of St Dunstan in the East, London* (1939), 126.

8 Welch, *Register of Freemen*, 27; John Withie, *The Names and Armes of them that hath beene Alldermen of the Warde of Alldersgate, 1451–1616* (1878), 15; Will of James Bacon, P.R.O., Prob. 11/55/28.

9 Gladys Scott Thomson, 'Three Suffolk Figures: Thomas Wolsey, Stephen Gardiner, and Nicholas Bacon', *Proc. Suffolk Inst. Arch.* (1951), xxv, ii, 160. Blackman and Sharp are frequently mentioned in this capacity in Bacon's estate records and other family correspondence.

10 Scott Robinson, 'Chislehurst and its Church', *Archaeologica Cantiana* xiii (1880), 389–91; Robinson takes his account from Hasted's classic *History of Kent* (1801) which has proved no more explicit regarding documentation; *D.N.B.*

11 Alan Simpson, *The Wealth of the Gentry, 1540–1660* (Chicago, 1961), 31–2; Bacon to the Earl of Leicester, 1564, Huntington Library MS. HM 1340, ff 86r–87r.

12 Robert Reyce, *Suffolk in the XVIIth Century: the Breviary of Suffolk, 1618* (1902).

13 In a genealogical description of Bacon's background which is admittedly inaccurate in several verifiable instances, an anonymous antiquary held that Bacon, ' ... being brought by his father the Abbott's sheepe reeve at Schoole at lengthe being sent to be made a priest & being told yt hys crowne must be shaven, rather than he would abide that wch he so much mislyked he ran away'; B.L. Add. MS. 5523 ('Pedigrees of Suffolk Families'), ff 95–9.

14 Lord Campbell's assertion that Bacon was educated at home is extremely doubtful, for his parents could neither afford a tutor nor spare the time and energy themselves – assuming that they even had the skill to prepare Nicholas for the rigours of Cambridge. John Campbell, *The Lives of the Lord Chancellors and the Keepers of the Great Seal of England* ... (5th edn, 10 vols., 1868), II, 214; B.L. Add. MS. 5523, ff 95–9.

15 Joan Simon, *Education and Society in Tudor England* (Cambridge, 1966), 56; E. G. Rupp, *Studies in the Making of the English Protestant Tradition* (Cambridge, 1966), 11–12, 198; Irvin B. Horst, *The Radical Brethren* (Nieuwkoop, 1972), 49.

16 John Venn and J. A. Venn, *Alumni Cantabrigiensis* Pt I (4 vols., Cambridge, 1922–7), I, 65.

17 Erasmus to Henry Bullock, Aug. 31, 1516, quoted in full in J. B. Mullinger, *The University of Cambridge from the Earliest Times* (3 vols., Cambridge, 1873–1911), I, 513–16.

18 Mullinger, *University of Cambridge*, I, 560–75; H. C. Porter, *Reformation and Reaction in Tudor Cambridge* (Cambridge, 1958), 44–8, 58–60; William A. Clebsch, *England's Earliest Protestants, 1520–1535* (New Haven, 1964), 42–6, 270–71.

19 V. J. K. Brook, *A Life of Archbishop Parker* (Oxford, 1962), 49.

20 The poet John Skelton, perhaps showing the irritability of his declining years, wrote 'A Replycacion agaynst certayne yong Scholars adjured of late', including this delightfully damning passage, cited in Mullinger, *University of Cambridge*, I, 439; 'A lytell ragge of rhetoricke, / A lesse lumpe of logicke, / A pece or patche of philosophy, / Then forthwith by and by / They tumble so in theology, / Drowned in dregges of divinite, / That they juge them selfe able to be / Doctours of the chayre in the vintre / At the Thre Cranes / To magnifye their names.'

21 J. R. Tanner (ed.), *The Historical Register of the University of Cambridge* (Cambridge, 1917), 367.

22 Mary Bateson (ed.), *Grace Book B, Part II ... Accounts of the Proctors of the University of Cambridge, 1511–1544* (Cambridge, 1905), 277; C. M. Borough, (ed.), 'Calendar of Papers of the North Family from Wroxton Abbey ... ' (unpublished typescript, National Register of Archives, 1960), 13.

23 All five of Bacon's sons took B.A.s at Cambridge; Venn and Venn, *Alumni Cantabrigiensis*, Pt I, I, 64–5.

24 Will of Nicholas Bacon, Dec. 23, 1578, P.R.O., Prob. 11/6/1.

25 *D.N.B.*

26 Sir Cecil Carr (ed.), *Pension Book of Clement's Inn* (Selden Soc., LXXVIII, 1960), xviii–xxii.

27 W. R. Douthwaite, *Gray's Inn, its History and Associations* (London, 1886), xiii; cf. also the map by Ralph Aggas, *tempus* Elizabeth, printed in Reginald J. Fletcher, *The Pension Book of Gray's Inn, 1569–1669* (1901), I, facing p. xxxii.

28 The best contemporary account of the structure and procedures of the Inns of Court is in the first part of the report on the state of the Inns drawn up for Henry VIII by Bacon, Thomas Denton and Robert Cary, some time around 1540. It was first printed in Edward Waterhouse, *Fortescutus Illustratus* (1663), 543–9, and is reprinted in both D. S. Bland, 'Henry VIII's Royal Commission on the Inns of Court', *J. Soc. Public Teachers of Law* (1969), 183–94; and C. H. Williams (ed.), *English Historical Documents, 1485–1558* (1967), 563–8. Cf. also Fletcher, *Pension Book of Gray's Inn*, xxxiii–xxxiv; Kenneth Charlton, *Education in Renaissance England*

(1965), 172–3; and cf. below, 29–32.

29 Fletcher, *Pension Book of Gray's Inn*, xxvi–xxvii.

30 At first glance this seems open to question, and one reference gives the date of Bacon's promotion to ancient as 1540; 'Simon Segar's Admission Lists to Gray's Inn', B.L. Harleian MS. 1912, 175v. But the weight of evidence supports the date of 1536: Segar himself has 1536 in two other places in the same list (ff 190v, 204v). The earlier date has been accepted by Fletcher and others.

31 'Segar's Lists', f 175v.

Chapter II

1 Douglas Bush, *The Renaissance and English Humanism* (Toronto, 1939); W. G. Zeeveld, *Foundations of Tudor Policy* (1948); Fritz Caspari, *Humanism and the Social Order in Tudor England* (Chicago, 1954); James K. McConica, *English Humanists and Reformation Politics under Henry VIII and Edward VI* (Oxford, 1965).

2 Walter C. Richardson, *History of the Court of Augmentations, 1536–1554* (Baton Rouge, Louisiana, 1961), 41–2.

3 Sept. 29, 1538, *L. and P.* xiii, ii, 180.

4 Ibid., 521.

5 Richard Rich, for example, functioned in the capacity of the Chancellor of the Court well before his official appointment to that office in April 1536; Richardson, *Augmentations*, 65, 70.

6 Ibid., 43, 492.

7 Cranmer to Cromwell, Oct. 23, 1538, *L. and P.*, xiii, ii, 257. For months prior to this suit Cranmer and Cromwell had been engaged in a bitter fight to assert their control over the government of Calais, and purge the religious reactionaries who threatened to restore the Roman rite. The Deputy for Calais, the aged Viscount Lisle, had long made known his sympathy for the strong Catholic elements nominally in his charge. When, in August 1538, Cranmer had tried to gain a curacy for an Anglican cleric named Adam Damplip, Lisle foiled the attempt. Not content that Lisle should win the day, Cranmer suggested Bacon's appointment to the vacant town clerkship, and emphasized in so doing the known religious convictions of his candidate. Yet Cromwell, already edging out on the political tightrope from which he would shortly plummet, allowed Bacon's suit to rest in abeyance. All things considered, Bacon ought to have been thankful; the Archbishop of Canterbury had brought him to the attention of Thomas Cromwell – who was most likely already well aware of Bacon's mettle – and yet the young lawyer had been spared the oblivion which probably would have followed such an appointment. The whole problem of Calais in this period is summarized

in H. F. Chettle, 'The Burgesses for Calais, 1536–1558', *English Historical Review*, L (1935), 492–501. Cf. also Jasper Ridley, *Thomas Cranmer* (Oxford, 1962), 166–8.

8 *L. and P.*, XIV, ii, 311.

9 Ibid., XV, 5.

10 Ibid., XV, 539.

11 Richardson, *Augmentations*, Ch. I.

12 Patent Rolls, 38 Henry VIII, Pt 5, m. 23, cited in Richardson, *Augmentations*, 42, 386.

13 Ibid., 385–6.

14 Ibid., 42.

15 *Myll, King, Stradwyke and Hale* v. *Yonge*, Court of Augmentations, Proceedings, *tempus* Henry VIII, P.R.O., E. 315/23, f 57r.

16 Ibid., f 58.

17 Southwell named Bacon as one of the three supervisors of his will in 1559; P.R.O., Prob. 11/43/53. Pope left his 'most dearly beloved friend' a gilt whistle in the form of a dragon, and named him as one of two chief executors. Dr Roy Strong has recently suggested that it is this whistle, worn as a pendant, which appears in the National Portrait Gallery portrait of Bacon. *D.N.B.*, 'Pope, Thomas'; Roy Strong, *Tudor and Jacobean Portraits* (2 vols., 1969), I, 15–16. Cf. Plate 3.

18 Feb. 13, 1544/5, *L. and P.*, XIX, i, 244; Feb. 6, 1544/5, *L. and P.*, XXI, i, 320; Nov. 11, 1543, *L. and P.*, XVIII, i, 262; July 18, 1545, *L. and P.*, XX, i, 271.

19 Richardson, *Augmentations*, 89; June 25, 1541, *L. and P.*, XVII, 135; 2 Mar., 1545/6, *L. and P.*, XXI, i, 155.

20 The traditional date of 1540 has been upheld in recent decades by Sir Cecil Carr (ed.), *The Pension Book of Clement's Inn* (Selden Soc., LXXVIII, 1960), xxiii, and Cyril King, *Some Notes on the Ancient Office of Reader in the Middle Temple* (1957), but is challenged in D. S. Bland, 'Henry VIII's Royal Commission on the Inns of Court', *J. Soc. Public Teachers of Law* (1969), 183–94. It is difficult to imagine that Bacon could have gained appointment to such an important committee before he had been recognized by the royal court in some other capacity. As there is no indication of such recognition before 1538, it is hardly conceivable that the commission should have been formed prior to that date. And, as the whole idea of the Report smacks of Cromwell's hand, it is not likely that it was initiated after his fall in 1540. All of this is, of course, conjecture.

21 Edward Waterhouse, *Fortescutus Illustratus* (1663), 539–46; the Report has recently been reprinted in Bland, loc. cit., and, more accessibly, in C. H. Williams (ed.), *English Historical Documents*,

1485–1558 (1967), 563–73.

22 Much of the credit for identifying Denton and Cary, and for bringing to light the connection of the former with Elyot, must go to Dr Michael MacDonald of Mt Allison University, Nova Scotia. I am indebted to him for making his findings available to me prior to their appearance in print.

23 It is interesting to note in this context that an early nineteenth-century account of the history of the Inns of Court pirates directly from the Denton–Bacon–Cary Report in what purports to be a recollection of practices at the Middle Temple of the Tudor era; W. Herbert, *Antiquities of the Inns of Court and Chancery* (1804).

24 Dr Richard Schoeck has recently confirmed this assessment in his address before the symposium on 'Law and Order in Tudor England', held at the Folger Shakespeare Library, Washington, D.C., Nov. 24–25, 1972. His subject was 'The Literature of Social Protest'.

25 Denton's part is strongly emphasized by Dr MacDonald, who also infers that much of this contribution may stem from Denton's collaboration and friendship with Thomas Elyot.

26 Cf. below, 59–62.

27 Mary Bateson (ed.), *Grace Book B, Part II ... Accounts of the Proctors of the University of Cambridge, 1511–1544* (Cambridge, 1905), 227; C. M. Borough, 'Calendar of the Papers of the North Family from Wroxton Abbey ... ' (unpublished typescript, National Register of Archives, 1960).

28 *L. and P.*, XVI, 240, 500; *L. and P.*, XX, 324.

29 D. S. Chambers (ed.), *Faculty Office Registers, 1534–1549* (Oxford, 1966), 75.

30 Ibid., 210.

31 Bacon's surviving children by Jane in their probable order of birth were: Elizabeth (1541), Nicholas (1543), Anne (1545), Nathaniel (1546), Edward (1548) and a second Elizabeth (1551). It was not unusual in that age to use the same name for more than one child in a family.

32 For a full discussion of the Ferneley family and their connections, cf. below, 150–52 and Fig. 4, 151.

33 Alan Simpson, *Wealth of the Gentry, 1540–1660* (Chicago, 1961), Table 2, 46–50.

34 William Page (ed.), *Victoria History of the County of Suffolk* (2 vols., 1907–11), I, 662–4.

35 *L. and P.*, XX, i, 483.

36 'Parish Registers of Redgrave, Co. Suffolk' (unpublished MS. copy in possession of the Society of Genealogists, London), f 6r.

37 The observations that follow are based on the interesting and complete description of Redgrave, including illustrations and the author's reconstructed plans, in Ernest Sandeen, 'The Building Activities of Sir Nicholas Bacon' (unpublished Ph.D. dissertation, University of Chicago, 1959), 92ff, and also Figs. 2, 3 and 4. I am much indebted to Professor Sandeen for permission to examine his dissertation and utilize his drawings, and also for an offprint of his essay 'The Building of Redgrave Hall, 1545–1554', in *Proc. Suffolk Inst. Arch.* (1961), xxix, i, in which the issue is discussed in more accessible form.

38 William Murdin (ed.), *A Collection of State Papers … left by William Cecill Lord Burghley* (2 vols., 1740–59), II, 747.

Chapter III

1 *Return of the Members of Parliament* (1878), Pt I, 377.

2 Joseph Nicolson and Richard Burn, *The History and Antiquities of the Counties of Westmorland and Cumberland* (2 vols., 1777), I, 11, 43–4, 286–9; A. G. Dickens (ed.), *The Clifford Letters of the Sixteenth Century*, Surtees Soc., vol. 172 (1962), 21–6; M. E. James, 'The First Earl of Cumberland and the Decline of Northern Feudalism', *Northern History*, 1 (1966), 43–69.

3 Cf. the unpublished essay on Laybourne in the files of the History of Parliament Trust, to which access was kindly given by Professor S. T. Bindoff.

4 James, 'The First Earl of Cumberland', 43–69; Anthony Fletcher, *Tudor Rebellions* (1968), 41–2.

5 Unpublished essay on the constituency of Westmorland in the files of the History of Parliament Trust.

6 *Return of the Members of Parliament*, I, Appendix xxx; unpublished essay on the constituency of Dartmouth in the files of the History of Parliament Trust.

7 Ibid.; Duke was Clerk of the Court and Ridgeway served as King's Chamberlain in addition to his minor posts in the Augmentations; *L. and P.*, xx, i, 266, and xx, ii, 517.

8 Joyce Youings, *Devon Monastic Lands: Calendar of Particulars for Grants, 1536–1558* (Devon and Cornwall Record Soc., n.s., I, Torquay, 1955), xx–xxi.

9 Walter C. Richardson, *History of the Court of Augmentations, 1536–1554* (Baton Rouge, Louisiana, 1961) 140, n 83; *L. and P.*, xxi, ii, 414. Goodrich left Bacon a ring of 40s. value in his will, and named him one of his two executors; P.R.O., Prob. 11/45/15.

10 The standard works on the Court of Wards are H. E. Bell, *An Introduction to the History and Records of the Court of Wards & Liveries* (Cambridge, 1953), which deals particularly with the

history, administrative and judicial structure, and records of the Court, and Joel Hurstfield, *The Queen's Wards: Wardship and Marriage under Elizabeth I* (rev. ed., 1973) which treats a more specific period, and seeks to place the Court in the social and political setting of its time. The summary below rests on both sources.

11 The only extant copy of Bacon's 'Articles' is that which was re-submitted in the reign of Elizabeth, in which he mentions the earlier version. 'The Discourses of Sir Nicholas Bacon', B.L. Add. MS. 32, 379, ff 26-33. Bell, *Court of Wards*, 24. For a discussion of this and Bacon's other plans for educational reform, cf. below, 59-62. Cf. also Tittler, 'Education and the Gentleman in Tudor England ... ', *History of Education* (Feb. 1976), 1-10.

12 *C.P.R., Philip and Mary*, I, 2-3; Bell, *Court of Wards*, 117.

13 Proceedings and Decrees of the Court of Wards and Liveries, Philip and Mary, P.R.O., Wards 1/2/file 51. Cf. also files 55 and 71 for very similar examples.

14 Alan Simpson, *Wealth of the Gentry, 1540-1660* (Chicago, 1961), 86, n 3, and 113.

15 *C.P.R., Edward VI*, I, 81, 89; *C.P.R., Mary*, I, 24.

16 *C.P.R., Edward VI*, II, 136.

17 Ibid., V, 358.

18 Ibid., IV, 255.

19 J. Payne Collier (ed.), *Trevelyan Papers prior to A.D. 1558* ('Prince Edward's Household Accounts,' Camden Soc., vol. 67, Cambridge, 1857), 195, 203, 204, 205; W. C. Richardson (ed.), *The Report of the Royal Commission of 1552* (Morgantown, West Virginia, 1974), 134 and n 619.

20 I am indebted to Dr Michael MacDonald for pointing this out.

21 William Stanford, *An Exposicion of the Kinges prerogative collected out of the great abridgement of Justice Fitzherbert ...* (2nd edn, published by Richard Tottel, 1567), *S.T.C.* no. 23213. By sheer coincidence, and probably unknown to Stanford, Bacon had come into possession of Fitzherbert's own MS. book on the Statutes up to 27 Edward I shortly after the great justice's death in 1538. The collection includes handwritten copies of Magna Carta, the Pro-visions of Merton, Statutes of Marlborough, and other classics of the English legal tradition. The collection is now in B.L. Royal MSS. 10 A V, and bears the *ex libris* of both Fitzherbert and Bacon.

22 *D.N.B.*, 'Stanford, William'.

23 Reginald J. Fletcher, *Pension Book of Gray's Inn, I, 1569-1669* (1901), 497.

24 Ibid., xxx-xxxi, 497.

25 On Feb. 9, 1553, Anne is already referred to as Bacon's wife in a licence to grant a manor. Considering the impropriety of hasty remarriage, it is likely that Jane was already on her sickbed when the gloves were ordered and that they were intended to cheer her during her terminal illness. Simpson, *Wealth of the Gentry*, 40 and n 1; *C.P.R.*, *Edward VI*, V, 261.

In addition to a worthy entry in the *D.N.B.*, several more recent commentaries attest to Anne's accomplishments in some detail. These include M. St C. Byrne, 'The Mother of Francis Bacon', *Blackwood's Magazine*, vol. CCXXXVI (1934), 758–71; M. B. Whiting, 'The Learned and Virtuous Lady Bacon', *Hibbert J.*, XXIX (1931), 270–83; and Ruth Hughey, 'Lady Anne Bacon's Translations', *Review of English Studies*, vol. 10, 1934 (no. 38, April), 211. A comprehensive view of Sir Anthony and the Cooke family may be found in M. K. McIntosh, 'The Cooke Family of Gidea Hall, Essex' (unpublished Ph.D. dissertation, Harvard University, 1967), and the same author's article, 'Sir Anthony Cooke: Tudor Humanist, Educator, and Religious Reformer', *Proc. Amer. Phil. Soc.*, vol. 119, no. 3 (June 1975), 233–50.

26 McIntosh, 'Sir Anthony Cooke ... ', 241; B. W. Beckingsale, *Burghley. Tudor Statesman, 1520–1598* (1967), 27, 33–4.

27 McIntosh, 'Sir Anthony Cooke ... ', 239–40.

28 C. S. Lewis, *English Literature in the Sixteenth Century* (1944), 307.

29 *S.T.C.* no. 18766 and a later edition, no. 18768, cited in Hughey, 'Lady Anne Bacon's Translations', 211. Cf. also Irvin B. Horst, *The Radical Brethren* (Nieuwkoop, 1972), 121.

30 Lewis, *English Literature*, 627.

31 William Urwick, *Nonconformity in Herts.* [sic] ... (1884), 86–7; Patrick Collinson, 'The Puritan Classical Movement in the Reign of Elizabeth I' (unpublished Ph.D. dissertation, 3 vols., University of London, 1957), II, 1117–83.

32 Cf. J. Spedding, R. L. Ellis and D. D. Heath (eds.), *The Works of Francis Bacon* (14 vols., 1857–74), vols. VIII–XIV, *passim*, and Lambeth Palace Library Bacon MSS., especially nos. 647 and 648. I am much indebted to the Librarian of the Lambeth Palace Library for permission to consult these papers.

33 Anne (Gresham) Bacon to Lady Anne Bacon [?] 1572, Bacon–Townshend Collection, Folger Shakespeare Library MS. L.d. 15.

34 Parker to Lady Anne Bacon, Feb. 6, 1567/8, John Bruce and Thomas T. Perowne (eds.), *Correspondence of Matthew Parker* (Parker Soc., Cambridge, 1853), 309–16.

35 G. C. L. DuCann, 'Ghosts at Gray's Inn', *Graya*, I (1927), 27.

36 Simpson, *Wealth of the Gentry*, 46–7.

37 Cecil's plight is well summarized in Conyers Read, *Mr Secretary Cecil and Queen Elizabeth* (New York, 1955), 94–101.

38 Ibid., 96 and n 43.

39 Ibid., 100–101; Patrick Fraser Tytler, *England under the Reigns of Edward VI and Mary* (2 vols., 1839), II, 192–6.

40 Read, *Mr Secretary Cecil*, 100–101; John Strype, *Annals of the Reformation* (4 vols., Oxford, 1824–40), IV, 489. Strype's account of *where* Cecil caught up with Mary should not, however, be taken seriously.

41 Both the route and chronology of Mary's flight are contentious, and there is little agreement among those, including Froude, Pollard and Beatrice White, who have attempted to describe it. The most convincing reconstruction of the meagre sources is H. F. M. Prescott, *Mary Tudor* (rev. edn, 1953), 165–71.

42 *C.P.R., Philip and Mary*, II, 12.

43 Bacon was elected Treasurer in October 1552, at which time he may actually not have been married, but he continued to serve at least to the end of 1555, when Gilbert Gerrard was elected to serve with him as co-Treasurer; Fletcher, *Pension Book of Gray's Inn*, I, 201, 216.

44 *C.P.R., Philip and Mary*, II, 24.

45 Ibid., 27.

46 C. H. Garrett, *The Marian Exiles* (Cambridge, 1938), 15–16, 125.

47 McIntosh, 'Sir Anthony Cooke', 343, n 70. Cf. also a payment of £50 made by Bacon to the Exchequer on Cooke's account at the very outset of the latter's exile in the summer of 1554; P.R.O., E.405/499/unpaginated.

48 Cited in Urwick, *Nonconformity in Herts.*, 83.

49 From Bacon's poem 'Made at Wymbleton', in *Recreations of his Age* (Oxford, 1919).

Chapter IV

1 George Puttenham, *The Arte of English Poesie* (1589), ed. G. D. Willcock and Alice Walker (Cambridge, 1936), 140.

2 'Thinkeinge alsoe with howe good will / The Idle tymes whiche yrkesome be / You have made shorte throwe your good skill / In readeinge pleasante thinges to me, / Whereof profitte we bothe did se, / As wittenes can if they coulde speake / Bothe your Tullye and my Senecke.' From the poem 'Made at Wymbleton', in *Recreations of His Age* (Oxford, 1919).

3 Seneca, *Oedipus*, in *Seneca's Tragedies* (Loeb ed., 2 vols., Cambridge, Mass., 1958), I, 508–9, lines 882–91. The Gorhambury *sententiae* are preserved in the form in which Bacon presented them to Lady Lumley after they had been incised at Gorhambury;

B.L. Royal MS. 17 A. xxiii. I am greatly indebted to Dr Elizabeth McCutcheon for the typescript of her paper 'The Great House Sententiae of Sir Nicholas Bacon', which she delivered at the Second International Congress of Neo-Latin Studies in Amsterdam, Aug. 21, 1973.

4 'An Ode of Horace turned at the desier of my Ladye his Lo: wyfe', in *Recreations of His Age*.

5 William Wightman compiled and edited Thomas Phaer's uncompleted nine-volume edition of Virgil's *Aeneid*; he dedicated the whole to Bacon in thanks for his support of the project. Wightman's act of gratitude was not without its irony, for Phaer had died a Catholic and had intended to dedicate the work to Mary Tudor. Bishop Kennett's Collections, B.L., Lansdowne MS. 981, f 143. Cf. also *D.N.B.*, 'Phaer, Thomas'. The work itself is listed as *The nyne fyrst bookes of the Eneidos* (1562), *S.T.C.* no. 24800.

6 Bacon to young Nicholas Bacon, Mar. 6, 1569/70, Bacon MSS., University of Chicago, no. 4071.

7 Cf. for example, B.L. Royal MSS., 10 AV.

8 E. R. Sandeen, 'The Origins of Sir Nicholas Bacon's Bookplate', *Transactions of the Cambridge Bibliographical Soc.*, II, v (1958), 373–6.

9 Walter Hamilton, *Dated Bookplates* (3 vols., 1894–5), I, ii, 4; Egerton Castle, *English Bookplates* (1892), 28–33; Sandeen, 'Origins'; Karl Emich Count zu Leiningen-Westerburg, *German Bookplates*, trans. G. R. Dennis (1901), 104ff, 127–30.

10 Thomas Digges (ed.), *A Geometrical Practical Treatize named Pantometria* ... (2 edn, 1591); cf. especially the dedicatory preface. Cf. also *D.N.B.*, 'Digges, Leonard'.

11 Kenneth Charlton, *Education in Renaissance England* (1965), 213; E. G. R. Taylor, *The Mathematical Practitioners of Tudor and Stuart England* (Cambridge, 1954), 173; *D.N.B.*, 'Blundeville, Thomas'.

12 Only the latter of these reports survives, but the covering letter to Cecil refers to the first submission. Bacon to Cecil, May 17th, 1561, B.L. Add. MS. 32379, ff 26–33. Cf. also Ch. III, n 11.

13 B.L. Add. MS. 32379, ff 26–33.

14 An English edition of Castiglione's *Courtier* was completed by Bacon's brother-in-law Thomas Hoby and published in 1561, the same year in which Bacon sent his proposal to Cecil, and an Italian version seems to have been circulated and read in England by the mid-1530s, so that Bacon may well have known the work. Pearl Hogrefe, *The Sir Thomas More Circle* (Urbana, Illinois, 1959), 59–60.

15 See the excellent summary of the controversy regarding education and the idea of 'true nobility' in Hogrefe, *The Sir Thomas*

More Circle, Ch. II.

16 Bacon to Cecil, May 17, 1561, B.L. Add. MS. 32379, ff 26–33. The analogy regarding horses and dogs was commonly used in this context, and provides an interesting clue to the evolution of the idea. Thomas Starkey, probably drawing on Italian sources, observed that 'gentlemen study more to bring up good hounds than wise heirs'; *A Dialogue Between Reginald Pole and Thomas Lupset*, ed. K. M. Burton (1948), 171. Ascham, writing a few years after Bacon, echoes the allusion, but not so pithily; Ascham, *The Scholemaster*, ed. R. J. Schoeck (Toronto, 1966), 30.

17 Only Bacon's revised orders for the school, drawn up in 1576, have survived; Norfolk and Norwich Record Office MS. 10129, item 2.

18 Ascham, *The Scholemaster*, 12–14; Folger Shakespeare Library MS. V.a. 197, f 66.

19 *C.P.R.*, *Edward VI*, III, 191, 192, 436.

20 Joan Simon, *Education and Society in Tudor England* (Cambridge, 1967), 323; N. Carlisle, *A Concise Description of the Endowed Grammar Schools in England and Wales* (2 vols., 1818), I, 513–18. In order to sustain the St Albans school financially, Bacon hit upon the novel idea of securing for it a 'wine charter', and thus it received the revenues from a monopoly on the sale of wine in the borough of St Albans. Oxford and Cambridge were the only other educational institutions thus privileged. A. R. M. Stowe, *English Grammar Schools in the Reign of Queen Elizabeth* (New York, 1908), 19–20.

21 W. K. Jordan, *The Charities of London, 1480–1660* (1960), 266; Bacon's will, probate copy, Bacon MSS., University of Chicago, no. 4371.

22 Fowle, Rector of St Mary's, Redgrave, by Bacon's presentation and the first chaplain of the Bacon household whose identity has come down to us, was an early organizer of classes in Suffolk. He was eventually suspended for nonconformity. Fowle long remained a friend of Nathaniel Bacon and other members of the family. Patrick Collinson, 'The Puritan Classical Movement in the Reign of Elizabeth I' (unpublished Ph.D. dissertation, 3 vols., University of London, 1957), II, 1262; John Venn and J. A. Venn, *Alumni Cantabrigienses*, Pt I (4 vols., Cambridge, 1922–7), ii, 167; Folger Shakespeare Library, MSS. L.d. 295 and L.d. 136.

23 Robert Johnson served as Bacon's chaplain at Gorhambury, organized prophesyings in Hertfordshire from about 1570, and was suspended for his failure to subscribe to the Act of Uniformity in 1571. His identity has been carefully distinguished from two

namesakes by Professor Collinson. Collinson, 'Puritan Classical Movement', 108, 168–9, 186, 333–7. Cf. also William Urwick, *Nonconformity in Herts* ... (1884), 80–82; and S. E. Lehmberg, 'Archbishop Grindal and the Prophesyings', *Historical Magazine of the Protestant Episcopal Church*, XXXIV (June 1965), ii, 101.

24 Walsall preceded Johnson as the Bacon chaplain at Gorhambury, and tutored Anthony and Francis Bacon. His record as a theological radical is less pronounced than Fowle's or Johnson's, but his 'Sermon preached at Paul's Crosse' in October 1578 – probably one of the sermons which Bacon annually endowed – and his letters leave little doubt as to his convictions. Joseph Foster, *Alumni Oxonienses* (4 vols., Oxford, 1891–2), IV, 1564; Millar Maclure, *The Paul's Cross Sermons, 1534–1642* (Toronto, 1958), 211; Raynham Hall Muniments, on loan to Norfolk and Norwich Record Office, p. 7; Virgil B. Heltzel, 'Young Francis Bacon's Tutor', *Modern Language Notes*, LXIII, vii, 483–5.

25 Sturmius to Lord Burghley, Dec. 5, 1577, *C.S.P., Foreign Series, Elizabeth*, IX, 354–5. Sturmius (1507–89) settled in Strasburg where he maintained an academy for students and a meeting place for other reformed theologians. He later acted as an agent for the English privy council. Sturmius has been called the 'bellweather of the pedagogical flock' both in Germany and in England for his ideas on education and for his practical Ciceronian training. T. W. Baldwin, *William Shakespere's Small Latine & Lesse Greeke* (12 vols., Urbana, Illinois, 1944), II, 22–3; *Biographie Universelle Michaud* ... (45 vols., Paris, n.d.), XXXIX, 365–7.

26 Before his appointment as Elizabeth's ambassador to France, Paulet spent several years as the governor of the openly presbyterian community in Jersey. Anthony Bacon studied with Daneau as well, but not before the death of his father. Octavius Ogle (ed.), *Copy-Book of Sir Amias Paulet's Letters* (1866), introduction, and 77–8, 129–30; A. F. Scott Pearson, *Thomas Cartwright and Elizabethan Puritanism* (Cambridge, 1925), 158.

27 *D.N.B.*, 'Beaumont, Robert'; H. C. Porter, *Reformation and Reaction at Tudor Cambridge* (Cambridge, 1958), 101, 106; Wilfred Prest, *The Inns of Court Under Elizabeth and the Early Stuarts* (Totawa, New Jersey, 1972), 139.

28 Bacon to young Nicholas Bacon, Mar. 6, 1565, Bacon MSS., University of Chicago, no. 4071.

29 Norfolk and Norwich Record Office MS. 10129, items 2 and 3; Bacon's will, probate copy, Bacon MSS., University of Chicago, no. 4371.

30 Nicholas Bacon, *The Recreations of His Age* (first edition printed Oxford 1903, but not issued until 1919). The published edition

was taken by Dr Daniel, Provost of Worcester College, Oxford, from a MS. copy of the poems in the collection of Rev. Maurice Howard Marsden, Rector of Moreton, Dorset. Several MS. copies exist elsewhere. These seem to have been copied by Bacon's admirers during his lifetime and for some decades after his death, if handwriting is any guide, but there is no indication that Bacon himself sought to publish the collection.

31 *Songes and Sonnettes written by the ryght honorable Lorde Henry Hawarde late Earl of Surrey, and other* (published by Richard Tottel, 1557), *S.T.C.* no. 13860. The best modern edition is Hyder Edward Rollins (ed.), *Tottel's Miscellany 1557–1587* (2nd edn, 2 vols., Cambridge, Mass., 1965).

32 Bacon's 'Of a Snowe balle': 'A wanton wenche vppon a colde daye / With Snowe balles prouoked me to playe: But theis snowe balles soe hette my desyer / That I maye calle them balles of wylde fyer. Whoe woulde haue thoughte in this colde snowe / Cupyde woulde hide his fonde fyrye towe, Or that from water shoulde breede brandes fyrye, Or colde and moyste shoulde cause hotte and drye? What place is free from Loues slye workeinge / If vnder snowe his fyer lye lurkeinge? Noe snowe nor thinge this fyer can quenche / But the like fyer of this like wenche.'

Spenser's *Amoretti*, Sonnet XXX: 'My loue is lyke to yse, and I to fyre; how comes it then that this her cold so great / is not dissolu'd through my so hot desyre, but harder growes the more I her intreat? Or how comes it that my exceeding heat / is not delayd by her hart frosen cold: but that I burne much more in boyling sweat, and feele my flames augmented manifold? What more miraculous thing may be told / that fire which all thing melts, should harden yse: and yse which is congeald with sencelesse cold, should kindle fyre by wonderfull deuyse? Such is the powre of loue in gentle mind, that it can alter all the course of kynd.' Taken from J. C. Smith and E. de Selincourt (eds.), *The Poetical Works of Edmund Spenser* (1912), 567. I am indebted to Miss Deborah Johnson for suggesting Spenser's poem.

33 George Puttenham, *The Arte of English Poesie* (1589), ed. G. D. Willcox and Alice Walker (Cambridge, 1936), 139–40.

34 Thomas Nashe, *Pierce Pennilesse his supplication to the Devell*, Vol. I of *The Works of Thomas Nashe* (5 vols., Oxford, 1958), ed. R. B. McKerrow, 194. I am greatly indebted to Fr Germain Marc'hadour for bringing this reference to my attention.

35 Ben Jonson, 'Timber, or Discoveries', in J. E. Spingarn (ed.), *Critical Essays of the Seventeenth Century*, Vol. I, 1605–1650 (1908), 26.

36 The importance of rhetoric as an integral part of legal training at

the Inns of Court has been emphasized in a seminal article by Dr Richard Schoeck, 'Rhetoric and Law in Sixteenth Century England', *Studies in Philology*, L (Apr. 1953), 110–27. Cf. also K. R. Wallace, 'Rhetorical Exercises in Tudor Education', *Quarterly J. Speech*, XXII, i (Feb. 1936), 28–50, especially 33–34.

37 J. E. Neale, *Elizabeth I and Her Parliaments, 1559–1581* (New York, 1958), 185.

38 Jan. 15, 1562/3, Peter Osborn to Sir Thomas Challoner, commenting on Bacon's address at the opening of the second Elizabethan Parliament, P.R.O., S.P. 70/48/90. Cf. also George Williams, *The Senecan Amble* ... (1948), which seems to have withstood the proffered revision by Earl Miner, 'Patterns of Stoicism in Thought and Prose Style, 1500–1700', *Publications of the Modern Language Association*, Vol. 85, v (Oct. 1970), 1023–34.

39 Apr. 2, 1571, Huntington Library MS. EL 2579, f 46r.

40 Ibid., f 27.

41 Bacon to Cecil, June 17, 1560, P.R.O., S.P. 52/4/15.

42 Gorhambury was largely built between March 1563 and September 1568, at a basic cost – i.e., not including raw materials – of £3,177 11s. 9d. Bacon MSS., Lambeth Palace Library, vol. 647, f 34, item 6.

43 The following commentary on the construction and appearance of Gorhambury rests largely on Ernest R. Sandeen, 'The Building Activities of Sir Nicholas Bacon' (unpublished Ph.D. dissertation, University of Chicago, 1959), Ch. VIII, 128–56.

44 According to Francis Bacon, the last Bacon to own Gorhambury, the Queen and Sir Nicholas had the following exchange upon the occasion of her first visit, in 1572: 'The Queen: "My Lord, what a little house have you gotten." Bacon: "Madam, my house is well, but it is you that have made me too great for my house." ' Her objection, echoed – as Sandeen recounts – at her first sight of Cecil's Theobalds, allegedly caused Bacon to build the great gallery, which was ready for her second visit in 1577. Francis Bacon, 'Apothegms', in James Spedding, R. L. Ellis and D. D. Heath (eds.), *The Works of Francis Bacon* (14 vols., 1857–74), VII, 144; Sandeen, 'Building Activities', 145–7.

45 Ibid., 137–44.

Chapter V

1 On the basis of a letter in B. L. Cotton MSS. (Vespasian F. xiii, f 257), Conyers Read felt that both Elizabeth and Cecil at first wanted Heath to continue in office, although Read acknowledged the unlikelihood of such a desire on their parts. Heath himself clearly wanted no part of serving under Elizabeth, although he

remained a member of the privy council after resigning as Chancellor. Conyers Read, *Mr Secretary Cecil and Queen Elizabeth* (New York, 1955), 122.

2 Christina Garrett, *The Marian Exiles* (Cambridge, 1938), 124–6; letter from John Jewel to Peter Martyr, Jan. 26, 1559, in Rev. Hastings Robinson (ed.), *The Zurich Letters* (Parker Soc., 3 vols., Cambridge, 1842–7), I, 8.

3 The evidence for Plowden's alleged candidacy for the woolsack is well summarized in Geoffrey de C. Parmiter, 'Edmund Plowden and the Woolsack, a Query', *The Downside Review* (Oct. 1972), vol. 90, no. 301, 251–9. Cf. also Robert Tittler, 'Plowden and the Woolsack: A Reply', *The Downside Review* (Jan. 1974), vol. 92, no. 306, 62–6.

4 J. E. Neale, 'Sir Nicholas Throckmorton's Advice to Queen Elizabeth on her Accession to the Throne', *English Historical Review*, LXV (1950), 91–8. Throckmorton suggested the names of the incumbent Nicholas Heath, Dr Nicholas Wotton, Anthony Cooke, Lord Rich, a Mr Carell (possibly Sir John Carell, a Sussex Catholic recusant) and Justice Dyer. For the Master of the Rolls he considered Thomas Denton – Bacon's old colleague who in fact had died shortly before Throckmorton wrote – Richard Goodrich and Sir Richard Sackville. Neale infers that Throckmorton wrote on November 18th, the day after Elizabeth's accession, and was probably away from court at the time.

5 *C.S.P. Domestic, Edward VI, Mary and Elizabeth*, 116.

6 Cecil as much as admitted his support for Bacon's appointment in a letter written some five years later when, in a falling out between the two, Cecil reminded Bacon of all that he had done for him. Cecil to Bacon, July 21, 1563, B.L. Add. MS. 102, ff 69r–70v.

7 Parker to Bacon, Dec. [?], 1558, and Dec. 20, 1558, in John Bruce and Thomas T. Perowne (eds.), *The Correspondence of Matthew Parker* (Parker Soc., Cambridge, 1853), 50–53.

8 From December 5th to 23rd Elizabeth remained at Somerset House and used it as the base of her operations; J. E. Neale, *Queen Elizabeth* (1934), 65. The precise date of Bacon's appearance is uncertain. Sanders gives it as December 15th, the day of Elizabeth's coronation, but we know that Bacon was then ill; this may represent instead the date of the Queen's invitation; G. W. Sanders, *Orders in Chancery* (2 vols., 1845), I, i, 20. A patent of 1561, granted in another context, refers to December 21st; *C.P.R., Elizabeth*, I, 39. Most other sources point to the 22nd, which is probably correct; *C.S.P. Domestic, Edward VI, Mary, and Elizabeth*, 116; John Campbell, *The Lives of the Lord Chancellors and*

the Keepers of the Great Seal of England ... (1st edn, 7 vols., 1845–7), II, 88. Unfortunately, none of the surviving copies of Bacon's acceptance speech is dated.

9 Again the precise date is uncertain, although it seems clear that Bacon was knighted before he became Lord Keeper; William Shaw, *The Knights of England* (3 vols., 1906), II, 70.

10 R. C. Braddock, 'The Royal Household, 1540–1560' (unpublished Ph.D. dissertation, Northwestern University, 1971), 171.

11 Cooke's humourless and zealous Protestantism evidently explains why he never attained major office under Elizabeth nor earned the Queen's friendship. M. K. McIntosh, 'The Cooke Family of Gidea Hall, Essex' (unpublished Ph.D. dissertation, Harvard University, 1967), 88.

12 *C.P.R., Elizabeth*, I, 39, 51.

13 5 Eliz. c. 18.

14 Numerous copies of this oration exist, including Huntington Library MS. EL 2579, f 1; National Library of Wales MS. 10905, f 13; Exeter College, Oxford, MS. 127, f 34; and Folger Shakespeare Library MS. V.a. 197, f 12v. I have quoted from the first of these copies, although the wording is almost identical in the others.

15 *C.P.R., Elizabeth*, II, 6.

16 The standard work on the Tudor Chancery is W. J. Jones, *The Elizabethan Court of Chancery* (Oxford, 1967), which makes extended reference to the Chancery before as well as during Elizabeth's reign.

17 Among the many discussions of the emergence of the principles of equity in the sixteenth century, three recent contributions provide particularly lucid summaries: Stuart E. Prall, 'The Development of Equity in Tudor England', *Amer. J. Legal History* (vol. 8, 1964), 1–19; D. E. C. Yale 'Introduction', and Samuel Thorne, 'Preface', in Edward Hake, *Epieikeia*, ed. D. E. C. Yale (New Haven, 1953); D. E. C. Yale (ed.), *Lord Nottingham's 'Manual of Chancery Practice' and 'Prolegomena of Chancery and Equity'* (Cambridge, 1965), especially editor's introduction, 16–24.

18 Yale (ed.), *Lord Nottingham's 'Manual'*, 14.

19 Prall, 'The Development of Equity', 3–4; Thorne's 'Preface' in Hake, *Epieikeia*, vi.

20 Christopher St Germain, *The Dyalogue in Englishe, between a Doctour of diuinitie and a Student in the lawes of England* (published by Richard Tottel, 1554), *S.T.C.* no. 21571, especially 25r–33v.

21 This is particularly evident in Bacon's 'Speech welcoming Mr Justice Manwood to the office of the Chief Baron of the Exchequer', delivered in Michaelmas Term, 1578; Huntington

Library MS. EL 2579, ff 56r–57v.

22 Cf., for example, Bacon's judgement in *Danyell, Jackson and Gregg* v. *Richardson* (1575), in Sanders, *Orders*, I, 54–54a.

23 The dispute arose from the Chancery case of *Tavernor* v. *Cromwell*. There are several MS. copies of this speech, of which I have used Folger Shakespeare Library MS. V.a. 143, 107–8. The applicability of this defence of the prerogative caused it to be published, anonymously, in 1641; Wing no. 367.

24 P.R.O., S.P. 12/44/52; Folger Shakespeare Library MS. V.a. 197, f 66.

25 More was, as is generally known, one of the early practitioners of a markedly different attitude both towards the institution of the family and towards the fellowship of man.

26 Cf., for example, Seneca's 'de Clementia', in Moses Hadas (ed. and trans.), *The Stoic Philosophy of Seneca* (Garden City, New York, 1958), 137–66. For Bacon's familiarity with Seneca, cf. above, 57.

27 This has been suggested in correspondence with Professor James S. Cockburn of the University of Maryland, to whom I am grateful. Even this puritan attitude, however, may well be grounded on the classical and humanist writings of which most puritan lawyers were well aware. It is worthy of note in this context that Calvin himself was well versed in those classical writings in which leniency and clemency were especially emphasized. Cf., for example, F. L. Battles and A. M. Hugo (eds.), *Calvin's Commentaries on Seneca's 'de Clementia'* (Leiden, 1969), *passim*, in which Calvin's first published work is discussed in fine detail.

28 Cf. William Holdsworth, *A History of English Law*, ed. A. L. Goodhart and H. G. Hanbury (7th edn, 13 vols., 1956), I, 423–8.

29 B. L. Harleian MS. 6853, vols. 7–10; *C.P.R. Elizabeth*, V, 324.

30 Bacon to Walsingham, Sept. 21, 1574, B. L. Lansdowne MS. 621, ff 29v–30v. In the end Walsingham went over Bacon's head and secured his suit from the Queen; B. L. Lansdowne MS. 163, ff 145–6.

31 The orders of 1566 are in P.R.O., C.220/Bundle 15/article 1, printed in Sanders, *Orders*, I, 28–33. Orders for 1573 in P.R.O., C.220/Bundle 15/articles 2 and 6; Sanders, *Orders*, I, 45–50. Orders for 1576 in P.R.O., C.220/Bundle 15/article 7.

32 Jones, taking his source from Sanders's *Orders*, dates this 1574, but the patent roll entry by which Bacon promulgated this reform is dated Nov. 23rd, 1573; Jones, *Elizabethan Chancery*, 130; P.R.O., C.66/1110/MS. 6–8.

33 A biographical analysis of the Masters appointed by Bacon may be found in Tittler, 'The Political Activities of Sir Nicholas Bacon

in the Reign of Elizabeth' (unpublished Ph.D. dissertation, New York University, 1971), Appendix II, 339-43.

34 Holdsworth, *History of English Law*, I, 410-11.

35 Sanders, *Orders*, I, 27; Jones, *Elizabethan Chancery*, 382.

36 Egerton, who became Lord Keeper in 1596, ruled that the Court would not consider suits of less than £10 value, or suits for goods and chattels worth less than £20; Sanders, *Orders*, I, 69-72.

37 Ibid., I, 20-24.

38 *Guildeford* v. *Thompson* (1561), cited in W. J. Jones, 'Conflict or Collaboration? Chancery Attitudes in the Reign of Elizabeth I', *Amer. J. Legal History* (vol. 5, 1961), 26 and n 68; *Cooper* v. *Fanshawe* (1576), *Easte* v. *Bittenson* (1578) and *Meanell* v. *Fenton* (1578), cited in Jones, *Elizabethan Chancery*, 342-3.

39 Jones, 'Conflict or Collaboration?', 19-26; Jones, *Elizabethan Chancery*, 78.

40 Jones, 'Conflict or Collaboration?', 27-9.

41 Ibid., 24-5; B.L. Harleian MS. 39, ff 177-8; B.L., Lansdowne MS. 621, f 16.

42 Sanders, *Orders*, I, 54a.

43 P.R.O., C.66/1110/MS. 6-8.

44 Huntington Library MSS. EL 2579, ff 49-52, and HM 1340, ff 46v-52r.

45 Professor Elton has noted that the justices of the assize were used similarly in the reign of Henry VIII; G. R. Elton, *Policy and Police* (Cambridge, 1972), 217, 240-41, 253-4. For a more detailed discussion of the justices of the assize, cf. James S. Cockburn, *A History of English Assizes, 1558-1714* (Cambridge, 1972), Ch. 8, and 188ff. Cf. also Gladys Jenkins, 'Ways and Means in Elizabethan Propaganda', *History*, XXVI (1941), 109.

46 Cf., for example, Bacon's speech at the end of Trinity Term, 1559, and at the end of Hilary Term, 1565; Huntington Library MSS. EL 2579, ff 13r-15r, and HM 1340, ff 26r-30v.

47 Dec. 29, 1575, P.R.O., S.P. 12/105/93; an undated copy may be found in the Yelverton MSS., B.L. Add. MS. 48018, ff 46v-52r.

48 These figures are the same in two independent sources: a handbook on Chancery, probably written in the early seventeenth century by William Lambarde, B.L. Stowe MS. 415 f 4, also in the Yelverton MSS., B.L. Add. MS. 48056, p. 12; and a list of payments to the Lord Chancellor *tempus* Mary, in B.L. Stowe MS. 571. Bacon's original patent for office stipulated a per diem total for service in Chancery of £542 12s., but included in that sum an undetermined amount for payment of the Masters, rendering the figure useless for our purposes; *C.P.R.*, *Elizabeth*, I, 39. Dr Simpson, relying exclusively on Bacon's receivers' accounts at the

University of Chicago, arrives at the lower total figure of £960 (or £961 in leap years). The discrepancy between his figure and my own arises in part because Bacon, and hence Simpson, did not count the wine allowance of £72, and considered the wax allowance of £16 under a separate heading. If the sum of these two figures is added to Simpson's rounded figure of £960, the total is £1,048. Alan Simpson, *The Wealth of the Gentry, 1540–1660* (Chicago, 1961), 62–3, 114.

49 This figure is derived from the totals for each year as listed in Simpson, *Wealth of the Gentry*, 114.

50 This estimate emerges in part from the discussion and estimates presented by G. E. Aylmer, *The King's Servants: the Civil Service of Charles I, 1625–1640* (1961), 160–82, 208, 222. Aylmer estimates the Lord Keeper's income in the 1620s as anywhere from £3,000 to £6,000 or more, while that of a Lord Chancellor is said to run from £3,000 up to £12,000. These figures not only take into account the inflation in the fruits of office, but include several kinds of remuneration not listed by Dr Simpson.

51 Ibid., 179; Joel Hurstfield, 'Political Corruption in Modern England: the Historian's Problem,' reprinted in *Freedom, Corruption and Government in Elizabethan England* (1973), 137–62, especially 139.

52 The first of these charges is known only through Bacon's refutation of it in 1577; B.L. Lansdowne MS. 621, f 102. Plowden's allegations are reported at second hand in Bishop White Kennett's collections, B.L. Sloan MS. 1565, f 141.

53 B.L. Lansdowne MS. 621, f 102.

54 Cf. above, 69.

55 Joel Hurstfield, 'Corruption and Reform Under Edward VI and Mary: the Example of Wardship,' in *Freedom, Corruption and Government*, 163–82, especially 165–8.

56 *C.P.R.*, *Philip and Mary*, I, 2–3; H. E. Bell, *An Introduction to the History and Records of the Court of Wards and Liveries* (Cambridge, 1953), 117; cf. above, 43.

57 Cf. above, 76.

58 *First Report of the Commissioners appointed to inquire into the Municipal Corporations of England and Wales* (Parliamentary Papers Series, 1835), Appendix, Pt IV, 2129–32.

59 Thomas Fuller, *Worthies of England*, ed. John Freeman (1952), 482; Bromley cited in Jones, *Elizabethan Chancery*, 39.

60 From the Queen's speech to Egerton upon his coming to office, May 6, 1596, Bodleian Library, Oxford, Tanner MS. 82, f 92.

61 Hake, *Epieikeia*, 143.

Chapter VI

1 The most reliable studies of the alignments in the early Elizabethan privy council are Wallace T. MacCaffrey, 'Elizabethan Politics, the First Decade, 1558–1568', *Past and Present* (no. 24, 1963), 25–42; MacCaffrey, *The Shaping of the Elizabethan Regime, 1558–1572* (Princeton, 1968), especially Ch. II.

2 Mason was an old friend and colleague of Cecil's and, to a lesser extent, Bacon's, from the 1540s, and Petre had been Cecil's friend and political mentor; B. W. Beckingsale, *Burghley. Tudor Statesman* (1967), 33, 35, 48, 59, 64. Bacon, Winchester and the Earl of Pembroke were credited by Cecil as being his only supporters at the council board while he was away in Scotland during the spring of 1560, but Pembroke was more usually known as a follower of Robert Dudley; Conyers Read, *Mr Secretary Cecil and Queen Elizabeth* (New York, 1955), 211; MacCaffrey, *Elizabethan Regime*, 202, 242. Mildmay is said by his biographer to have been perhaps Cecil's closest friend on the council, and he was frequently linked with Bacon as well; Stanford Lehmberg, *Sir Walter Mildmay and Tudor Government* (Austin, Texas, 1964), 76–7. Bedford was also an old associate of Bacon and Cecil, as his father had been before him; *D.N.B.*

3 These and the impressions following emerge from scrutiny of the State Papers, Patent Rolls, and *Acts of the Privy Council.*

4 J. E. Neale, *Queen Elizabeth* (1934), 67.

5 V. J. K. Brook, *A Life of Archbishop Parker* (Oxford, 1962), 1–12, 16, 48–51.

6 John Strype, *The Life and Acts of Matthew Parker* (3 vols., Oxford, 1821), I, 71.

7 Bacon to Parker, Dec. 9, 1558, John Bruce and Thomas T. Perowne (eds.), *Correspondence of Matthew Parker* (Parker Soc., Cambridge, 1853), 49; Parker to Bacon, n.d. [between Dec. 10 and 20, 1558], ibid., 50–52; and cf. further letters of similar nature, ibid., 52–3, 53, 57–63, 68. Parker finally accepted the office on Sept. 9, 1559; Bacon to Parker, Sept. 9, 1559, Corpus Christi College, Cambridge, MS. 114, p. 125.

8 Many copies of this speech have survived; I have used Huntington Library MS. EL 2579, ff 1–5. Cf. also J. E. Neale, *Elizabeth I and her Parliaments* (2 vols., 1953–7), I, 51–68.

9 Ibid., I, 59.

10 Ibid., I, 59–67.

11 Ibid., I, 67–9.

12 William P. Haugaard, *Elizabeth and the English Reformation* (Cambridge, 1968), 96–7.

13 Neale, *Parliaments*, I, 57, 59, 61; Marjorie McIntosh, 'The Cooke

Family of Gidea Hall, Essex' (unpublished Ph.D. dissertation, Harvard University, 1967), 90. Cecil may have previously nominated Cooke for a seat at Stamford in 1553, which Cooke did not take; ibid., 69.

14 Haugaard, *Elizabeth and the English Reformation*, 96–100; Neale, *Parliaments*, I, 69–70.

15 The best summary of the disputation is still W. H. Frere, *The English Church in the Reigns of Elizabeth and James* (1904), 22–5. Cf. also C. S. Meyer, *Elizabeth I and the Religious Settlement* (St Louis, 1960), 142–5.

16 P.R.O., S.P. 12/3/52.

17 Neale, *Parliaments*, I, 75.

18 Ibid., I, 79.

19 Ibid., I, 80–81.

20 Huntington Library MS. EL 2579, ff 8–11.

21 Meyer, *Elizabeth and the Religious Settlement*, 89, 107–10; John Strype, *Annals of the Reformation* (4 vols., Oxford, 1824–40), I, i, 244–8; McIntosh, 'The Cooke Family of Gidea Hall, Essex', 88–9.

22 John Venn and J. A. Venn, *Alumni Cantabrigiensis*, Pt I (4 vols., Cambridge, 1922–7), II, 167; John LeNeve, *Fasti Ecclesiae Anglicanae* (3 vols., Oxford, 1854), II, 499.

23 B.M. Cotton MS. Titus F, I, ff 64r–68v, and Huntington Library MS. EL 2579, ff 31r–34v.

24 The following is based upon Patrick Collinson, *The Elizabethan Puritan Movement* (Berkeley, 1967), 181–3. Cf. also an excellent English statement in favour of rural deaneries written anonymously – though probably by Thomas Becon, Chancellor of the diocese of Norwich – in 1578, reprinted in Historical Manuscripts Commission, *Calendar of the MSS. of the Marquis of Salisbury* (18 vols., 1883–1965), II, 195–8.

25 Collinson, *Elizabethan Puritan Movement*, 182.

26 Huntington Library MS. EL 2579, ff 46v–51v.

27 The best discussions of early Elizabethan foreign relations are in Read, *Mr Secretary Cecil*, Chs. VII, VIII, XI, XII; R. B. Wernham, *Before the Armada* (New York, 1966), Chs. 18–20; and MacCaffrey, *Elizabethan Regime*, Ch. 6.

28 The treaty is printed in Patrick Forbes (ed.), *A Full View of Public Transactions in the Reign of Elizabeth* (2 vols., 1740–41), I, 68–81.

29 Huntington Library MS. EL 2579, ff 1–5v.

30 Wernham, *Before the Armada*, 247–51; Neale, *Queen Elizabeth*, 91–5.

31 Cecil to Sir Ralph Sadler and Sir James Crofts, Nov. 3, 1559, B.L. Add. MS. 33592 (Sadler Papers, Vol. II), ff 1–2; Neale, *Queen Elizabeth*, 93.

32 Cecil to Sadler, Nov. 12, 1559, B.L. Add. MS. 33592, f 78.
33 Read, *Mr Secretary Cecil*, 158–9.
34 Cecil to Sadler and Crofts, Oct. 31, 1559, B.L. Add. MS. 33591, ff 249–50.
35 P.R.O., S.P. 12/7/73, f 191.
36 Several copies of this speech have survived. I have used Folger Shakespeare Library MS. V.a. 197, ff 19–31.
37 The Privy Council to the Queen, Dec. [?] 24, 1559, P.R.O., S.P. 12/7/73, ff 185–91.
38 Huntington Library MS. EL 2579, ff 25–8. These magistrates performed administrative as well as judicial functions, and were a crucial link in the promulgation and enforcement of government policy at the local level. Bacon utilized such Star Chamber speeches quite regularly as a means of keeping the justices well informed of policy. Cf. James S. Cockburn, *A History of English Assizes, 1558–1714* (Cambridge, 1972), 8–10, 153, 178–81.
39 Wernham, *Before the Armada*, 256; Read, *Mr Secretary Cecil*, 162.
40 Ibid., 173–4. The 'Commission to treat with the King and Queen of France' (May 25, 1560) is printed in *C.S.P., Foreign, Elizabeth*, III, 78.
41 John Sheres to Cecil, May 25, 1560, *C.S.P., Foreign, Elizabeth*, III, 79–80.
42 Norfolk to Cecil, June 7, 1560, ibid., III, 107.
43 Read, *Mr Secretary Cecil*, 170–71.
44 Bacon to Cecil, June 17, 1560, P.R.O., S.P. 54/4/15.
45 The Latin quotation may be translated as 'Don't do anything which cannot be undone at a later time.'
46 The Treaty of Edinburgh was concluded on July 6th, 1560; *C.S.P., Foreign, Elizabeth*, III, 173ff.
47 The best summaries are J. E. Neale, *The Age of Catherine de Medici* (1943), Chs. II and III, and N. M. Sutherland, *The Massacre of St Bartholomew* ... (1973), Ch. I.
48 Wernham, *Before the Armada*, 265; Read, *Mr Secretary Cecil*, 246–52.
49 Wernham, *Before the Armada*, 266; Read, *Mr Secretary Cecil*, 257–60.
50 Jean Héritier, *Catherine de Medici* (New York, 1966), 221–2; Read, *Mr Secretary Cecil*, 258–9.
51 Ibid., 259.
52 Huntington Library MS. EL 2579, ff 1–5v.
53 Cf. above, 95.
54 'Speeches of the Lord Keeper Sir Nicholas Bacon', B.L. Harleian MS. 398 ff 44v–46v.
55 P.R.O., S.P. 12/5/22, f 92.
56 Sir Thomas Smith to Cecil, July 4, 1563, P.R.O., S.P. 70/60/973.
57 Cecil to Smith, July 15, 1563, B.L. Lansdowne MS. 102 (Burghley

Papers), f 36.

58 'A Speech used by my Lord Keeper to the Q. Ma in presence of my LL. of Arundel, Bedford, Pembroke, and my L: Robert, and of the Controller, the Secretarye, and mr. Mason [20 July] 1563 at Grenwich', B.L. Add. MS. 33271, ff 18ff. A copy may be found in B.L. Harleian MS. 398, ff 46v–47v.

59 Cecil's searing and indignant reproach is dated July 21st, and refers to Bacon's speech as having been delivered the previous day. Cecil to Bacon, July 21, 1563, B.L. Lansdowne MS. 102 (Burghley Papers), ff 69r–70v. The letter is discussed, though out of its proper context, in Fr Francis Edwards, S.J., 'I am no Clerk', *The Month*, n.s., 31 (1964), 211–18.

60 Cf. letters from Lord Admiral Clinton to Cecil, Sir Francis Knollys to the Queen, and Lord Wentworth to the Privy Council, July 31, 1563; *C.S.P.*, *Domestic, Elizabeth*, 229; Read, *Mr Secretary Cecil*, 259.

Chapter VII

1 S. T. Bindoff, 'The Making of the Statute of Artificers', in Bindoff, Hurstfield and Williams (eds.), *Elizabethan Government and Society* (1961), Ch. III, especially 79–94.

2 *Acts of the Privy Council*, n.s., VII, 27–8.

3 Bindoff, 'Statute of Artificers', 81. The 'Considerations delivered to the Parlyamente' is found among the Cecil papers at Hatfield House, vol. 152, f 96–9, and has been printed by the Historical Manuscripts Commission in the *Calendar of the MSS. of the Marquis of Salisbury* (18 vols., 1883–1965), I, 162–5.

4 Bindoff, 'Statute of Artificers', 83.

5 Ibid., 83–7.

6 Ibid., 87–94.

7 Ibid., 89–94.

8 Ibid., 89.

9 Ibid., 83, 89.

10 Ibid., 90–91; *C.P.R.*, *Elizabeth*, II, 621–2.

11 J. E. Neale, *Elizabeth I and her Parliaments* (2 vols., 1953–7), I, Ch. I.

12 The two Catholics were Sir Edward Saunders, Chief Justice of the Queen's Bench and Sir Anthony Browne, Chief Justice of the Common Pleas, both of whom were Marian appointees. Bindoff, 'Statute of Artificers', 81. Cf. above, 70, and Ch. V, n 8.

13 H.M.C., *Salisbury*, I, 162–5.

14 Cf. above, 59–60.

15 Bindoff, 'Statute of Artificers', 89.

16 Cf. above, 62.

17 Cf. above, 60.

18 Cf. above, 61.
19 Cf. above, 30.
20 Huntington Library MS. EL 2579, ff 13r–15r.
21 Cf. above, 79, and Ch. V, n 43 and 44.
22 Huntington Library MS. EL 2579, ff 13v–14r.
23 Cf., for example, 1 Eliz. c. 16; 5 Eliz. c. 6; 5 Eliz. c. 12; 8 Eliz. c. 15.
24 Bindoff, 'Statute of Artificers', 84–5.
25 *Acts of the Privy Council*, n.s., VII, 28.
26 Rich and North had been privy councillors under Henry, Edward and Mary – although Rich hardly served after 1553 – while Mildmay was sworn to the council in February 1559; *D.N.B.*, 'Rich, Richard' and 'North, Edward'; Stanford Lehmberg, *Walter Mildmay and Tudor Government* (Austin, Texas, 1964), 48.
27 The committee of June 28, 1559 included Bacon, Winchester, Cecil, Parry, Cave, Sackville, Mildmay and Gerrard; *C.P.R.*, *Elizabeth*, I, 119–20.
28 P.R.O., S.P. 12/5/22, f 92. I am indebted to Katherine Wyndham of Bedford College, London, for pointing out that this scheme did catch on shortly thereafter.
29 'The Discourses of Sir Nicholas Bacon', B.L. Add. MS. 32 379, ff 34r–35v.
30 *C.P.R.*, *Elizabeth*, II, 92–3.
31 Returns to the committee are scattered, but the best evidence of its work, and of Bacon's contribution, are found both in the P.R.O. and in the Bacon Papers at the University of Chicago. In the former, cf. especially S.P. 46/27/70 (Oct. 14, 1561), and S.P. 46/13/251 (Oct. 18, 1563). Among those audits at the University of Chicago which pertain to the work of this committee, the following are endorsed in Bacon's hand: no. 4519 (a summary of the totals for various officials, dated January 22, 1563 [/4], and described by Bacon, significantly enough, as 'ffrom my l Tresurer'); no. 4509 (debts of the Duchy of Lancaster and the Court of Wards, May 6 [1563]); no. 4514 (n.d., arrears of the Exchequer). The remainder, mostly endorsed by Cecil, were presumably conveyed by him to Bacon as in the case of no. 4519 above, and thus remain in Bacon's papers. Two other documents, dated October 18th, 1563, and December 6th, 1563, respectively, indicate Bacon's personal activity in gathering information regarding expenses; P.R.O., S.P. 46/16/161–2, and S.P. 46/27/188.
32 *C.P.R.*, *Elizabeth*, II, 92–3; Bacon MSS., University of Chicago, cf. for example, nos. 4516 and 4517 (Admiralty Accounts, May 10, 1563 and June 13, 1563), and no. 4506 (Account of the Treasurer at Berwick, among others, May 5, 1563).

33 The authoritative treatment of the debasement itself is J. D. Gould, *The Great Debasement* (Oxford, 1970), but this excellent work stops short of treating the recoinage of 1560–61. For the latter, cf. C. W. C. Oman, 'The Tudors and the Currency, 1526–1560', *T.R.H.S.*, n.s., IX (1895), 167–88; A. E. Feaveryear, *The Pound Sterling* (2nd edn, rev. Victor Morgen, Oxford, 1963), 73–86; Conyers Read, 'Profits in the Recoinage of 1560–61', *Economic History Review*, VI (1935–6), 186–94; and Raymond de Roover, *Gresham on Foreign Exchange* (Cambridge, Mass., 1949), 173–218, *passim*.

34 Commission dated Dec. 31, 1558; *C.P.R., Elizabeth*, I, 68–70.

35 Ibid., I, 66–7. The text of the letters creating this committee indicates that the Queen had already determined upon the course of recoinage. The commissioners included Lord North, Thomas Parry, Ambrose Cave, Edmund Peckham and Walter Mildmay, in addition to Cecil himself.

36 These reports to Cecil are as widely scattered as they are numerous. Important representative examples include the following: opinion of Thomas Stanley (Master of the Mint), n.d., P.R.O., S.P. 15/9/71 and S.P. 12/13/27, ff 68–9; opinion of William Humphrey, B.L. Harleian MS. 660, f 25; opinion of Mr Fitzherbert, B.L. Lansdowne MS. 4, f 19; opinion of the Queen, S.P. 12/11/6.

37 P. L. Hughes and Rev. J. F. Larkin, *Tudor Royal Proclamations* (3 vols., New Haven, 1964–9), II, no. 471 (Sept. 27, 1560).

38 B.L. Add. MS. 40061 (Redgrave Hall Papers), ff 20r–21v, 24r–25v, 26r–27v, 28r–29v and 32, are all undated memoranda regarding the impact which the recoinage was expected to have on Ireland, and are all endorsed in Bacon's writing. A more general memorandum on the process for recalling base coinage in the same MS. volume, again noted in Bacon's hand, is dated April 15, 1559; ibid., ff 11–12v. It thus appears that all these plans were submitted at about the same time to Bacon so that he might screen them for Cecil's consideration.

39 Bacon to Cecil, Oct. 22, 1560, P.R.O., S.P. 12/12/26, ff 47–48v.

40 Cf. the 'Report and Opinion of the Queen's Commissioners on the Controversy of the Mint', May 24, 1578, signed by Bacon, Burghley, Sussex, Hatton, Leicester, Walsingham and Mildmay; B.L. Lansdowne MS. 26 (Burghley Papers), ff 24–5; copy in B.L. Lansdowne MS. 48, f 53.

41 Bindoff, 'Statute of Artificers', 87; P.R.O., S.P. 12/17/100–101.

42 Cf. above, 79.

43 Cf. above, 75–6ff.

44 The digest, though anonymous, may very likely be attributable to

Bacon as Professor Bindoff suggests; Bindoff, 'Statute of Artificers', 90.

45 Cf. above, 79–80.

46 Bindoff, 'Statute of Artificers', 90–91.

47 Sir Nicholas Bacon to his son Nathaniel, incorrectly dated Apr. 24, 1571, Bacon MSS. University of Chicago, no. 4118. Internal evidence shows that the letter should be dated 1572. Cf. below, 164.

48 *D.N.B.*, 'Seckford, Thomas'.

Chapter VIII

1 Wallace T. MacCaffrey, *The Shaping of the Elizabethan Regime* (Princeton, 1968), 95–103; Conyers Read, *Mr Secretary Cecil and Queen Elizabeth* (New York, 1955), 198–202.

2 Ibid., 199–200.

3 B. W. Beckingsale, *Burghley. Tudor Statesman* (New York, 1967), 220; Wallace T. MacCaffrey, 'Place and Patronage in Elizabethan Politics', in Bindoff, Hurstfield, and Williams (eds.), *Elizabethan Government and Society* (1961), 110; MacCaffrey, *Elizabethan Regime*, 101; Read, *Mr Secretary Cecil*, 124.

4 Fr Francis Edwards, S.J., 'I am no Clerk', *The Month*, n.s., vol. 31 (1964), 211–18.

5 MacCaffrey, *Elizabethan Regime*, 101, 202; 'Reasons ag. the E. of Lecst' [1566], Cecil Papers, B.L. microfilm M485/40, f 28.

6 Samuel Haynes, (ed.), *A Collection of State Papers ... left by William Cecil* (2 vols. 1740–59), II, 755; MacCaffrey, *Elizabethan Regime*, 138; Beckingsale, *Burghley*, 105.

7 J. E. Neale, *Queen Elizabeth* (1934), 123.

8 Ibid., 124.

9 J. E. Neale, *Elizabeth I and her Parliaments* (2 vols., 1953–7), I, 101–13; 'An Oration made in the tyme of the ... Parliamente in the name of the Nobles and Lords ... unto the Queenes highnes ... moueinge hur maiestye to Mariage', Huntington Library MS. EL 2579, ff 35r–36v.

10 There have been several misconceptions regarding the details of Hales's identity, and especially the assertion, repeated by Neale and others, that he acted as Clerk of the Hanaper in Chancery at the time his tract was written; Neale, *Queen Elizabeth*, 129. He is most correctly identified in A. J. Slavin, 'Sir Ralph Sadler and Master John Hales at the Hanaper ... ', *B.I.H.R.*, XXXVIII (May 1965), 31–47. Cf. also *D.N.B.*, 'Hales, John'; and the correction to the same (anonymous), in *B.I.H.R.*, I, (1923), 63–4; and G. T. Peck, 'John Hales and the Puritans during the Marian Exile', *Church History* (X, 1941), 159–77. The most comprehensive treat-

ment of his celebrated tract is Mortimer Levine, *The Early Elizabethan Succession Question, 1558–1568* (Stanford, 1966), although some of Levine's assertions are brought into question below.

11 MacCaffrey, *Elizabethan Regime*, 163–70; Neale, *Queen Elizabeth*, 131.

12 Levine, *Elizabethan Succession Question*, 63–8.

13 Ibid., 15–16.

14 Cf. above, 100.

15 Neale, *Queen Elizabeth*, 130; Levine, *Elizabethan Succession Question*, 68–9.

16 Ibid., 69; Cecil Papers, Hatfield House, vol. 154, ff 55–8, a list of questions to be put to Hales.

17 Cf. 'A Speache used in councell on the ende of Midsomer Terme, 1562 ... alsoe spoken to hur maiestye at Grenwiche in July following', Huntington Library MS. EL 2579, ff 28–30v.

18 These points are the product of modern speculation rather than contemporary evidence; Levine, *Elizabethan Succession Question*, 77.

19 The interrogation was conducted by Sir John Mason on May 2, 1564; Cecil Papers, B.L. microfilm M485/40, ff 63–64v.

20 Cecil to Smith, Apr. 27, 1564, B.L. Lansdowne MS. 102, f 89; same to same, May 1, 1564, B.L. Lansdowne MS. 102, f 93.

21 P.R.O., E 407/53/unpaginated. It is also interesting to note here that Bacon even played a minor part in the early stages of the investigations; Dudley, Northampton, and Mason to Cecil, Apr. 26, 1564, B.L. Harleian MS. 6990, f 62.

22 Bacon to Elizabeth, July 7, 1564, Huntington Library MS. HM 1340, f 63; P.R.O., E 407/53/unpaginated.

23 Guzman de Silva to Philip, July 22, 1564, *C.S.P., Spanish, Elizabeth*, I, 369.

24 P.R.O., E 407/53/unpaginated. Cf. also a reference to Bacon participating in the privy council meeting of August 5th in the minutes of the meeting of the 8th; *Acts of the Privy Council*, n.s., VII, 147.

25 Bacon to Cecil, Nov. 16, 1564, B.L. Harleian MS. 1877, f 25.

26 P.R.O., E 407/53/unpaginated.

27 Bacon to Cecil, Nov. 27, 1564, Huntington Library MS. HM 1340, f 85v.

28 Cecil Papers, B.L. microfilm M 485/40, f 62.

29 Because it is the most detailed, Levine's summary is the best expression of the traditional presumption of Bacon's guilt, though Neale and others have accepted the same views; Levine, *Elizabethan Succession Question*, 74–8, 83–4; Neale, *Queen Elizabeth*, 129–30.

30 Bacon to Cecil, Jan. 25, 1560, in Haynes, *State Papers*, I, 409–10; Guzman de Silva to Philip, Feb. 4, 1566, *C.S.P.*, *Spanish, Elizabeth*, I, 517; Burghley to Sir Francis Walsingham, July 9, 1571, in Dudley Digges (ed.), *The Compleat Ambassador* (1655), 115–16.

31 *D.N.B.*, 'Hales, Christopher'.

32 Slavin, 'Sadler and Hales', 33–8, *passim*.

33 Edward Hales was the son of John Hales, Baron of the Exchequer under Henry VIII, and cousin of Christopher Hales, the grandfather of our John Hales; W. B. Bannerman (ed.), *Visitations of Kent* (Harleian Soc., 1923), 56, 78. His patent was dated May 8, 1549, and surrendered June 18, 1567; *C.P.R., Edward VI*, V, 406; *C.P.R., Elizabeth*, IV, 72.

34 A jurisdictional dispute over the care of the records in the Tower was carried on between Hales and William Cordell, Master of the Rolls, until it was settled in the latter's favour in 1581. Until then Hales himself kept charge of these records, including the many important Chancery enrolments among them; W. J. Jones, *The Elizabethan Court of Chancery* (Oxford, 1967), 6, 66–8.

35 Levine, *Elizabethan Succession Question*, 77; de Silva to Philip, July 22, 1564, *C.S.P., Spanish, Elizabeth*, I, 369; N. Doleman [pseud. for Fr Robert Parsons, S.J.], *Conference about the Next Succession to the Crowne of England* (1594), *S.T.C.* no. 19398, Pt II, 1–2.

36 *C.P.R., Philip and Mary*, IV, 191–2; Sadler to Cecil, Jan. 11, 1573, B.L. Lansdowne MS. 16 (Burghley Papers), f 78; Slavin, 'Sadler and Hales', 39.

37 Hales to Cecil, Jan. 27, 1566, B.L. Lansdowne MS. 8 (Burghley Papers), ff 8–9.

38 Bacon to the lords of the privy council, Jan. 13, 1565, B.L. Harleian MS. 5175, ff 98–99. A copy of the same, but dated a few days later, may be found in the Cecil Papers, B.L. microfilm M 485/40, f 86.

39 Hales to Cecil, Jan. 27, 1566, B.L. Lansdowne MS. 9, ff 8–9.

40 Levine, *Elizabethan Succession Question*, 79; *D.N.B.*, 'Fleetwood, William'.

41 William Camden, *Annales, or the History of the Most Renowned and Victorious Princess Elizabeth* ... (3rd edn, 1635), *S.T.C.* no. 4501, 58. It should be noted that modern interpreters of Leicester, including Eleanor Rosenberg, Patrick Collinson and Wallace MacCaffrey, have generally sought to revise Camden's negative approach. Yet such efforts, however valid, do not serve to discredit Camden in regard to this particular issue: the evidence seems, in fact, to vindicate his opinion.

42 MacCaffrey, *Elizabethan Regime*, 168–70; A. F. Steuart (ed.), *Memoires of Sir James Melville of Halhill* (1929), 98.

43 Ibid., 98.
44 Read, *Mr Secretary Cecil*, 314-15.
45 Ibid., 314-15.
46 MacCaffrey, *Elizabethan Regime*, 170; Read, *Mr Secretary Cecil*, 315.
47 Cecil to Smith, Nov. 26, 1564, B.L. Lansdowne MS. 102 (Burghley Papers), ff 103-4.
48 Bacon to Cecil, Nov. 26, 1564, B.L. Harleian MS. 5176, ff 97-8.
49 Camden, *Annales*, 58.
50 Bacon to Leicester, n.d., B.L. Harleian MS. 1877, f 27; Bacon to Leicester, Dec. 28, 1564, Huntington Library MS. HM 1340, f 86; Bacon to Leicester and Cecil, Apr. 5, 1565 [misdated 1564, a date which internal evidence rules impossible], P.R.O., S.P. 12/33/42, ff 97r-99v.
51 Smith to Cecil, Apr. 10, 1565, *C.S.P., Foreign, Elizabeth*, VII, 330.
52 Royal commission dated October 25th, 1566; B.L. Cotton MS. Titus F I, f 98v. Bacon in fact returned to his duties on November 8th; ibid., f 99.
53 This tradition was cited in Robert Naunton, *Fragmentia Regalia* (1641), and reprinted from there in *Somers Tracts* (2nd edn, 13 vols., 1809-15), I, 266, n 3.
54 B.L. Cotton MS. Titus F I, f 98v.

Chapter IX

1 Wallace T. MacCaffrey, *The Shaping of the Elizabethan Regime* (Princeton, 1968), 185-8; Mortimer Levine, *The Early Elizabethan Succession Question, 1558-1568* (Stanford, 1966), 165-7.
2 Neville J. Williams, *Thomas Howard, Fourth Duke of Norfolk* (1964), 61, 63-4, 85.
3 Ibid., Ch. V; A. H. Smith, *County and Court: Government and Politics in Norfolk, 1558-1603* (Oxford, 1974), Ch. II.
4 Williams, *Thomas Howard*, 87.
5 MacCaffrey, *Elizabethan Regime*, 135; J. E. Neale, *Queen Elizabeth*, (1934), 83-8; Conyers Read, *Mr Secretary Cecil and Queen Elizabeth* (New York, 1955), 326, 333-4; Guzman de Silva to Philip, Feb. 4, 1565/6, *C.S.P., Spanish, Elizabeth*, I, 517.
6 MacCaffrey, *Elizabethan Regime*, 193-4.
7 J. E. Neale, *Elizabeth I and her Parliaments* (2 vols., 1953-7), I, 129-64.
8 Huntington Library MS. EL 2579, f 41; Neale, *Queen Elizabeth*, 135, 173.
9 B.L. Cotton MS. Titus F, ff 100ff; Neale, *Parliaments*, 135.
10 Ibid., 173; Huntington Library MS. HM 1340, f 84; Cecil Papers, Hatfield House, vol. 183, f 163.
11 MacCaffrey, *Elizabethan Regime*, 226.

12 Lady Antonia Fraser, *Mary, Queen of Scots* (1969), Chs. 16–17.
13 *C.S.P., Scotland, Elizabeth*, II, 339–42.
14 Ibid., II, 342–3.
15 *Loc. cit.*; Throckmorton to Cecil, July 1, 1567, P.R.O., S.P. 52/14/2.
16 Fraser, *Mary*, 368.
17 Ibid., 385–7; MacCaffrey, *Elizabethan Regime*, 254–62; P.R.O., S.P. 12/47/36.
18 'Transacta Inter Angliam et Scotiam, 1568–1570', B.L. Cotton MS. Caligula C, I f 297; MacCaffrey, *Elizabethan Regime*, 262–4.
19 The best account of the Westminster Conference is Gordon Donaldson's aptly titled *The First Trial of Mary, Queen of Scots* (1969), especially Ch. 5. Cf. also B.L. Cotton MS. Caligula C, I, *passim*.
20 Thus, for example, he dealt brusquely with Moray, for whom he doubtless had sympathy, after one of the Earl's important presentations; Dec. 6, 1568, B.L. Cotton MS. Caligula C, I, ff 320–21. For the earlier hearings at Westminster, concerning the Settlement of Religion, cf. above, 88–90.
21 Donaldson, *First Trial of Mary*, Ch. 7, especially 191–5.
22 B.L. Cotton MS. Caligula C, I, ff 368–9 and 373–4.
23 R. B. Wernham, *Before the Armada* (New York, 1966), 290–96.
24 Conyers Read, 'Queen Elizabeth's Seizure of the Duke of Alva's Payships', *J. Modern History*, v, iv (Dec. 1933), 443–64; MacCaffrey, *Elizabethan Regime*, 279–83; Wernham, *Before the Armada*, 296–7; de Spes to Alva, Dec. 21, 1568, *C.S.P., Spanish, Elizabethan*, II, 90; same to same, Dec. 27–30, 1568, ibid., 91–3.
25 Read, 'Seizure of Alva's Payships', 450, n 21; Wernham, *Before the Armada*, 298–9.
26 Bacon to Cecil, Jan. 5, 1568/9, P.R.O., S.P. 12/49/10.
27 [Jan. ?] 8, 1568/9, Cecil Papers, Hatfield House, vol. 155, f 80.
28 Read, 'Seizure of Alva's Payships', 450, 452; *C.S.P., Spanish, Elizabeth*, II, 122–32; Alva to Philip, Mar. 10, 1569, ibid., II, 132–3.
29 Read, 'Seizure of Alva's Payships', 450, n 21; Read, *Mr Secretary Cecil*, 440–43.
30 Parker to Cecil, Mar. 25, 1565, B.L. Harleian MS. 5176 (Burghley Papers), f 149; Grindal to [?] Cecil (Mar. 25, 1566), P.R.O., S.P. 15/13/40; John Strype, *Life and Acts of Matthew Parker* (3 vols., Oxford, 1821), I, 428–9.
31 Parker to Lady Anne Bacon, Feb. 6, 1569, in John Bruce and Thomas T. Perowne (eds.), *Correspondence of Matthew Parker* (Parker Soc., Cambridge, 1853), 309–16; V. J. K. Brook, *A Life of Archbishop Parker* (Oxford, 1962), 226–8; Albert Peel (ed.), *The*

Seconde Parte of a Register ... (2 vols., Cambridge, 1915), I, 242-3; Patrick Collinson, 'The Puritan Classical Movement in the Reign of Elizabeth I' (unpublished Ph.D. dissertation, 3 vols., University of London, 1957), II, 1262.

32 Guzman de Silva to Philip, July 10, 1568, *C.S.P., Spanish, Elizabeth*, II, 52; and same to same, July 17, 1568, ibid., II, 58; de Spes to Philip, Oct. 23, 1568, ibid., II, 79.

33 Read, *Mr Secretary Cecil*, 440-54; MacCaffrey, *Elizabethan Regime*, 305-9; 314-21; Williams, *Thomas Howard*, Ch. 9.

34 Read, *Mr Secretary Cecil*, 443, 446-50; MacCaffrey, *Elizabethan Regime*, 310-21; Williams, *Thomas Howard*, 160-65.

35 Ibid., 165; de Spes to Philip, Oct. 8, 1569; *C.S.P., Spanish, Elizabeth*, II, 198-200.

36 La Mothe Fénélon to Charles IX, Oct. 18, 1569, in A. Teulet (ed.), *Correspondance diplomatique de la Mothe Fénélon* (7 vols., Paris, 1838-40), II, 285; Williams, *Thomas Howard*, 194-5.

37 De Spes to Philip, Oct. 31, 1569, *C.S.P., Spanish, Elizabeth*, II, 206.

38 Cf., for example, Christopher Norris to the Lord Keeper and Mr Secretary Cecil, Feb. 14, 1570, B.L. Cotton MS. Caligula C, I, ff 377-9.

39 Fénélon to Charles IX, Nov. 1, 1569, in Teulet (ed.), *Correspondance de Fénélon*, II, 308-13.

40 [?] Chester to Cecil, [?] Mar., 1570, P.R.O., S.P. 12/67/1.

41 Neville Williams, 'The Risings in Norfolk of 1569 and 1570', *Norfolk Arch.*, XXXII (1961), 73-81.

42 'A determination by the Q Maity', Mar. 14, 1570, B.L. Cotton MS. Caligula C, I, ff 323-4.

43 [Sir Francis Englefield] to [?], Apr. 11, 1570, P.R.O., S.P. 15/18/38 and 15/18/278-9.

44 MacCaffrey, *Elizabethan Regime*, 359, 378-80; *D.N.B.*, 'Lumley, John'.

45 MacCaffrey, *Elizabethan Regime*, 378-80; W. C. Dickinson, *Scotland, from the Earliest Times to 1603* (1961), 347; J. E. Neale, *The Age of Catherine de Medici* (1962 edn), 71-3; Wernham, *Before the Armada*, 306.

Chapter X

1 The fourth delegate was Lord Howard of Effingham, who had not joined his cousins in the 1569 revolt. His presence on this delegation was probably more to lend dignity than voice. The most reliable source for this meeting, and the one upon which my account is based, is 'Transacta Inter Angliam et Scotiam', B.L. Cotton MS. Caligula C, II, ff 204-7. Cf. also Ross's statement in *C.S.P., Scotland*, III, 158-61.

2 Conyers Read, *Lord Burghley and Queen Elizabeth* (1960), 23.

3 A. Teulet (ed.), *Correspondance diplomatique de la Mothe Fénélon* (7 vols., Paris, 1838–40), III, 169–70; Read, *Lord Burghley*, 23, 25; Elizabeth to Sussex, May 31, 1570, B.L. Cotton MS. Caligula C, II, f 320.

4 Fénélon to Sieur de Vassal, [?] May, 1570, in Teulet, *Correspondance de Fénélon*, III, 187.

5 Same to same, ibid., III, 188–9; J. A. Froude, *History of England* (12 vols., New York, 1872), 63–4; Read, *Lord Burghley*, 25.

6 J. E. Neale, *Queen Elizabeth* (1934), 191; Read, *Lord Burghley*, 22 and n 18. The latter correctly dates the posting of the bull as May 25th; Froude *et al.* had placed it ten days earlier.

7 Read, *Lord Burghley*, 24.

8 Fénélon to Sieur de Vassal, in Teulet, *Correspondance de Fénélon*, III, 187; Froude, *History of England*, 63–5. The sequence of these events is not precise in Fénélon, the only primary source, and Froude for one acknowledged his difficulty in reconstructing it. Although my own reconstruction of the events does not concur with Froude, it seems the most logical in the context of these events, and incorporates the correct rendering of when the bull of excommunication was actually posted, which Froude had mistaken.

9 Read, *Lord Burghley*, 25–9.

10 De Spes to Philip, Jan. 16, 1571, *C.S.P., Spanish, Elizabeth*, II, 290; John Chisholme to the Laird of Grange, Feb. 24, 1571, *C.S.P., Scotland*, III, 485–7.

11 'Short answeres to ye foure princypall poyntes before rembryd', Feb. 21, 1571 (in Bacon's hand and endorsed by Cecil), ibid., III, 484.

12 Wallace T. MacCaffrey, *The Shaping of the Elizabethan Regime* (Princeton, 1968), 390.

13 Cf., for example, an account of the sessions of March 12th and 20th, in which Bacon and Burghley respectively raised the issue; de Spes to Philip, Mar. 14, 1571, *C.S.P., Spanish, Elizabeth*, II, 298; 'Account of the Conference at Grenwich … ', Mar. 20, 1571, *C.S.P., Scotland*, III, 505–8.

14 Read, *Lord Burghley*, 25–9.

15 N. M. Sutherland, *The Massacre of St Bartholomew* … (1973), 141–2, 152–5, and Ch. IX–X, *passim*; Read, *Lord Burghley*, 30–32; MacCaffrey, *Elizabethan Regime*, 391–6.

16 Burghley to Walsingham, July 9, 1571, in Dudley Digges (ed.), *The Compleat Ambassador* (1655), 115. Strype reports the same comment with slightly different wording; John Strype, *Annals of the Reformation* (4 vols., Oxford, 1824–40), II, i, 57.

17 B.L. Sloan MS. 1786, ff 18–24; Inner Temple, Petyt MS. 538, vol. 49, f 14v. A copy with slightly different wording is reprinted in J. Payne Collier (ed.), *The Egerton Papers* ... , (Camden Soc., XII, 1840), 50–59. Only the Petyt MS. copy bears a date, and its assertion of 1570 must be taken as any time up to March 25, 1571, new style. Both the logic of events and Professor Mac-Caffrey's assertion that only Cecil, Walsingham, Buckhurst and Leicester knew of the scheme until quite late point to Bacon's authorship in the opening months of (new style) 1571; Mac-Caffrey, *Elizabethan Regime*, 392.

18 Collier, *loc. cit.*

19 Elizabeth to Walsingham, Mar. 24, 1571, and June 8, 1571, in Digges, *Compleat Ambassador*, 62–6, 106–8; Sutherland, *Massacre of St Bartholomew*, 152–83.

20 Burghley to Walsingham, July 9, 1571, in Digges, *Compleat Ambassador*, 115–16.

21 Leicester to Walsingham, [?] Aug., 1571, ibid., 129; de Spes to Philip, Aug. 18, 1571, *C.S.P., Spanish, Elizabeth*, II, 229–330.

22 Burghley to Walsingham, July 9, 1571, in Digges, *Compleat Ambassador*, 115–16; de Spes to Philip, Aug. 23, 1571, *C.S.P., Spanish, Elizabeth*, II, 330–31.

23 Burghley to Walsingham, Sir Thomas Smith and Sir Henry Killigrew, Feb. 13, 1571/2, in Digges, *Compleat Ambassador*, 154–9; Neale, *Queen Elizabeth*, 225.

24 R. B. Wernham, *Before the Armada* (New York, 1966), 316–17.

25 Burghley received the first inklings of the plot as early as April 1571, but its full details were not entirely known to him until October; Read, *Lord Burghley*, 38–42.

26 Parliament opened on the unusually late date of May 8th in 1572; J. E. Neale, *Elizabeth I and her Parliaments* (2 vols., 1953–7), I, 242.

27 Cited in ibid., I, 246.

28 *D.N.B.*, 'Bell, Robert'; Neale, *Parliaments*, 248–52.

29 Neale, *Parliaments*, I, 244. The friendship of Norton and Bacon is best illustrated by the letter of condolence from the former to Anthony Bacon, written the day after the Lord Keeper's death, in which the former reminisces somewhat regarding his friendship with the elder Bacon; Feb. 20, 1579, B.L. Add. MS. 33, 271, f 42r.

30 Neale, *Parliaments*, I, 278–80. For Digges's relationship to Bacon, cf. above, 58.

31 Neale, *Parliaments*, I, 262–3, 268–73, 277–8.

32 Neville J. Williams, *Thomas Howard, Fourth Duke of Norfolk* (1964), 243, 248, 253.

33 Neale, *Parliaments*, I, 273–4, 308–11.

34 Cited in ibid., 309.

35 Neale, *Queen Elizabeth*, 224-5.

36 Ibid., 241.

37 MacCaffrey, *Elizabethan Regime*, 452-3.

38 Only Sadler, born a year before Bacon, was older; ibid., 448.

39 Bacon to Burghley, July 12, 1572, B.L. Lansdowne MS. 14 (Burghley Papers, 1572), f 176. The spelling has been modernized.

40 Francis Bacon, 'Apothegms', in James Spedding, R. L. Ellis and D. D. Heath (eds.), *The Works of Francis Bacon* (14 vols., 1857-74), VII, 144; cf. above, 215, n 44.

Chapter XI

1 Cf., for example, the will of Thomas Bacon, 'gent.', of 'Heggessett' (Hessett), Suffolk, proven Mar. 10, 1547, P.R.O., Prob. 11/31/41; Bacon purchased the wardship of his nephew William Rede, son of William Rede and Anne Ferneley, for the substantial sum of £66 13s. 4d.; Alan Simpson, *The Wealth of the Gentry, 1540-1660* (Chicago, 1961), 86, n 3.

2 Tooley, distantly related to Bacon, was one of the foremost merchants of Ipswich in the entire century. He had willed an almshouse to the borough, but the legal complications surrounding the bequest baffled the borough elders for several years until, at the suggestion of the benefactor's widow, Bacon was called in to settle the matter in 1562. John Webb, *Great Tooley of Ipswich* (Ipswich, 1962), 158, 163-4, 184, n 13.

3 From the 'Annals of the Town Council', Dec. 23, 1575, reprinted in Nathaniel Bacon, *The Annalls of Ipswiche* (1654), ed. W. H. Richardson (Ipswich, 1884), 308.

4 May 13, 157[2 or 5], Bacon to the Bailiffs and Commonality of Ipswich, Ipswich and East Suffolk Record Office MS. HD 36: 2672/art. 57.

5 Nathaniel Bacon, *Annalls of Ipswiche*, 261-2, 269.

6 Cf. below, 164.

7 Bacon to young Nicholas Bacon, Mar. 18 and 22, 1573, Bacon MSS., Chicago, nos. 4125 and 4126. Jermin served as Sheriff of Norfolk and Suffolk – the offices were combined until 1575 – in 1558 and 1572, is listed on at least one of the surviving lists of the J.P.s for Suffolk for this period, and was one of the commissioners for the musters in 1569. Hamon LeStrange, *Norfolk Official Lists* (Norwich, 1890), 19-20; Return of Suffolk J.P.s for 1569, P.R.O., S.P. 12/60/62, f 172-3; B.L. Harleian MS. 309, f 107.

8 Nathaniel Bacon to Bacon, n.d., Bacon MSS., Folger Shakespeare Library MS. L.d. 72; Bacon to Bassingbourne Gawdy, Nov. 4, 1576, Bodleian Library, Oxford, Tanner MS. 50 ('Gawdy Papers'), f 1b. Cf. also A. H. Smith, 'The Elizabethan Gentry of

Norfolk; Office Holding and Faction' (unpublished Ph.D. dissertation, University of London, 1959), 161-3. I am grateful for permission to use this thesis.

9 Simpson, *Wealth of the Gentry*, Ch. II.

10 For a full and lucid discussion of Stiffkey and its construction, cf. E. R. Sandeen, 'The Building Activities of Sir Nicholas Bacon' (unpublished Ph.D. dissertation, University of Chicago, 1959), 157-232. I am grateful for permission to use this thesis.

11 Bacon's continuing and profound interest in his lands and buildings is perhaps the single greatest preoccupation of his surviving correspondence; it is particularly evident in the Bacon MSS. at the University of Chicago.

12 Simpson, *Wealth of the Gentry*, 114; Lilian J. Redstone, 'The Liberty of Bury St Edmunds', *Proc. Suffolk Inst. Arch.* (1911), xv, ii, 200-211.

13 Bacon to Sir Clement Higham *et al.*, Nov. 29, 1562, Bury St Edmunds and West Suffolk Record Office MS. c4/1.

14 Unpublished essay in the files of the History of Parliament Trust on parliamentary representation in St Albans. I should like to thank Miss Norah Fuidge for access to this and other essays.

15 Essays on Eye and Sudbury, ibid.; 'accounts of Thomas Rysham, *alias* Barbor, Mayor' of Sudbury, cited in Ethel Stokes and Lilian J. Redstone, 'Calendar of the Muniments of the Borough of Sudbury', *Proc. Suffolk Inst. Arch.* (1909), xiii, iii, 20.

16 Walter C. Metcalfe (ed.), *The Visitations of Suffolk* (Exeter, 1882), 21, 137; Simpson, *Wealth of the Gentry*, 34-6.

17 Bacon's intervention in settling the Tooley bequest at Ipswich, and his intercession on behalf of an indigent kinsman in the same town are excellent examples. Cf. above, 149 and n 2-4.

18 Probably at Bacon's instigation, Doyley served as J.P. for Oxfordshire and Buckinghamshire, and as a member of several *ad hoc* commissions appointed by the privy council. He died of the plague in 1576 while still quite young. W. H. Turner, *The Visitations of the County of Oxford* ... (Harleian Soc., 1871), 325; *C.P.R., Elizabeth*, V, 196, 223, 246; *Acts of the Privy Council*, n.s., IX, 25, 135, 392.

19 This windfall resulted from rather odd circumstances. The three Buttes brothers, Sir William, Thomas and Sir Edmund, married the three daughters and co-heiresses of Sir Henry Bures, and Anne was the only child of all three marriages. She thus brought with her the total inheritance of both the Bures and the Buttes families, and linked Nicholas with her powerful uncles as if he were their own son.

20 J. W. Burgon, *The Life and Times of Sir Thomas Gresham* (2 vols.,

1839), II, 469-70. Cf. also a patent of denization for Anne 'wife of Nathaniel Bacon', July 5, 1569; *C.P.R., Elizabeth*, IV, 349.

21 Bacon to Gresham, Apr. 3, 1577, Bradfer-Lawrence MSS., Norfolk Record Office MS. VII b. (1), unfoliated.

22 Metcalfe, *Visitations of Suffolk*, 109; *Burke's Peerage* (104th edn, 1967), 142. The suggestion of Edward's later marriage is derived from the painting of the family tree, dated 1578, in which Edward is shown unmarried (Plate 2).

23 Whereas Nicholas received Redgrave, Nathaniel was given Stiffkey during his father's lifetime, and Anthony – the first of the Lord Keeper's sons by Anne Cooke – received Gorhambury. Edward, like the youngest child Francis, received little in the way of land: the small Suffolk manor of Bramfield and a few tenements in London. Perhaps he had acquired, or was about to acquire, some land as part of his wife's dowry.

24 Cf. the revealing letter from Edward to Nathaniel, written from Paris, in which the former related how his father finally had his treasurer Mr Kemp pay out £20, and how he had received from 'my ladie [i.e., Lady Anne] great good speache'. But he also adds that his father disapproved of his travelling companions and refused to give him the advice regarding the journey which had been requested. In the end Edward had to receive further financial assistance from his cousin Robert Bacon. Aug. 13, [?] 1575, Folger Shakespeare Library MS. L.d. 37.

25 Walter Rye, *Visitation of Norfolk* (Harleian Soc., 1891-5, 2 vols.), I, 320-21; Dashwood and Bulmer, *Visitation of Norfolk* (2 vols. Norwich, 1878-95), I, 103-6; Smith, 'Elizabethan Gentry of Norfolk', Appendix II, 381.

26 Cf. the undated letter from Bacon to Woodhouse printed in full in Simpson, *Wealth of the Gentry*, 14-15. Cf. also letter from Bacon to young Nicholas Bacon, June 19, 1571, Bacon MSS., Chicago, no. 4114; Francis Wyndham to Nathaniel Bacon, Dec. 14, 1574, and May 26, 1575, Raynham Hall MSS. (4)5 and (4)6, on loan to Norfolk and Norwich Record Office from Lord Cromwell and used with permission.

27 Bacon to young Nicholas Bacon, Feb. 23, 1571, Bacon MSS., Chicago, no. 4112; Simpson, *Wealth of the Gentry*, 59; A. Hassell Smith, *County and Court: Government and Politics in Norfolk, 1558-1603* (Oxford, 1974), Appendix I, especially 355.

28 Cf., for example, his role in investigating the Hubbart pirate episode, below, 165-6.

29 *D.N.B.*; R. W. Ketton-Cremer, 'A Drawing for Blomefield's Norfolk: the Tomb of Judge Francis Wyndham', *Norfolk Arch.*, xxv (1934), ii, 170-79; Rye, *Visitation of Norfolk*, 100-101; Smith,

County and Court, Appendix I, especially 355. For a discussion of the Norfolk shire election of 1572, cf. below, 162–4.

30 Cf. the seminal work on the puritan concept of marriage and the family by Levin L. Schücking, trans. Brian Battershaw, *The Puritan Family; a Social Study from the Literary Sources* (Leipzig, 1969), especially Pts I, II and IV. The humanist attitude is nowhere better exemplified than by the well-known family life of Sir Thomas More and, in times closer to Bacon's age, by the household of his father-in-law Anthony Cooke.

31 Bacon to Nathaniel Bacon, n.d., Raynham Hall MS. (4)1.

32 Bacon to young Nicholas Bacon, Feb. 23, 1571, and Mar. 6, [?] 1569, Bacon MSS., Chicago, nos. 4112 and 4071.

33 Bacon to young Nicholas Bacon, Dec. 11, 1567, Bacon MSS., Chicago, no. 4084.

34 Cf. above, n 26.

35 Francis Wyndham to Nathaniel Bacon, May 26, 1575, Raynham Hall MS. (4)6.

36 Raynham Hall MSS. (4) *passim.*

37 Francis Wyndham to Nathaniel Bacon, Dec. 2, 1576, in H. W. Saunders (ed.), *The Official Papers of Sir Nathaniel Bacon of Stiffkey, Norfolk* (Camden Soc., 3rd series, xxvi, 1915), 185.

38 Anne Bacon to Lady Anne Bacon, n.d., Folger Shakespeare Library MS. L.d. 15.

39 Francis Wyndham to Nathaniel Bacon, Dec. 10, 1576, Raynham Hall MS. (4)13.

40 The reference was either to 'yor mother' – a frequent device for 'mother-in-law', but clearly not in reference to the Lord Keeper's own wife who stayed at Redgrave on very few occasions – or to 'yor wief and her mother'; Bacon to young Nicholas Bacon, Bacon MSS., Chicago, nos. 4089, 4093, 4094, 4124, 4125.

41 Smith, *County and Court*, 57–61.

42 Rosemary O'Day, 'The Ecclesiastical Patronage of the Lord Keeper, 1558–1642', *T.R.H.S.* (5th series, xxiii, 1973), 89–90.

43 Ibid., 92–4; Tittler, 'The Political Activity of Sir Nicholas Bacon in the Reign of Elizabeth, 1558–1579' (unpublished Ph.D. dissertation, New York University, 1971), 344–55.

44 Albert Peel (ed.), *The Seconde Parte of a Register* (2 vols., Cambridge, 1915), I, 242–3; Patrick Collinson, 'The Puritan Classical Movement in the Reign of Elizabeth I' (unpublished Ph.D. dissertation, 3 vols., University of London, 1957) II, 1261; R. G. Usher, *The Presbyterian Movement in the Reign of Queen Elizabeth* (Camden Soc., 3rd series, VIII, 1905), 66.

45 Collinson, 'Puritan Classical Movement', I, 108, 161, 168–9, 186, 333–7; S. E. Lehmberg, 'Archbishop Grindal and the Prophesy-

ings', *Historical Magazine of the Protestant Episcopal Church*, XXXIV, ii, 101; John Strype, *The Life and Acts of Matthew Parker* (3 vols., Oxford, 1821), II, 69ff; William Urwick, *Nonconformity in Herts* ... (1884), 80–82.

46 Matthew Parker to Lady Anne Bacon, Feb. 6, 1568, in John Bruce and Thomas T. Perowne (eds.), *Correspondence of Matthew Parker* (Parker Soc., Cambridge, 1853), 309–16; R. W. Dixon, *History of the Church of England* (6 vols., 1878–1902), VI, 192–3; V. J. K. Brook, *A Life of Archbishop Parker* (Oxford, 1962), 227–8.

47 Urwick, *Nonconformity in Herts.*, 82. Although the term 'Dutchman' as used in sixteenth-century England often referred to radical theological views rather than nationality, Thomas seems to have been born in Bois-le-Duc, Brabant.

48 Cf., for example, Bacon to young Nicholas Bacon June 18, 1567, Bacon MSS., Chicago, no. 4083, and same to same, Dec. 9, 1568, Bacon MSS., Chicago, no. 4092; these refer to appointments at Eccles, Suffolk, and Mettinghall, Suffolk, respectively.

49 Cf. above, 150 and n 15.

50 Cf., for example, suit from George Nunne, a Bacon retainer, for Bacon's help in securing him the position of undersheriff of Norfolk and Suffolk in 1569; Bacon to young Nicholas Bacon, Nov. 9, 1569, Bacon MSS., Chicago, no. 4099; suit from Thomas Jermin on behalf of Robert Ashfield for Bacon's help in obtaining the same post, Nov. 17, 1565, B.L. Add. MS. 27447 (Paston Correspondence), f 110.

51 Smith, *County and Court*, 81.

52 Anon., 'The Lord Lieutenancy of Suffolk under the Tudors', *Proc. Suffolk Inst. Arch.* (1928–9), XX, ii, 229. The Duke of Norfolk himself was the Lord Lieutenant.

53 These two areas, more specifically the Hundreds of Holt and North Greenhoe in Norfolk, and Bury St Edmunds, Hartesmere and Thednestry in Suffolk, are identified as puritan strongholds at this time by both Smith, 'Elizabethan Gentry of Norfolk, Office Holding and Faction' (unpublished Ph.D. dissertation, University of London, 1959), 165, 206, *passim*, and Collinson, *The Elizabethan Puritan Movement* (Berkeley, 1967), 174, 182–3, 187–8.

54 Cf. above, 61, 150, 19. It should be noted that the Duke of Norfolk was the Steward of the Eight and a Half Hundreds of Bury, but this is a distinct jurisdiction from the Liberty of Bury. On the other hand, the territory of each was largely co-terminous, and thus Bacon could not exercise his full rights until after Norfolk's execution. Lilian Redstone, 'The Liberty of Bury St Edmunds', *Proc. Suffolk Inst. Arch.* (1911), XV, ii, 200–211; Angela

Green, 'The Stewardship of the Eight and a Half Hundreds', *Proc. Suffolk Inst. Arch.* (1963), xxx, iii, 255–62.

55 Blackman and Sharp married Bacon's sisters Anne and Barbara respectively, and both acted as general messengers and *factotums* to the Lord Keeper from time to time. Simpson, *Wealth of the Gentry*, 28, n 3.

56 Andrews was born in Bury and after completing his studies at Oxford, Cambridge and the Middle Temple, he returned to settle there. Bacon appointed him a Governor of the Bury Grammar School, probably secured for him a parliamentary seat at Sudbury in 1563, and seats on the Suffolk commission of the peace in at least 1569 and 1575. In return, Andrews served the Lord Keeper in many ways, including the purchase of wardships for Bacon in his own name; Metcalfe, *Visitations of Suffolk*, 1; N. M. Fuidge, 'The Personnel of the House of Commons of 1563–1567' (unpublished M.A. thesis, University of London, 1950), III, 7–8; John Venn and J. A. Venn, *Alumni Cantabrigiensis*, Pt I (4 vols., Cambridge, 1922), I, 31; Lists of Suffolk J.P.s for 1569 and 1575, P.R.O., S.P. 12/60/172–3, and B.L. Stowe MS. 570, f 58–9; Norfolk Record Office MS. 13902, 28–F–2; Simpson, *Wealth of the Gentry*, 86, n 3.

57 Baldero (*c.* 1520–74) was Bacon's steward. He, too, was educated at Cambridge and Gray's Inn, and Bacon may have met him at the latter. He purchased wardships and performed other duties for Bacon, and the Lord Keeper secured for him the positions of escheator of Norfolk and Suffolk in 1561, and of foedary in Suffolk alone in 1568. For Baldero's dependent he secured a lesser office in his own retinue. Venn and Venn, *Alumni Cantabrigiensis*, I, i, 174; *C.P.R., Elizabeth*, IV, 240, 269; *List of Escheators for England and Wales* (List and Index Soc. LXXII, 1970), 91; Bacon to young Nicholas Bacon, Oct. 4, 1569, Bacon MSS., Chicago, no. 4098.

58 Kemp was also Bacon's nephew, having married the daughter of Barbara and Robert Sharp. Bacon signed over to him the lease of Burwell Rectory, Cambs., and appointed him a Deputy at the Court of Faculties. Kemp remained a Bacon follower after the Lord Keeper's death, and later sat as M.P. for Eye, which had virtually become a Bacon family seat. Simpson, *Wealth of the Gentry*, 27, 28, n 3; R. C. Gabriel, 'Members of the House of Commons, 1586–1587' (unpublished M.A. thesis, University of London, 1954), 461–2; *C.P.R., Elizabeth*, II, 168; unpublished essay in the files of the History of Parliament Trust on Kemp, examined by kind permission of Miss Fuidge.

59 Collinson, 'The Puritan Classical Movement', 889.

60 Smith, *County and Court*, 51–61.

61 Norfolk to Cecil, [?] 1566, P.R.O., S.P. 15/13/52. Cf. also Smith, *County and Court*, Ch. II.
62 Smith, *County and Court*, 32–3. J. E. Neale, *The Elizabethan House of Commons* (1949), 194–5; Neville J. Williams, *Thomas Howard, Fourth Duke of Norfolk* (1964), 75–6.
63 Although they did not necessarily owe office to the duke, seven sheriffs appointed between 1558 and 1572 were his tenants or retainers: John Appleyard (1559), Thomas Tindall (1561), William Paston (1565), Lionel Tolemache (1566), Edward Clere (1567), Christopher Heydon (1569) and Ralph Shelton (1571). Appleyard was a relative of Leicester, and Shelton – Henry Woodhouse's brother-in-law – was a puritan friend of the Bacons, but Clere, Appleyard and Paston rose to the duke's banner in 1569. Smith, *County and Court*, 35; Hamon LeStrange, *Norfolk Official Lists*, 19–20; Williams, *Thomas Howard*, 49, 180; P.R.O., S.P. 12/71/61.
64 Smith, 'Elizabethan Gentry of Norfolk', 12–28, 53–61, 328–32.
65 Smith, *County and Court*, Ch. VIII.
66 Ibid., 167–73.
67 Smith, 'Elizabethan Gentry of Norfolk', 3, 72, and Ch. I, *passim*.
68 The following observations are drawn largely from Dr Smith's statistical analysis of the Norfolk commissions of the peace; Smith, *County and Court*, Appendix II, 357–9.
69 Ibid., loc. cit.; cf. also B.L. Stowe MS. 570, f 51; P.R.O., S.P. 12/96/58–9.
70 Neale, *The Elizabethan House of Commons*, 27.
71 The returns for 1571 are found in the MSS. of Lord de Tabley, and I am greatly indebted once again to Miss Norah Fuidge and the History of Parliament Trust for access to a copy of this list. Identification of these individuals follows from Williams, *Thomas Howard*, *passim*, and Neale, *The Elizabethan House of Commons*, 194–5. In contrast, Bacon seems not to have influenced the choice of any M.P.s in Norfolk in 1571, and only two – the seats for Eye – in Suffolk, though it is possible that the burgesses for Sudbury were his nominees in 1571 as we know them to have been in 1572; History of Parliament Trust folder on Eye.
72 B.L. Add. MS. 48018 (Yelverton Papers), f 282.
73 Cf. for example, the exchange between Clere and Richard Southwell, Apr. 16 and [?] Apr. 1572, B.L. Add. MS. 27960 (Clere Family Correspondence), f 9; Smith, *County and Court*, 316.
74 Bacon to young Nicholas Bacon incorrectly dated April 24, 1571, Bacon MSS., Chicago, no. 4118. The date is clearly 1572, based on the contents of the letter, and because the Parliament of 1571 opened on April 2nd: a date clearly incongruous with the

reference in this letter to elections being held after the 24th.

75 Bacon to young Nicholas Bacon, Bacon MSS., loc. cit.

76 *Return of the Members of Parliament* (1878), Pt I, 411.

77 Cf. above, 161.

78 Commissions of August 1577 for Suffolk include Nathaniel Bacon, Francis Wyndham and Drue Drury – the last-named a puritan ally of the Bacons; P.R.O., S.P. 15/25/48.

79 The commission appointed in October 1578 by the privy council to investigate the protracted dispute between the pro-Catholic Bishop Freke of Norwich and his puritan Chancellor Thomas Becon, a holdover from Parkhurst's administration, included among others Nathaniel Bacon, Philip Parker (a patron of the Dedham classis of ministers and an associate of the Bacons), William Blennerhasset (whom Parkhurst had brought to the Lord Keeper's attention as a puritan worthy of local office) and Drue Drury. P.R.O., S.P. 12/126/3. For the entire episode, cf. S.P. 12/127, 12/126, and 15/25, *passim*, and Smith, 'Elizabethan Gentry of Norfolk', 175–84. On Parker, cf. Collinson, 'The Puritan Classical Movement', I, 359, n 3; on Blennerhasset, cf. Cambridge University Library MS. Ee.II, 34 (Parkhurst Correspondence), f 68b.

80 Nathaniel Bacon to Bacon, Aug. 24, 1576, Bacon MSS., Folger Shakespeare Library, L.d. 74. This is obviously the second letter from Nathaniel on this subject, but the first seems not to have survived.

81 Smith, 'Elizabethan Gentry of Norfolk', 193; Dashwood and Bulmer, *Visitation of Norfolk*, II, 122–3; Captain John Smith to Dr Wilson, Jan. 29, 1576, Historical Manuscripts Commission, *Calendar of the MSS. of the Marquis of Salisbury* (18 vols., 1883–1965), II, 126.

82 Folger MS. L.d. 74.

83 Bacon to Nathaniel Bacon, Aug. 28, 1576, Bacon MSS., Folger L.d. 140.

84 Conyers Read, *Mr Secretary Walsingham and the Policy of Queen Elizabeth* (3 vols., Oxford, 1925), I, 325–31.

85 Folger MS. L.d. 140.

86 Lincoln to the Lord Keeper (in which reference is made to the letter from Bacon to Lincoln which has not survived), Aug. 24, 1576, Folger MS. L.d. 403; same to same, Aug. 27 and 28, 1576, Folger MSS. L.d. 404 and 405; the lords of the privy council to Nathaniel Bacon, Aug. 27, 1576, Folger MS. L.d. 482.

87 Nathaniel Bacon to Bacon, Sept. 1, 1576, Folger MS. L.d. 75; Nathaniel Bacon to the privy council (undated, but assigned by Dr Robert Kenny to Sept. 6), Folger MS. L.d. 66; Lincoln to

Bacon, Sept. 13, 1576, Folger MS. L.d. 406.

88 Lincoln to Bacon, Aug. 24, 1576, Folger MS. L.d. 403.

89 Lords of the privy council to Nathaniel Bacon *et al.*, Sept. 14, 1576, Folger MS. L.d. 483.

90 Sir Francis Walsingham to Bacon, Sept. 17, 1576, Folger MS. L.d. 612.

Chapter XII

1 Patrick Collinson, *The Elizabethan Puritan Movement* (Berkeley, 1967), Pts III and IV, *passim.*

2 Ibid., 439–40; William Urwick, *Nonconformity in Herts* ... (1884), 75–96.

3 Theodore Beza to Heinrich Bullinger, Sept. 3, 1566, in Rev. Hastings Robinson (ed.), *The Zurich Letters* (Parker Soc., 3 vols., Cambridge, 1842–7), II, 127–36.

4 Cf. above, 61.

5 Patrick Collinson, 'The Puritan Classical Movement in the reign of Elizabeth I' (unpublished Ph.D. dissertation, 3 vols., University of London, 1957), I, 108, 161, 168–9, 186, 333–7; S. E. Lehmberg, 'Archbishop Grindal and the Prophesyings', *Historical Magazine of the Protestant Episcopal Church*, XXXIV, ii, 101.

6 Urwick, *Nonconformity in Herts.*, 80–82.

7 Johnson to Parker, Aug. 14, 1571, Inner Temple, Petyt MS. 538, vol. 47, f 32; in John Strype, *The Life and Acts of Matthew Parker* (3 vols., Oxford, 1821), II, 69ff.

8 Collinson, 'The Puritan Classical Movement', I, 146–9.

9 The best summaries of Grindal's difficulties are in Lehmberg, 'Archbishop Grindal', and Collinson, *Elizabethan Puritan Movement*, 191–201.

10 William Nicholson (ed.), *The Remains of Edmund Grindal, D.D.* (Parker Soc., Cambridge, 1843), ii–iii; *D.N.B.*, 'Grindal, Edmund'.

11 Grindal to Cecil, July 3, 1563, in Nicholson, *Remains of Grindal*, 272–3.

12 Grindal to Cecil, Sept. 15, 1568, in ibid., 299–300.

13 Cf. an undated – and undelivered – document entitled 'A Copy of a paper drawn up by A. Bp Grindall & Presented to ye Lds of ye Council ... ', B.L. Add. MS. 29546, ff 46–7.

14 Grindal to the lords of the privy council, Nov. 30, 1577, in Nicholson, *Remains of Grindal*, 392, n 2, (cited).

15 Huntington Library MS. EL 2579, ff 59–60.

16 [?] Dec. 1, 1577, Folger Shakespeare Library MS. V.a. 197, f 19.

17 The best modern accounts of Anglo-Dutch relations during the 1570s include Conyers Read, *Mr Secretary Walsingham and the*

Policy of Queen Elizabeth (3 vols., Oxford, 1925), especially I, Chs. V–VII; Conyers Read, *Lord Burghley and Queen Elizabeth* (1960), especially Chs. V, X and XI; R. B. Wernham, 'English Policy and the Revolt of the Netherlands', in J. S. Bromley and E. H. Kossmann (eds.), *Britain and the Netherlands* (1960), 29–41; R. B. Wernham, 'Elizabethan War Aims and Strategy', in Bindoff, Hurstfield and Williams (eds.), *Elizabethan Government and Society* (1962), 340–68; R. B. Wernham, *Before the Armada* (1966), Chs. 23–4; and Charles Wilson, *Queen Elizabeth and the Revolt of the Netherlands* (1970).

18 Cf. J. B. Black, 'Queen Elizabeth, the Sea Beggars, and the Capture of Brielle, 1572', *English Historical Review*, XLVI (1931), 30–47.

19 Peter Geyl, *The Revolt of the Netherlands* (1958), 136.

20 Wernham, *Before the Armada*, 327–8.

21 This tradition is most concisely stated by Neale and Wernham; Wernham, ibid., 320–21, and 'English Policy and the Revolt of the Netherlands', 29–31; J. E. Neale, *Queen Elizabeth* (1934), 232–3.

22 Such attempts are best represented by the frontal attack in Wilson, *Queen Elizabeth and the Revolt*, especially Ch. I and Conclusion. But cf. also the review of Wilson's work by G. D. Ramsay, *English Historical Review*, LXXXVI (July 1971), 568–71.

23 Read, *Walsingham*, I, 314–15.

24 Ibid., I, 316–18.

25 Ibid., I, 314–15; J. M. Kervyn de Lettenhove and L. G. van Severen, *Relations Politiques des Pays Bas* ... (11 vols., Brussels, 1882–1900), VIII, 121–3.

26 Antonio de Guaras to [?] Zayas, Jan. 9, 1576, *C.S.P.*, *Spanish, Elizabeth*, II, 518–19.

27 On this theme, cf. especially Conyers Read, 'Walsingham and Burghley in Queen Elizabeth's Privy Council', *English Historical Review*, XXVIII (Jan. 1913), 34–58, especially 36–8.

28 Ibid., 34–7; Read, *Walsingham*, I, *passim*.

29 Ibid., I, 316–17.

30 *C.S.P.*, *Foreign, Elizabeth*, XI, 222.

31 Read, *Burghley*, 164–6, in which Burghley's opinions are quoted in full.

32 'The some of the opinion of the Counsell upon the request of the Hollanders ... ', Jan. 16, 1576, in de Lettenhove and van Severen, *Relations Politiques*, VIII, 121–3.

33 'Answer given to the Hollanders [by the Queen]', Jan. 15, 1576, printed in full in *C.S.P.*, *Foreign, Elizabeth*, XI, 229–30, and in de Lettenhove and van Severen, *Relations Politiques*, VIII, 118–20.

Although this reply is dated a day earlier than the final council memo of the 16th, it is clear from the wording that Elizabeth acted here in full knowledge of the council's advice.

34 Wilson, *Queen Elizabeth and the Revolt*, 39–40; Read, *Walsingham*, I, 327–31.

35 Ibid., I, 333–5.

36 Nathaniel Bacon to Bacon, Aug. 24, 1576, Folger MS. L.d. 74; cf. above, 165–6.

37 Walsingham to Bacon, Sept. 17, 1576, Folger MS. L.d. 612.

38 Geyl, *Revolt*, 145–50; Read, *Walsingham*, I, 336–7.

39 Geyl, *Revolt*, 150–51. Orange, however, did not approve of the negotiations with Don John, and refused to accept the Perpetual Edict; ibid., 151; Read, *Walsingham*, I, 338.

40 Geyl, *Revolt*, 150.

41 Read, *Walsingham*, I, 335–6; John Stow, *The Chronicles of England* (1580), *S.T.C.* no. 23333, 1187.

42 Read, *Walsingham*, I, 345–6; Geyl, *Revolt*, 151–3.

43 Ibid., 153–4.

44 Aug. 2, 1577, *C.S.P., Foreign, Elizabeth*, XII, 54–5, and 'Instructions from Davison to Henry Gilpin', Aug. 11, 1577, in de Lettenhove and van Severen, *Relations Politiques*, IX, 452–3.

45 Antonio de Guaras to [?] Zayas, Sept. 20, 1577, *C.S.P., Spanish, Elizabeth*, II, 544–5. For Bacon's role, cf. his letter of September 15th to the Queen. This was erroneously attributed to Burghley by the cataloguer of the copy in B.L. Harleian MS. 286, f 21, and that erroneous attribution was picked up in de Lettenhove and van Severen, *Relations Politiques*, IX, 575–6 (where a further error was made when the B.L. folio number was given as 51 rather than 21), and from there by Read, *Walsingham*, I, 353, n 1. As two other copies make clear, it is without doubt Bacon's letter. Both are dated from Gorhambury, and the Huntingdon Library copy is found in a collection of his letters and specches; Huntington Library MS. HM 1340, ff 88–90, and P.R.O., S.P. 12/115/24.

46 Geyl, *Revolt*, 76, 87, 101, 146–8.

47 Read, *Walsingham*, I, 355–7.

48 Ibid., I, 356, and Walsingham to Davison, Oct. 20, 1577, in de Lettenhove and van Severen, *Relations Politiques*, X, 41–3.

49 Read, *Walsingham*, I, 360.

50 Bacon to the Queen, Nov. 20, 1577, Huntington Library MS. HM 1340, ff 90v–91v.

51 Read, *Walsingham*, I, 361–3.

52 Geyl, *Revolt*, 160.

53 Walsingham to Bacon, Feb. 4, 1578, B.L. Cotton MS. Vespasian

F, xii, f 217. A privy council letter written, signed and dated on February 4th, indicates that the council was then at Hampton Court, with both Walsingham and Bacon attending; Folger MS. L.a. 705.

54 Read, *Walsingham*, I, 365.

55 *Loc. cit.*

56 The Queen to Duke Casimir, July 30, 1577, *C.S.P.*, *Foreign*, *Elizabeth*, XII, 47–9; [The Queen] to Mr Hoddeson, ibid., 86.

57 Davison to Leicester, Oct. 19, 1577, in de Lettenhove and van Severen, *Relations Politiques*, X, 281; Davison to Burghley, Nov. 18, 1577, *C.S.P.*, *Foreign*, *Elizabeth*, XII, 324–7.

58 Bacon to the Queen, Sept. 15, 1577, S.P. 12/115/24; cf. also n 45.

59 Wilson, *Queen Elizabeth and the Revolt*, 60–64; Read, *Walsingham*, I, 374–6.

60 Read, *Walsingham*, I, 374–6.

61 Ibid., 375–6.

62 Ibid., 376.

63 Burghley's Memorial (undated, but placed *c.* May 12th by de Lettenhove and van Severen, which seems roughly accurate); de Lettenhove and van Severen, *Relations Politiques*, X, 465–7.

64 Bacon to the Queen, May 6, 1578, Huntington Library MS. HM 1340, f 92.

65 Reprinted in full in Read, *Walsingham*, I, 377.

66 Read, 'Walsingham and Burghley in Queen Elizabeth's Privy Council', 29–33.

67 Bacon to Walsingham, July 24, 1578; Huntington Library MS. HM 1340, f 93r; copy in Corpus Christi College Library, Cambridge, MS. 543, f 6.

Epilogue

1 Matthew Parker to Bacon, Dec. [?] and 20, 1558, in John Bruce and Thomas T. Perowne (eds.), *The Correspondence of Matthew Parker* (Parker Soc., Cambridge, 1853), 50–53.

2 Bacon had to be replaced during part of the Parliaments of 1566 and 1571, and at the Chancery in 1559 and 1575. Huntington Library MS. EL 2579, f 41; *C.P.R.*, *Elizabeth*, V, 276; *C.P.R.*, *Elizabeth*, I, 19; William Cordell to Lord Burghley, Sep. 1, 1575, Cecil Papers, Hatfield House, vol. 160, f 54. I am indebted to Miss Clare Talbot, Librarian at Hatfield House, for access to this document.

3 Ibid.

4 Francis Wyndham to Nathaniel Bacon, Dec. 30, 1575, in H. W. Saunders (ed.), *The Official Papers of Sir Nathaniel Bacon of Stiffkey*, *Norfolk* (Camden Society, 3rd series, XXVI, 1915), 186–9.

5 M. B. Pulman, *The Elizabethan Privy Council in the Fifteen-Seventies* (Berkeley, 1971), 166.

6 'Report and Opinion of the Queen's Commissioners on the Controversy of the Mint', signed by Bacon and six others, May 24, 1578, B.L. Lansdowne MSS. 48, f 53, and 26, ff 24-5.

7 Cf. the indenture drawn up and signed by the Lord Keeper and his son Edward on the one hand and the Company of Cursitors on the other, for the rental of Cursitors' Hall, which Bacon had built; Dec. 23, 1578, P.R.O., C. 220/Bundle 15/art. 13.

8 Recounted fully in E. R. Sandeen, 'The Building Activities of Sir Nicholas Bacon' (unpublished Ph.D. dissertation, University of Chicago, 1959), 235-9; cf. also Corpus Christi College, Chapel MSS., B, Pt I.

9 Cf., for example, the dedications of Thomas Twyne, *The Garlande of Godly Flowers* (1574), *S.T.C.* no. 24408, and Jacobus Falckenburgius, *Jacobi à Falckenburgk ... Britannia ...* (1578), *S.T.C.* no. 10674.

10 The poet George Gascoigne, a distant relation by marriage, sent Bacon a New Year's card in January 1578 which is of some interest to literary scholars as well as to historians. It contains a pen drawing of an unbroken colt and an accompanying poem ('Before the sturdye colte / will byde the bytt ... ') to wish the Lord Keeper a 'goode newe yeare and many to gods goode pleasure' and, incidentally, to seek his favour; Raynham Hall MSS, on loan from Lord Cromwell to the Norfolk and Norwich Record Office, unpaginated. Cf. also C. T. Prouty, *George Gascoigne* ... (New York, 1942), 90, n 56, and 293-304. On the same New Year Bacon and Elizabeth exchanged gifts. He sent her £13 6s. 8d. in gold, and she sent him a 'double bowl of silver and gilt, keel', of 34¾ oz. weight; Nichols, *Progresses of Queen Elizabeth* (3 vols., 1823), II, 65, 81.

11 Nichols, *Progresses*, II, 57-8. The possibility that the Queen paid a visit in 1573, as tendered by Nichols (I, 309), still exists, but little hard evidence may be found to support that tradition.

12 The following is reconstructed from the table of expenditures for the visit which is found in the Lambeth Palace Library, MS. 647, item 9, ff 42-3. I am indebted to the Librarian, Mr E. G. W. Bill, for permission to examine this manuscript.

13 Alexander Nowell to Michael Shaller, Aug. 4, 1576, St Paul's Cathedral MS. W.D. 32 ('Michael Shaller's Notebook'), f 6, and copy, f 11.

14 Indenture between the Lord Keeper and his son Nicholas on the one hand, and Alexander Nowell and the Chapter of St Paul's on the other hand; June 13, 1577, Norfolk and Norwich Record Office MS. 13902, 28-F-2.

15 Nowell to Shaller, July 29, 1581; St Paul's MS. W.D. 32, f 7. The first Earl actually died in December 1569, and Bacon had even been one of the executors of his will, but the second Earl took twelve years to erect a monument; *D.N.B.*, 'Herbert, William'.

16 Payne Fisher, *The Tombes, Monuments, and Sepulchral Inscriptions in St Paul's Cathedral* (1684), Wing. no. F 1042, 91–3; Sir William Dugdale, *The History of St Paul's Cathedral* (2 vols., reprinted 1818), I, opposite p. 50.

17 Dugdale, *St Paul's* I, opposite p. 56.

18 Eric Mercer, *English Art, 1553–1625* (Oxford, 1962), Plate 84b.

19 John Stow, *The Chronicles of England* (1580), *S.T.C.* no. 23333, 1194.

20 J. Spedding, R. L. Ellis and D. D. Heath (eds.), *Works of Francis Bacon* (14 vols., 1857–74), VII, 183.

21 Cecil Papers, Hatfield House, vol. 229 ('Burghley's Journal'), entry for Feb. 20, 1579; George Whetstone, *A Remembraunce of the Woorthie and well imployed life of ... Sir Nicholas Bacon ...* (1579), *S.T.C.* no. 25343.

22 Reprinted in translation in Payne Fisher, *Tombs of St Paul's*, 92.

23 Thomas Norton to Anthony Bacon, Feb. 20, 1579; Hopkinson MSS., Bradford Central Library, Bradford, Yorkshire, XVIII, ff 126–7.

24 Cf., for example, W. H. Dixon, *Personal History of Francis Bacon* (1861), 50–51, and William Urwick, *Nonconformity in Herts.*, 85, in which Dixon's reference is cited to substantiate the same point.

25 Dr Alan Simpson presented a full and detailed account of Bacon's lands, revenues, and receipts from office; Alan Simpson, *The Wealth of the Gentry, 1540–1660* (Chicago, 1961), 109–14. Bacon's investment in commerce and industry accounted for a fraction of his total wealth. They included very modest investments in the Muscovy Company and the Company of Mineral and Battery Works, both of which Dr Simpson has recorded, and a somewhat more active role in a substantial salt-mining operation in South Wales; Simpson, *Wealth of the Gentry*, 88–9; M. B. Donald, *The History of the Company of Mineral and Battery Works, 1565–1604* (1961), 35, 37, 74; A. J. Gerson, 'The Organization and Early History of the Muscovy Company', in A. J. Gerson (ed.), *Studies in the History of English Commerce ...* (New York, 1912), 118; William Wightman, Receiver of South Wales, to Edward Herbert of Montgomeryshire, [?] 1566/7, calendared in W. J. Smith (ed.), *Herbert Correspondence ...* (Cardiff, 1963), 49.

26 Simpson, *Wealth of the Gentry*, 90, and table C, 114. It is instructive to compare these figures to the total bequests of Sir Walter Mildmay, whose position and length of service at court was

roughly equivalent to Bacon's, but who left bequests of £6,282 in cash and plate; Stanford Lehmberg, *Sir Walter Mildmay and Tudor Government* (Austin, Texas, 1964), 307.

27 Simpson, *Wealth of the Gentry*, 90.

28 This final version of December 23rd, 1578, includes sections from previous wills, dated June 2nd, 1575, and September 11th, 1577, and there had probably been several versions before that which are not mentioned in the final draft. I have used the probate copy of the will, Bacon MSS., University of Chicago MS. no. 4371, probated February 24th, 1579, four days after the Lord Keeper's death. For Bacon's inquisition post mortem, or those parts which can be made out through stain and mildew, cf. P.R.O., C.142/191/90.

29 The whole funeral is reconstructed by Dr Simpson, *Wealth of the Gentry*, 22–7.

30 Dr Simpson has found evidence for two different cost estimates, for £919 12s. 1d. and £1,000 respectively, and I find one for a much higher total – £2,230 18s. 10d. – but the latter includes several items not strictly related to the funeral. Simpson, *Wealth of the Gentry*, 27, n 1; executors' account drawn up by Nathaniel and young Nicholas Bacon, Raynham Hall MSS., box 1, item 35, and a copy, item 44.

31 Seneca, 'de Clementia', in John W. Basore (ed.), *Seneca, Moral Essays* (Loeb edition, 3 vols., Cambridge, Mass. 1958), I, 356–449; cf. also F. L. Battles and André M. Hugo, *Calvin's Commentary on Seneca's 'de Clementia'* (Leiden, 1969), for interesting insight into the Calvinist reception of Seneca's essay.

32 Cf. Anthony Esler, *The Aspiring Mind of the Elizabethan Younger Generation* (Durham, North Carolina, 1966), *passim*.

Index

Bacon, Nicholas (son), 63, 149, 154,
156, 158–62, 164, 237
Bacon, Robert (father), 16–18, 201
Bacon, Thomas (brother), 17–18, 43
Baldero, Francis, 159, 240
Barker, Richard, 62
Barnes, Robert, 20
Beaumont, Robert, 57, 62
Beccles, Suffolk, 82
Bedford, Francis Russell, 2nd Earl
of, 84–5, 116, 136, 221
Bedford, John Russell, 1st Earl of,
40–41
Bell, Robert, 144
Beza, Theodore, 169
Bindoff, Prof. S. T., 12, 102–8,
112–13
Blackman, Robert (brother-in-law),
18, 159, 202, 240
Blundeville, Thomas, 58–9
bookplates, 58
Bothwell, James Hepburn, Earl of,
129–30
bribery and corruption, 80–82
Bromley, Sir Thomas, 82–3
Browne, Sir Anthony, 102, 120, 224
Browne, John, 170
Bucer, Martin, 92
Buchanan, George, 191
Buckhurst, Thomas Sackville, Lord,
142–3
Bures family, 152
Burghley, see Cecil, William
Bury St Edmunds, 16, 34, 150, 159,
239; Abbey and Abbey School,
18–19; Grammar School, 61,
158–9, 202
Buttes, Sir William, 154, 166, 236
Buttes family, 152, 154, 156, 236

Calais, 25, 93, 96, 98, 204–5
Cambridge, University of, 19–21,
32, 78, 212; Bacon donates books
to, 58; Bacon's sons at, 62, 106;
Benet (Corpus Christi) College,
19–21, 61–2, 106, 187
Camden, William, 9, 123, 125
Cartwright, Thomas, 170

Cary, Robert, 30, 32, 203, 206; see
also Denton–Bacon–Cary Report
Castiglione, Baldassare, Count, 60,
62, 211
Cateau-Cambrésis, Treaty of (1559),
93–4, 98
Catelyn, Robert, 126
catholics: in East Anglia, 160–65;
under Elizabeth, 88–90, 127–8,
132, 135
Cave, Ambrose, 225–6
Cecil, Mildred (née Cooke), 97
Cecil, William, later Lord Burghley,
23, 41, 59, 69, 195–7, 215; and
domestic affairs, 106, 110–11,
136–7, 225–6; and foreign
affairs, 94–7, 99–100, 133–5, 176,
178, 183–4, 186; and marriage/
succession question, 116, 119–21,
123–4, 128–9, 143; under Mary,
52–4; and Mary Stuart, 139–42,
145; relations with Bacon, 21, 35,
49–50, 70, 84–6, 88, 97, 125,
133–7, 145–6, (disagreement over
Newhaven) 99–100, 216
Chancery, Court of, 71–80, 83, 113,
122–3, 195, 217
Charles, Archduke, 121, 128
Charles IX, King of France, 128,
137
Cheke, John, 41, 50, 57
Chester, Chamberlain of, 78
Cinque Ports, 78
Clere, Sir Edward, 163
Clifford family, 38–40
Clinton, Edward, Lord, see Lincoln
Coinage, 103, 108, 111–12, 187
Condé, Prince de, 98
'Considerations delivered to the
Parliament, 1559', 103–6, 113–14
Cooke, Anne (second wife), 49–54,
57, 61–2, 150, 156, 169, 209;
poem to, 56
Cooke, Sir Anthony, 41, 49–50, 69,
91, 104, 106, 209, 216–17, 222,
238; in exile, 54; in parliament,
88, 104; tomb, 190
Cordell, William, 104, 113, 164, 229